Here to Stay, Here to Fight

Here to Stay, Here to Fight

A *Race Today* Anthology

Edited by Paul Field, Robin Bunce,
Leila Hassan and Margaret Peacock

First published 2019 by Pluto Press
345 Archway Road, London N6 5AA

www.plutobooks.com

British Library Cataloguing in Publication Data
A catalogue record for this book is available from the British Library

ISBN   978 0 7453 3977 1   Hardback
ISBN   978 0 7453 3975 7   Paperback
ISBN   978 1 7868 0483 9   PDF eBook
ISBN   978 1 7868 0485 3   Kindle eBook
ISBN   978 1 7868 0484 6   EPUB eBook

This book is printed on paper suitable for recycling and made from fully managed
and sustained forest sources. Logging, pulping and manufacturing processes are
expected to conform to the environmental standards of the country of origin.

Typeset by Stanford DTP Services, Northampton, England

Simultaneously printed in the United Kingdom and United States of America

Contents

List of Figures

Acknowledgements

This book has its origins in the work of the *Race Today* Collective, a small organisation – in the Jamesian sense – based in Brixton from 1974 to 1991. The editorial team which put this collection together, and which worked closely with several members of the original Collective, would like to express their warmest thanks to all of the librarians and archivists who helped us access copies of *Race Today*, the *Race Today Review*, and the various pamphlets produced by the Collective in the 1970s and 1980s. The staff of the Black Cultural Archives in Brixton, the London School of Economics library in Portugal Street, the staff in the West Room, at Cambridge University Library, the staff at the Bishopsgate Institute Library, and at the Library of SOAS in Bloomsbury, and the Radzinowicz Library in Cambridge, have been unfailingly helpful. Their expertise and advice has been invaluable to this project.

The staff at the George Padmore Institute in Stroud Green Road have been especially helpful. In fact, without the ongoing aid of Sarah Garrod, whose work includes preserving and cataloguing *Race Today*, this volume would not have been possible. We are indebted to Sarah as on many occasions she helped locate articles from the pages of *Race Today*, and thank her for her expert assistance.

We must also record our gratitude to Sarah White, also of the George Padmore Institute and New Beacon Books, who put us in touch with contributors to *Race Today*, and who kindly gave us permission to reproduce her own and John La Rose's articles in this volume.

We owe particularly heartfelt thanks to Sandra Field, for the many hours spent patiently reading and helping to transcribe many of these articles, for which we are immensely grateful.

We are no less obliged to all of those who helped us contact the many writers whose work appears in this volume. Getting permission for every piece was an enormous task, and no mean feat, as many of these articles were written more than forty years ago and their authors are based on three different continents. Thanks to David Renton and Tim Hempstead at Garden Court Chambers, and to Professor David McNally and Tyler Shipley for their help making contact with the authors of some of these pieces.

We would like to offer our thanks to Gerry Adams for his permission to publish 'Pawn Shops and Politics', which is taken from his book *Fall Memories*, originally published by Brandon, now an imprint of The O'Brien Press. Thanks to Michael O'Brien at The O'Brien Press and to Olive Sharkey and Sinn Fein's staff and volunteers for their help. Our thanks to Monica McKinley whose interviews with Toni Morrison and Ntozake Shange, which originally appeared in the 1985 *Race Today Review*, are reproduced here; and to Bandung Productions which conducted the interview with Jayaben Desai and Arthur Scargill, which appeared in the June–July issue of *Race Today* from 1987.

We are indebted to Ishmahil Blagrove and 'Rice N Peas Films' for access to their wonderful archive of photographs, several of which appear in this volume.

In Cambridge, this project has been supported by the Principal, Fellows and staff of Homerton College. Scanning and digitising the original pages of *Race Today*, would not have been possible without their resources.

Above all, we owe our gratitude to the many contributors whose articles, reviews, interviews, poetry and prose make up this volume, to the family of Darcus Howe who supported this project, and to the members of the *Race Today* Collective,

Jean Ambrose
Barbara Beese
Michael Cadette
Eden Charles
Farrukh Dhondy
Mala Dhondy (née Sen)
Patricia Dick
Leila Hassan
Claudius Hilliman
Darcus Howe
Linton Kwesi Johnson
Akua Rugg
Marva Spencer
Lorine Stapleton (née Burt)

and to Olive Morris who helped find *Race Today* a home in the summer of 1974.

This book is dedicated in memory of Darcus Howe
(26 February 1943–1 April 2017).

Introduction

Leila Hassan, Robin Bunce and Paul Field

From 1974 to 1988, *Race Today*, the journal of the *Race Today* Collective, was at the epicentre of the struggle for racial justice in Britain. *Race Today* was ground-breaking in terms of its reports and analysis of struggles by Black and Asian workers in the UK against police and state racism. These insights flowed from the work of the Collective, work which was not merely journalistic. For the Collective was a campaigning organisation, which supported grass-roots movements, movements which sought to advance the struggle for Black Power, the fight for women's liberation, and the anti-colonial campaign to free the 'Third World'. *Race Today* placed race, sex and social class at the core of its analysis of events in Britain, and across the world. *Race Today*'s writers reflected the magazine's global reach, as the magazine included contributors such as C.L.R. James, who lived above the journal's offices in Railton Road, Brixton; Darcus Howe and Leila Hassan, the magazine's editors; and writers, activists and intellectuals such as Mala Sen, Barbara Beese, Akua Rugg, Linton Kwesi Johnson, Selma James, Farrukh Dhondy, John La Rose, Martin Glaberman, Walter Rodney, Maurice Bishop, Bukkha Rennie and Franklyn Harvey.

While *Race Today* was widely read and influential in the 1970s and '80s, the magazine is now hard to access, as only a handful of archives contain the complete run. This anthology aims to bring the insightful journalism and fearless activism of the *Race Today* Collective to the attention of a new generation at a time when the struggle for racial justice has never been more urgent. With the struggle against police brutality and racism gaining new impetus through the Black Lives Matter movement, with the Far Right on the march again in the UK, US and Europe, there is an appetite among younger activists to learn about the recent history of Black radicalism in Britain, a history which *Race Today* chronicled, and in which the Collective played an essential part.

TOWARDS RACIAL JUSTICE

From its inception, the *Race Today* Collective lent its organisational weight to dozens of grass-roots justice campaigns including those to free the Brockwell Park Three, the Bradford Twelve, and George Lindo. The biggest test of the Collective's strength occurred in 1981. In the wake of the New Cross fire, they conceived and organised the Black Peoples Day of Action, a mass protest which saw 20,000 people, the vast majority Black, march through London, chanting 'Thirteen Dead and Nothing Said'.

Similarly, the Collective and its journal were instrumental in helping to organise the largest squat in British history in London's East End. Through their work with the Bengali Housing Action Group (BHAG), the Collective achieved the seemingly impossible. An entire community was re-housed by the GLC following a 3-year campaign of direct action in which dozens of Bengali families squatted vacant property. Turning to the rights of workers, the journal published eyewitness accounts and analysis of Imperial Typewriters and Grunwick strikes by Asian workers against sweatshop employers. The Collective also covered the insurrections led by Black youth at Carnival in 1976, and the uprisings which began in Brixton in April 1981 before spreading to sixty other cities. When Black youth rose up again in Brixton and Broadwater Farm in 1985, *Race Today* provided a voice for the dispossessed.

Race Today saw culture and politics as inseparable. Writers such as Howe, Johnson, Dhondy and Rugg argued that liberation movements and cultural movements emerged hand-in-hand. From this perspective, the magazine sought to provide a platform for self-expression of Black people, women, workers and others oppressed by capitalism and imperialism. Through its cultural arms – Creation for Liberation and the International Book Fair of Radical and Third World Books – and through their participation in a mass band at Notting Hill Carnival, *Race Today* and its sister publication *Race Today Review* brought the work of Black artists such as Toni Morrison, Grace Nichols, Mickey Smith, Lorna Goodison, Ntozake Shange and Jean 'Binta' Breeze to public attention.

ORIGINS

As Linton Kwesi Johnson explains below, it was Howe's appointment as editor on 6 November 1973, which set *Race Today*, formerly the liberal monthly publication of Chatham House's Institute of Race Relations, on a radical new course. A well-known Black Power activist, and one of the Mangrove Nine, Howe was a controversial choice. Howe's selection was a consequence of the revolution in the Institute's political outlook. His appointment was made possible after the Institute's staff under the leadership of A. Sivanandan, its former librarian, succeeded in wresting control from its paternalistic Council and transformed it into an anti-racist organ-isation. The *Guardian* noted that Howe's editorship 'promises to steer the magazine yet further from its academic origins towards the front line of racial politics'.*

In August 1974, this wish to place *Race Today* on the front line of the emerging struggle for racial justice, led Howe to break with the Institute completely. Assisted by Olive Morris, the core of what would become the *Race Today* Collective relocated the magazine to a squat at the heart of Britain's Black community in Brixton, South London. Freed from all constraints, *Race Today* became the journal of a 'small organisation'. The *Race Today* Collective was established in 1974 along explicitly Jamesian lines. Taking inspiration from James et al.'s *Facing Reality* (1958), the new Collective recognised that as a truly revolutionary socialist group, it was not their role to act as a self-appointed vanguard to the working class. Rather, the Collective sought to establish a paper (and small publishing house) which like the 'paper of the Marxist organization', described by James, would 'recognize and record' the struggles of the working class.† Writing in *Race Today*, Howe argued that a paper 'can only do this by plunging into the great mass of the people and meeting the new society that is there.' Howe described this task in his first editorial in recognisably Jamesian terms:

> Our task is to record and recognise the struggles of the emerging forces as manifestations of the revolutionary potential of the black population. We recognise too the release of intellectual energy from within the black community, which always comes to the fore when the masses of the oppressed by their actions create a new social reality.(January 1974).

FACING REALITY

Race Today reflected a Jamesian approach to writing. Its articles fore-grounded the authentic voices of protagonists, reflecting on and recording their own struggles. Martin Glaberman, one of James's American comrades, noted that James liked to remind people of Trotsky's criticism of the US Socialist Workers Party newspaper. The paper was produced as a means of advancing the Party line, and therefore

---

* *The Guardian*, 6 November 1973.
† C.L.R. James and Grace Lee Boggs with Cornelius Castoriadis, *Facing Reality* (2006) originally published under James's pseudonym 'J.R. Johnson' (Detroit, MI: Cor-respondence Publishing Company, 1958), p. 159.

Each of them [the paper's journalists] speaks for the workers (and speaks very well) but nobody will hear the workers. In spite of its literary brilliance, to a certain degree the paper becomes a victim of journalistic routine. You do not hear at all how the workers live, fight, clash with the police or drink whiskey.*

Jamesians, by contrast, went out of their way to ensure that the voice of working people appeared in their own newspaper *Correspondence*. Raya Dunayevskaya, another of James's comrades, coined the phrase 'full fountain pen' to describe the process of interviewing workers, typing up their words and then taking back the transcript to them to correct and verify before publication. It was this intimate relationship with, and involvement in working-class struggles and communities, which enabled *Correspondence* to discuss issues such as popular culture, music, cinema, sports and family life a decade before the New Left embraced such topics (Worcester, 1998).†

In a similar vein, the *Race Today* Collective gave expression to the Black cultural explosion which occurred in the 1970s and '80s through a myriad of cultural media: Linton Kwesi Johnson via his dub poetry and music; Farrukh Dhondy through his novels and plays; C.L.R. James through his sports writing, literature and literary criticism; Jean Binta Breeze and Mikey Smith in their spoken poems. The Collective even formed their own masquerade band known as '*Race Today* Mangrove Renegade Band' with the support of mas players from Ladbroke Grove. They went on to win Best Costume in 1977, 1978 and 1979 at the Notting Hill Carnival. In 1977, the *Race Today* masquerade band celebrated insurgent national liberation movements in Africa with a mass entitled 'Forces of Victory'. 'Viva Zapata', their 1978 mass, was a homage to the life of Emiliano Zapata, the Mexican revolutionary. Their 1979 'Feast of Barbarian' was rooted in Britain's own ancient tradition of resistance to foreign rule.

Race Today's coverage was always internationalist. It reflected the Collective's role as part of a global revolutionary movement, which linked Black Power in Europe and the US with national liberation movements in what was called 'the Third World'. True to James's revolutionary socialist politics, the journal rejected ethnic nationalism. Rather, the Collective argued that the militant struggles of the Black working class, youth, and

---

* Martin Glaberman, 'Remembering CLR James', *Against the Current* 72, January–February 1998.

† Kent Worcester, *C.L.R. James, A Political Biography* (Albany: State University of New York Press, 1996).

women against the state and employers had the potential to inspire the wider working-class movement to fight for power.

Consistent with this rejection of ethnic nationalism was the fact that *Race Today* embraced political blackness, which sought to unite all people of colour who had been exploited by colonialism, and oppressed by racism and capitalism. This was not unique to *Race Today*, for political blackness was a response to the experience of British imperialism. Consequently, 'blackness as a unifying political identity' (Wild, 2008)* was a feature of the wider Black Power movement in Britain, which successfully united South Asian, West Indian, and African migrants. Indeed, this concept of blackness was commonplace among Black and Asian radicals in Britain in the 1970s and '80s, even those who worked within mainstream organisations such as the Labour Party. Yet *Race Today* remains, perhaps, one of the best examples of this inclusive political blackness. It united Black and Asian activists in diverse struggles, united against racist violence, united in campaigns for decent housing, better schooling and for defence of the Notting Hill Carnival. Indeed, it is worth noting that consensus around political blackness collapsed soon after *Race Today*'s last issue.

Race Today's commitment 'to record and recognise' the struggle of the Black and Asian working class was set out in Howe's editorial of April 1974. Howe cited Karl Marx's *A Worker's Inquiry* (1880)† which set down a hundred questions to be asked of every worker as they 'alone can describe with full knowledge the misfortunes that they suffer', and provide 'an exact and positive knowledge of the conditions in which the working class – the class to whom the future belongs – lives and moves'. The April 1974 issue of *Race Today* contained multiple first-hand accounts of the working conditions and struggles of Asian workers in order to provide 'an exact and positive knowledge' about 'this section of the working class ... involved in successive strike actions in the past five years which now threaten to develop into a cohesive and powerful mass movement of Asian workers' (Howe, 1974). Likewise, *Race Today*'s interviews with Black nurses and women health workers in August 1974, following the first-ever strike by nurses in the UK, broke new ground by identifying how gender, race and class intersected in the increased exploitation of and discrimination against

---

* Rosie Wild, 'Black was the Colour of Our Fight: The Transnational Roots of British Black Power', in Robin D.G. Kelley and Stephen Tuck (eds), *The Other Special Relationship: Race, Rights, and Riots in Britain and the United States* (New York: Palgrave Macmillan, 2015).

† Karl Marx, *A Worker's Inquiry* (1880): *La Revue Socialiste*, https://www.marxists.org/archive/marx/works/1880/04/20.htm

Black nurses. Similarly, *Race Today*'s vivid account of the dramatic wildcat strikes at Ford's in Dagenham, was largely based on one of the assembly-line worker's diaries, and its description of the 1981 insurrection was in large part derived from verbatim accounts: the *Race Today* office, in Railton Road, Brixton, was on the front line of the uprising, and the Collective monitored the battle, recorded events and, after the insurrection was over, debriefed its leading participants.

THE LIFE OF THE COLLECTIVE

The Collective was originally based at 74 Shakespeare Road. As the magazine's influence grew, so did its premises. In 1980, the members of the Collective broke through a wall connecting their house on Shakespeare Road with a house on Railton Road, in order to establish a second squat. The new squat, 165 Railton Road, later became the offices of *Race Today*. During the 1980s, the ground floor of the Railton Road squat housed *Race Today*'s production team, the first floor comprised editorial offices, and James lived on the top floor. The basement was the venue for *Race Today*'s 'Basement Sessions', which facilitated self-education. Sometimes these sessions were reading groups. Indeed, an early set of sessions was devoted to James's *Nkrumah and the Ghana Revolution* (1977). On other occasions, the Basement Sessions were used to build bridges with other communities involved in their own acts of resistance. In 1984, to take one example, at Hassan's instigation, the Collective paid for the wives of striking coal miners to come to London and tell their stories.

Race Today's final issue was published in 1988, but the Collective endured into the early 1990s. Howe was keen, at least initially, to keep the organisation going. In a letter to the members of the Collective written in 1989 he argued that the organisation should continue as a basis for future interventions in British national life.* However, as Johnson recalls, James's death in 1989 'created a pall over everything. Some members were affected by it. I certainly was.' James's death, coupled with Howe's increasing involvement in television journalism, and his conviction that *Race Today* had 'exhausted the moment' brought the Collective to an end. The *Race Today* Collective was formally dissolved on 7 April 1991.

---

* University of Columbia Rare Books and Manuscript Library, Darcus Howe Papers, Letter to the Collective, 1989, Box VIII, Folder 4.

'HERE TO STAY! HERE TO FIGHT!'

The following pages contain some of the articles, speeches, interviews, prose and poetry published by the Collective. Much of the material comes from the pages of the 140 issues of *Race Today* published from 1974 to 1988, and the *Race Today Review*, which appeared annually from 1981. We have also referred to the pamphlets put out by the Collective which expanded on the material contained in the magazine. The book is divided into sections reflecting the breadth of the journal's coverage and political campaigns. Each section contains an introduction from a different writer setting the pieces that follow in a broader political context and there is a section at the end assessing the legacies of *Race Today* in 2019.

This book is the product of a group which includes some of the surviving members of the *Race Today* Collective including Leila Hassan – editor of the journal for much of the 1980s, members of Darcus Howe's family, Howe's biographers, and Howe's former comrades and colleagues. It forms part of a series of initiatives designed to ensure that the legacy and political work of Howe and the *Race Today* Collective are preserved for the benefit of future generations.

I

Race Today and British Politics

INTRODUCTION
Linton Kwesi Johnson

'Seize The Time' was the rallying call of Bobby Seale, co-founder of the Black Panther Party in the US, in his eponymous book. When appointed editor of *Race Today* in 1973, that is precisely what Darcus Howe and his staff did. *Race Today* was then a liberal monthly publication of the Institute of Race Relations. Soon after his appointment, Howe broke away from the IRR and established a new base in a squat in Brixton, South London, and set about the business of building a collective of Black and Asian activists – the *Race Today* Collective – and embarked on the transformation of the old *Race Today* into a new journal of autonomous activism, rooted in our communities, with an international perspective. Whether wittingly or not, Howe was aided and abetted in the coup by two active revolutionary intellectuals: Ambalavaner Sivanandan, the Sri Lankan-born, pugnacious former librarian and director of the IRR, and Trinidadian John La Rose, erudite publisher of New Beacon Books and the IRR's chairman. Farrukh Dhondy, Darcus Howe's comrade from the Black Panther Movement and RTC member, rightly describes him as a 'maverick', a street-wise activist with a sharp intellect; an experienced journalist known for his uncompromising stance against racial injustice and a successful defendant in the famous Mangrove Nine trial at the Old Bailey.

Howe's intervention was timely. It came at a time of growing militancy among the young Black population and a vacuum of radical and revolutionary Black political activity. The Black Power movement was in decline and the Labour Party was not seen as a vehicle for the advancement of racial justice. The strategy of the state was to neutralise independent Black political activity by institutionalising anti-racist struggles through race relations and community relations boards and councils run by the Home Office. With Darcus Howe at the helm, the new *Race Today* became an eloquent campaigning voice of independent Black political action that could not be ignored by the political classes. We sought to offer ideological

8

clarity, based on the conviction that working people had the capacity to organise their own struggles for change and win.

The period of the new *Race Today*'s existence (1973–88) was one of capitalist crises, and industrial and political upheavals; it was a time of intense class struggle and Britain's Black and Asian communities were very much involved. This period saw the rise of neoliberalism, ushered in by the Conservative Party under the leadership of Margaret Thatcher, who gained power with a racist anti-immigrant campaign. It was also a time of open rebellion against racist policing; a rise in racist and fascist attacks and murders, and an increase in independent campaigns for justice in Black and Asian communities. *Race Today* was at the forefront of the fight-back and the RTC was engaged in supporting the struggles on the factory floor, on the streets, in the schools and in the courts.

The 1970s and '80s saw the growth of community, social and cultural organisations in the Black communities. This period witnessed an explosion of Black British creativity in the arts, in sports and the growth of Black churches throughout the inner cities. These developments were documented in pages of *Race Today*. Moreover, Creation for Liberation, its cultural arm, provided a platform to promote and nurture this new explosion of artistic and cultural creativity. *Race Today* Publications were joint organizers of the International Book Fair of Radical, Black and Third World Books (1982–95) together with New Beacon Books and Bogle L'Ouverture Books. This was in line with our Black international perspective. The book fair brought together, publishers, booksellers, intellectuals, writers, poets, musicians, film-makers and activists from around the globe, and provided a platform to debate the burning cultural, political and social issues of the day in pursuit of ideological clarity and ways to advance our struggles.

John La Rose, a doyen of the anti-colonial movement in the Caribbean and a pioneer of the Black education movement in Britain, was the director of the book fair. He was a close ally of the RTC with a shared socialist vision of change. He co-founded the Black Parents Movement, an independent organisation that, over a decade, agitated for youth and parent power and was involved in many campaigns against racism in education and police injustice against Black youths. The BPM, the Bradford Black Collective and the RTC formed an Alliance offering mutual support and solidarity in the campaigns in which we were engaged. When the New Cross massacre of January 1981 happened, where 13 Black youngsters were murdered in a racist arson attack at a 16th-birthday party, the police responded with a systematic campaign of lies and disinformation, aided and abetted by sections of the press, in order to cover up facts and attribute that heinous crime to 'Black on Black' violence. The response of the Black communities was immediate and decisive. The intervention of the Alliance was crucial. At a mass meeting of Black community organisations and concerned Black citizens, the New Cross Massacre Action Committee was formed, with John La Rose as the chairman. Our intervention marked a turning point in race relations in Britain. The New Cross Massacre Action Committee ensured that the parents of the deceased got solid legal representation, ensured that they were at the centre of the campaign for justice, established a fact-finding committee to counter the Metropolitan Police's campaign of disinformation, thwarted their attempts to frame some of the youths who had survived the fire and organised fund-raising activities to offer financial assistance to the bereaved. Moreover, on 2 March 1981, we organized the Black People's Day of Action, which saw fifteen thousand people march through the streets of London demanding justice. Darcus Howe's organisational prowess was a significant factor in the mobilisation. It was the most spectacular expression of Black political power that this country had seen. It was indeed a watershed moment, that gave Black people a new sense of the power we had to fight back. By the end of the 1980s, in the aftermath of the Black insurrections of 1981 and 1985, the obstacles to racial integration became less formidable and we began to have representation in Parliament. *Race Today*'s contribution to that change was not insignificant.

'FROM VICTIM TO PROTAGONIST: THE CHANGING SOCIAL REALITY'
Darcus Howe, January 1974

Up to the late 1960s, the race question in Britain had been dominated by a liberal mystification of who and what black people are and consequently what they can and cannot do. The portrayal of the black population as 'helpless victims' has been the central thesis of this tendency, finding concrete expression in various statutory and non-statutory bodies which comprise the Race Relations Industry – the Race Relations Board, the Community Relations Commission, the Runnymede Trust and the 'old' Institute of Race Relations.

In opposition to this tendency, a small but articulate body of black activists posed the revolutionary potential of Caribbean and Asian peoples. The release of the creative power and popular energy from within the ranks tore apart the illusions of liberalism manifested in the 'victim theory' and gave concrete expression to self-activity of the masses of the black people as the motivating force in the fight against racism. That they are victims – yes – but only to the extent that they are in the process of becoming protagonists. Witness for example the battles waged in the communities on the police question, on education, on housing, on the shop floor (Asian workers mainly in the Midlands, Caribbean workers in the South of England).

To persist in the 'victim theory' in the face of all this is not merely to distort the social reality of the black population. It reveals the institutions of liberalism as prime agents of social control standing on the necks of the emerging forces in the black community. In the recent strike of Asian workers in the textile industry (Mansfield Hosiery), the local community relations officer enjoined the racist trade union leadership to mediate between the workers and management. Where before the Race Relations industry confined itself to mediating within communities, today they are moving to find a new lease of life in the mediating machinery within industry and therefore in presenting an image of management with a liberal face. White workers would rightly resent these harbingers of welfare meddling in matters that do not concern them, with the consequence of exacerbating the already tense racial divisions on the shop floor.

However, within the liberal institutions themselves, the presence of black workers on the political stage, created a serious crisis. The Institute of Race

Figure 1.1   Linton Kwesi Johnson and Darcus Howe at the First International Book fair of Radical, Black & Third World Books, Islington Town Hall, 1982.

Relations was particularly affected. The organisation broke at its seams, the liberals were dethroned as the progressives sought to respond to new developments within the black community itself. This process gave birth to the 'new' *Race Today* and its publishers, Towards Racial Justice.

Our editorial policy, therefore, has been formed and shaped out of the conflict between liberal mediation, of whatever colour, and the newly emerging social forces of black revolt. Our task is to record and recognise the struggles of the emerging forces as manifestations of the revolutionary potential of the black population. We recognise too the release of intellectual energy from within the black community, which always comes to the fore when the masses of the oppressed by their actions create a new social reality. *Race Today* opens its pages to the tendency which seeks to give a theoretical clarification to independent grass-roots self-activity with a view to furthering its development.

'WE DID NOT COME ALIVE IN BRITAIN'
John La Rose, Race Today, March 1976

Extracts from a speech given on 7 February 1976 at an event at Brixton Civic Centre to celebrate the second anniversary of the new Race Today:

What is happening in the last of England's remaining colonies – in Scotland, Ireland and Wales – will not be new to the worker emigrants from the Caribbean and more so to those sections who were active in the anti-colonial and anti-imperialist, nationalist struggles in the 1940s and 1950s. Some of the worker emigrants to Britain were active participants in the People's Progressive Party and the People's National Congress in Guyana, the Gairy Party, the Grenada Manual and Mental Workers Union, the Butler Party, the People's National Movement, the People's National Party, the Jamaican Labour Party, the St. Kitts Labour Party, the Antigua Labour Party, the Barbados Labour Party, the West Indian Independence Party and in trade unions and other more radical sections of the nationalist movement which were Marxist and stood for revolutionary social change. They were also active in trade unions and peasant organisations. All these groupings have also been the leavening here for the early cultural, social and political activity of blacks in Britain.

The encounter with white racism and the manoeuvres of the British capitalist power did not begin in England but in the Caribbean. 'Economically and politically the white man is supreme', Arthur Lewis wrote in *Labour in the West Indies. The Birth of a Workers Movement*, published in 1939 just after the strikes and uprisings from 1935–1938. Arthur Lewis continues:

> He owns the biggest plantations, stores and banks controlling directly and indirectly the entire economic life of the community. It is he whom the governor often nominates to his councils, and for his sons that the best government jobs are reserved. Socially, the whites in general consti-tute the aristocracy. They run their own clubs from which non-whites are excluded, and it is they who constitute the 'Court' life of 'His Majesty's representative, the Governor'.

That was as late as the 1930s, a period of serious crisis of modern capital-ism. This aspect of racism, which in effect is the preservation of economic and social privilege, was so naked in a colony that no one could mistake it. The Caribbean was white minority rule buttressing white economic exploitation and white minority privilege with gradations of colour-class-ing below. The black worker and peasant were generally at the bottom. Coming to Britain, the emigrants knew that, but they only knew white power at the top. What was new was racism from within the white working class. That was strange, especially for the radical nationalist and Marxist sections who believed in the international solidarity of the working class and who had received messages of solidarity from Britain. They, in particu-lar, had to come to terms with that new situation.

I remember attending a meeting of the North London West Indian Association where it was decided to change their symbol, which until that time, was a white hand clasping a black hand. They said nobody had wanted our black hand, so they were withdrawing it. That was in the early '60s. Ideology had to be reassessed in terms of experience.

On A New Terrain

The myth now has it that the black emigrants first came here in 1950/51 on the SS *Windrush*. What did we encounter here? In Britain, there was the declining League of Coloured Peoples, led by Dr Harold Moody and the Caribbean Labour Congress (London Branch). The CLC was a branch of the labour and trade union movement, the Caribbean Labour Congress, which had been formed in the '40s and which in the 1950s was split by the Cold War rift between the World Federation of Trade Unions and the International Confederation of free Trade Unions. These were the most prominent black organisations in Britain at the time. The CLC London Branch was dominated by Communist Party membership.

The emigrants also proceeded to form branches of the politics they had left behind – PPP-PNC branches among Guyanese, JLP-PNP among Jamaicans. With the ascendancy of the PNM in Trinidad from 1955, there was also the PNM London Branch. Politically active West Indians also joined all the left organisations in Britain, besides forming independent underground revolutionary organisations concerned with the struggle for workers' and people's power in the Caribbean.

It was an experience of naked colonialism, accustomed to struggling against the colonial power from abroad, now transferred into the heart of metropolitan oppression. Anti-colonialist politics, majority consciousness, even then as now not eroded, felt itself part of black people's struggles in Africa, the United States, Canada and Asia, and especially in the Caribbean. More attention was focused then on the United States, where the major black rebellions and struggles were taking place. But the Caribbean was there and became more seriously part of black preoccupation with the Rodney Affair in Jamaica in 1968, the Trinidad rebellion and uprising in 1970, Grenada, Martinique and Guadeloupe later, and since then.

In Britain, at the time therefore, the blacks developed two types of independent organisations: a) political organisations which were an extension of the radical nationalist and workers' struggles in the Caribbean, and b) community organisations like Brent International Friendship Association and others.

These alone could not provide coherence for the black population. There were the independent black churches which had been a bulwark against colonial, cultural and social domination. These were re-established here. 'Partners' or 'box' or 'sou-sou' were also formed to buy homes. The cricket club, the All Fours Club, all the varied social forms from our past experience were reproduced here.

The Notting Hill and Nottingdale riots in 1958/59 compelled the early black settlers, with encouragement from Norman Manley and Dr La Corbinere, West Indian Federal politicians, to coordinate their efforts and form the West Indian Standing Conference almost twenty years back. The federation of the West Indian islands then in existence, was also extended here to Britain. Some of the political activists from the '40s took the lead. The outlines of independent black political social and cultural organisation were already clear.

Emerging Struggles

I referred earlier to the experience in the North London West Indian Association and its decision in the early 1960s. This was what was new: the experience at the workplace, the struggle for jobs and job promotion. NLWIA picketed to get black bus inspectors in London Transport, as white workers went on strike to prevent black workers being employed. Police went 'nigger hunting'. A booklet called 'Nigger Hunting' was produced by the West Indian Standing Conference to prove this. The Police Federation denied it. Police harassed our home entertainments. Parents became anxious about an education system which they had once believed was superior to what they had left behind and which they now found wanting. Historically attached to education as a means of social mobility since the destruction of slavery in the 1830s, the black parent now had to reorient herself/himself to the experience of schooling in Britain. The black children's experience of schooling led to their rebellion against school, against their parents when they failed to understand, and society as a whole. But it was through the organisations which were first established that the struggles were fought, these community organisations which at the moment of crisis in 1958/59 joined to form the West Indian Standing Conference.

What I have to say now must be regarded as very important, politically and socially. It was through these same organisations that the group trips back to the Caribbean were organised. This was a novel emigration from the Caribbean, constantly in touch with its roots and interacting with the population at home, helping the youth and workers there to understand the nature of imperialism abroad. Not like the forced emigration from Africa, cut off at source. It was in the mid-1960s that the black youth intervened politically and pushed black politics and resistance in a more radical independent direction. From the visit of Stokely Carmichael in the summer of 1967 came the UCPA, the Black Panther Movement which later became the Black Workers Movement, the BUFP, the Black Workers Coordinating Committee, the BLF. There was also RAAS, the Black Dimension, Black Eagles and an important newspaper at that time, *The Hustler*.

Experience with revolutionary white left organisations, up to that time, had convinced black activists who had joined them, that they were petty bourgeois dominated. These organisations had the habits and prejudices of that group and were unable to grasp the issues about the wageless black youth, racism and education and amongst the working class; they were chronically racist themselves, sometimes in an unconscious way like the rest of the society. There was no turning back from independent revolutionary black politics.

By the end of the 1960s – 1969 to be exact – the Black Education Movement, the Black Schools Movement, CECWA (Caribbean Education and Community Workers' Association) had got under way. The publication of *How the West Indian Child is Made Educationally Sub-normal in the British Schooling System*, by Bernard Coard, exposed schooling for what it was, like the black youth had already exposed the police and the courts to society as a whole. The two movements did not coalesce. The black youth political organisations took up the issues raised by the Black Education Movement. The two movements coincided in some of their views and in the issues to be tackled but they travelled independent paths.

The Way Forward

What is new today is the decline of the black youth political organisations and the rise of internal neo-colonial practices directed at blacks, workers and middle strata, through the NCCI (National Committee for Commonwealth Immigrants), later to become the CRC, and soon to be the RRC – police liaison systems being one clear example.

And now emerging from all those struggles and experiences has come the Black Parents' Movement, which, so far, has attempted to form an unconditional alliance with the combative black youth – the students, the waged and the wageless unemployed in their daily struggles against the police, the schools and the state. This new movement suffers from some of the same ideological weakness which we have experienced in the Caribbean and here. And *Race Today*, in the last two years, has been foremost in attempting to clarify these experiences ideologically so that we can collectively struggle and find our way forward.

The weakness of the black workers' struggles, so far, does not reside in a lack of conception of their sense of power. This historic sense of power and organisation has scored many victories here in the courts, in the schools, in employment, in various kinds of activities and institutions we have established etc. Our weaknesses are those of the past carried over into the present.

The important struggle we have before us is a struggle over ideology. It is no longer enough to respond against the individual grievance but to be clear that the individual grievance is part of a system of grievances with which we are familiar. And that those grievances are not individual acts of oppression simply, but part of a system of oppression which we must oppose and destroy root and branch, here and in the Caribbean.

The black workers are not yet attuned to a sense of struggle for power in this society. The way forward by now must be clear from our anti-colonial and anti-imperialist radical and revolutionary struggles at home. And now here. It will involve class struggle within each ethnic group and across ethnic groups as in the Caribbean; and simultaneously within and across nationalities – English, Irish, Scottish, Welsh and other minorities. The left groups in Britain, dominated by an unconscious racism, what we called a certain kind of political symbolism used as cosmetics, ignored and failed to support nationalist demands in Britain. That can no longer be ignored.

A revolutionary nationalism *will* emerge in Scotland and Wales as it already has in Ireland, as it emerged in Vietnam and in the Caribbean. The multi-ethnic, multi-national, revolutionary class alliance will emerge not only from what revolutionary blacks do, but from what others do as well. Guinea Bissau, Mozambique, Angola are examples of how such alliances are formed and triumph.

Nearly all modern European states are multi-ethnic, multi-national societies, centralised. Our international perspective, the black international perspective, will derive from what I have called elsewhere the 'Black People in the World' condition. It's our experience here in Britain which shaped this development. But it will be bolstered by our relationships with Caribbean/Black communities in Canada, the US and of course in the Caribbean. We blacks have been the leavening for a new perspective in Britain. And it is what Aimé Césaire, the poet, calls our total vision from below that has enabled us to behave here in Britain, in the US, Canada and Africa like we have so far.

'WE ARE THE MAJORITY AT FORD'S'
Race Today, November 1976

Of the 23,000 workers at the Ford's Dagenham estate 60% are black – West Indian and Asian. In the Body Plant we are 70% of the labour force of 6,000 workers. And in the Paint, Trim and Assembly Plant (PTA) we are 60% of a labour force of 5,000 workers. The car industry, for the capitalists, is a major source of wealth and power in the international economy. It is equally so for the British section and Ford's is King in Britain.

The production of cars at Ford's Dagenham estate brings wealth and power to some 40 other industries whose products are essential to the production of the motor car.

It is not only the capitalist who derives power from the car industry. At Dagenham, the sole power is not Henry Ford. To be in the majority at such a crucial point in the national economy is not only to have power against the Ford management, but also to be powerful in relation to those who govern us. Ford's Dagenham has now to be added to the various points of power we have accumulated in Britain, from which we launch the struggle to win what we need here in Babylon.

And the black workers at Ford's Dagenham estate are at the centre of the rebellion taking place here. We introduced ourselves to the nation on the night shift of Tuesday, September 28, 1976. The night shift clocked in at 9.45 pm. This is the Body Plant. 4,000 black workers have left their homes in the black community for the wage the eight-hour shift would bring them. For the next eight hours, the workers would press and assemble the body of the motor car – doors, roofs, wing and floor panels.

By 11.30 pm, the rumour is in circulation that there is a dispute among the door-setters. There are 12 door-setters on the night shift (B-shift). The management has tried to introduce new equipment on this section, even though it was agreed years ago that no new techniques are introduced on the night shift. In short, the door-setters are asked to do more work for the same money. They refuse it.

The management resurrects the old weapon. They must divide the door-setters from the rest of the workers in the Body Plant. It is layoff time. The entire plant is ordered home. They will only be paid for the hours they have worked. It is past midnight now and transportation from the company estate to the black community is at a minimum. It is naked punishment – all night in the plant and no wages to show for it.

The shop stewards, elected shop-floor representatives of the Transport and General Workers Union, call a meeting. Not much is resolved here. Attempts are made to close the gates and have a sit-in organised. And then it all exploded. Cups from the canteen are thrown at management officials. They flee. Fires are lit and two post office vans are overturned. The directors' dining room is smashed to smithereens. Police and firemen arrive and the men refuse to let them in. Hoses are turned on the police. The windows of the administrative block are broken and equipment destroyed. At the end of it all management gives an estimate – £20,000 worth of damage.

The following is a diary of subsequent events:

Wednesday, September 29
Day shift refuses to come out in support of night shift workers. The night shift has a meeting and rejects management proposals. A strike is on.

Tuesday, October 12
Back to work.

Thursday, October 14
Four part workers are sacked for their involvement in the riot. 72 men stop work.

Friday, October 15
72 men return and a strike call is rejected. Another man is sacked and five are suspended without pay for five days. This brings the total of dismissals to five and suspensions to seven. Eight door-hangers come out in support.

Monday, October 18
Seven door-hangers who come out in support are sacked as fears of further layoffs increase.

Monday, November 17
A report appears that Paul Thornborough, a 'scab' who did one of the door-hanging jobs, is expelled from the TGWU. In effect this means that he cannot work at Ford's.

'Since January 1973, the men in the PTA have been laid off 35 times! Very large numbers of workers have left Fords, in disgust at the loss of earnings due to frequent layoffs – but among those who remain, the anger is building up. At the moment there is an official strike call in the PTA Plant to get a new layoff agreement. The demand has come up in the factory for 40 hours pay, work or no work. The demand has come directly from workers.' – PTA Convenor

The fight against layoffs is an old one, going back 20 years. There is a dispute between management and a section of workers in the plant and all the workers are sent home without pay. The workers have, through their representatives, demanded a guaranteed wage, work or no work. It is this struggle that the black workers have taken up.

'WHAT'S TO BE DONE WITH POWELL?'
Race Today, February 1977

Powell is the one politician in Britain who has a battery of amplifiers and an army of shorthand writers to transmit and record his cries from the wilderness of political isolation. Time and again he returns to the theme of immigration, and the theme of the political threat posed by the existence of black people in the cities of Britain and in key sections of the British economy. He is the one voice among the party politicians of Britain on whom the lessons of Notting Hill and the political potential of the uprising of black workers is not lost.

Listen to the man: 'The coloured population of over two million ... which is predominantly concentrated in the central areas of the metropolis and other key urban and industrial centres of England does possess ... a power which would not accrue to a mere random sample of two million persons similarly located but not perceived or perceiving themselves as distinct from the rest.'

Enoch has not always sung this hymn to black political power. As a Minister in the pre-Labour government of the '50s and early '60s, Powell's Ministry of Health was actually responsible for importing and maintaining blacks from the West Indies, from India and Pakistan in the National Health Service. In 1964, when the Immigration Bill, which limited and controlled the movement of workers from the ex-colonies to the homeland of capitalism, was being debated, Powell was silent. Then, in 1968 he made his 'rivers of blood' speech, attempting to tap, in the mass of the working class, those elements of opinion and support which would attack black people, our presence and our rights in this country, in a nationalist revival.

Today, Powell is not dreaming a nightmare. He is not conjuring from a fevered imagination the blood that may stain the green grass of England's pleasant land. He is describing, as an enemy describes, the strength of a section of the working class which has proved its ability and intention to turn this potential into visible and viable political power. Listen again: 'I have been describing the forces which invest the New Commonwealth immigrant and immigrant-descended population in England with the sort of power which cannot, in the nature of things, remain unexerted. The consequences of New Commonwealth immigration are not static, they are dynamic ... The picture is not that of a province or corner of the country occupied by a distinct and growing population, though that would be perilous enough. It is of the occupation, more and more intense, of key areas – and, it may be added, of key functions – in the heartlands of the Kingdom.'

Powell makes it clear, to critics and admirers alike, that he acknowledges this power of black people with extreme reluctance. The antidote for him is the force of white nationalism that exists in the working class. There are two alternatives he poses, to this drive of black working-class power: the state must take a stand and not be driven to affording the black population any concessions, real or sham. It must make no acknowledgement or concessions through fear. The frustrations of the white working class must be turned into a movement to stop the blacks.

Harping on the second and final solution, Powell predicts 'civil war'. The whites must not join us in our assault on the police in Notting Hill, in our demand for an extension of the social wage, in the struggle around housing, in our refusal to do shit work, in our opposition to the social contract in industrial employment. They must fight us. They must not stand by bemused or confused by the battle, between blacks and the state. They must unite behind the slogan to chuck us out of the country so as to promote the conditions for civil war and heavy state intervention.

Apart from this call to civil war, Powell has nothing to offer the white masses whom he addresses through the loudhailers of the British press. His economic policy of the nineteenth-century free market cuts no ice. As an Irish MP (he represents the protestants of South Down at Westminster), he has failed to represent the anti-British sentiments of the Irish Protestant members of the Westminster Parliament who want to break away from direct British rule. He is the most popular leper in Conservative politics, flirting through his black speeches, with fringe groups like the National Front, who draw power from his sentiments, and votes from his endorsements of their programmes of repatriation.

Powell has been the most famous loser in the Conservative Party, refusing to serve under Heath, being denounced now by the newcomers in Conservative politics such as Winston Churchill Jr. who have accepted the influence of the black vote in their constituencies and are seeking to organise it under Conservative Asian and West Indian leadership.

What's to be done about Powell? Various organisations within the race relations industry have called for his prosecution under the Race Relations Act. A Labour MP has construed his words as provocation likely to lead to a breach of the peace. The editorials in the press, following his speech, concluded that Powell had put himself beyond the pale of respectable politics and debate by seeking to stimulate antagonism between blacks and whites.

And yet, prosecutions under any Act will not stop Powell. Neither will denunciations of his logic in the *Guardian* or criticisms of his views in the *Spectator*. Here is a man whose political power and future depends on the white working-class reaction to his call to arms, against the black population. He has described the potential of the black movement in terms which no politician has dared to use. The defeat of Powell means the defeat of the nationalism that is still part of the exploitable cultural consciousness of sections of the white working class. That defeat cannot be brought about by any 'ideological' effort, by any 'raising of consciousness' through leaflets and resolutions. It can only be brought about when white workers recognise, as a contribution to their own struggles, the power, the method, the very mood of blacks who make a move on the streets of Notting Hill, in the Asian ghettoes of London, on the shop floors of factories, in the industrial centres of Babylon.

'ENTER MRS THATCHER'
Darcus Howe, February 1978

The following speech was delivered by Darcus Howe at the public meeting held to commemorate the first anniversary of the Bradford Black Collective.

I do not believe there is anybody in this room, who can recall a moment in the history of our presence in this country, when the political focus of the entire nation has been trained so mercilessly and murderously on blacks. That is the moment in which we live, and that is the moment I want to assess.

It is difficult in these matters to say when and where it all started, but we have got to grasp a moment to see and understand the reality of our present position.

Right Wing Groups

About four years ago, there emerged in this society a cluster of political groups, whose one linkage between themselves was that they wanted blacks out of this country. You had the National Front, you had the British Movement, you had a party in Leeds, another in Blackburn and so on; but the one unifying link between them was the fact that they wanted to inflict political punishment on the black community in this country. They would hold demonstrations; some of their thugs would attack you at night when you are walking the streets; they would carry slogans saying your head is smaller than theirs and therefore you are inferior; they would contest some elections; they got some votes. They won one local councillor out of that whole organised formation. I think he was Kingsley Read in Blackburn. I'm not sure, correct me if I'm wrong. They didn't seem to be getting much support. In politics, if you are in one of those organisations I have described, one thing you aim to achieve is political power on the terrain in which you organise. They didn't seem likely to win political power in the near future.

There emerged some whites, who said that these groups are a cancer on the body politic, and they must be attacked, and if they demonstrated they must be fought. That is what has been called the 'anti-fascist movement'. We intervened, now and then. In Lewisham, there were some young blacks who threw some stones. In Wolverhampton, when the young blacks in the club heard that the National Front were coming to pay them a visit, they waited, and the Front didn't come. The youths said, 'well, if you ain't coming, we are going to look for you'. Those were the major interventions, not the whole black community, not everybody, but it seemed we had a measure of that situation and the groups didn't appear, as a body of people, likely to hold the reins of political power in this country ...

Thatcher And the Labour Party

Enter Mrs Thatcher, and the entire political atmosphere is transformed. She is the leader of the Conservative Party that is in opposition in the House of Commons, and she is likely to hold the central reins of political power in November. She has got behind her a national organisation that is steeped and deeply rooted in the British political tradition. She has blonde hair and blue eyes. She will be able to set in motion the armed forces of the state. She will be able to legislate sanctions against us. A lot of people in her political organisation would have gone to university, and have brothers and sisters and cousins who are at the head of the British military. If you go through MI5 and MI6, she will have some connections there. You have to know in politics whom you are dealing with. I want this meeting to be clear, Madam Chair, about precisely what we are up against.

She has got some connections in the White House with the peanut man up there; she has got some friends who are prime ministers of different countries all over the world, and she is a part of an organisation with international links. So when she talks, know precisely that is what is in the background.

Then, there is the Labour Party. She has got them too. I don't believe there is any person in this room who could be sincere that the Labour Party would be a vehicle for our freedom. I have observed one thing about politics in Britain in regard to blacks. The Labour Party, because it says it is for the working class, and because we are working class, can't initiate certain things. They get the Tories to do it and then follow them afterwards. The first time that we were seriously attacked in this country was with the passing of the first Immigration Act, legislated by a Conservative government. The Labour Party, in opposition, said, 'we won't have anything to do with that, you are anti-black, you don't like black people and we are for them.' Immediately they got into power, they passed another Immigration Act. She has got them too. They might not have as many friends as she has got in the military, and in the armed sections of the state, but they have got some people who live next door to you, they've got some power inside the factory where you work, they've got some power inside the community where you live. So you are dealing with two political organisations, one which is very clear that it is against you, the other, which is posing as though it is for you, but you know is against you. And now, the Liberal Party. We don't have to talk about them because, like the National Front, they are a bit remote from state power. You have these three organisations, therefore, and a cluster of political groups. I believe those to be the array of forces, political forces, that are now trained against us.

In The Beginning

I do not want people to believe, nor will I ever propagandise that it began with the forces I have been describing. If you believe that it began with this lot, you know what you are likely to say: 'Margaret Thatcher is evil, so is Jim Callaghan, so is Steel in the Liberal Party and Kingsley Read and John Tyndall, and if we get some nice people, everything is going to be alright.' I don't want you to believe that: 'That if we get some blacks and put them in the exact positions where those people are, everything is going to be alright.'

I don't want you to believe that. The only way you could go beyond that is if you understand that what we are dealing with is a system of exploitation of which those are only the political organisers. And if you are to recall your own history, you would have met them before. I am addressing this meeting in English. I never knew any other language. It means I have been around these people all my life. This is not the first time that we are in confrontation with them. This is not the first time that they are focusing on us, oh no, not at all. You must recall the past, specifically to understand that this is but another stage in the implementation of a system of economic exploitation over blacks.

Only white workers believe, and I am always astounded that they do, that the people who have been governing them in Parliament governed them alone. How many of you here are old enough to remember carrying a flag in the colonies on the Queen's birthday, and the Union Jack on Empire Day and so on? These people governed large sections of the globe and we were all subjects in that system of exploitation. I believe that our presence in this country today is a direct result of that relationship. Maggie Thatcher, I knew her before. She was Baldwin, she was Churchill, she was Ramsay McDonald, she was Ernest Bevin, she was all those in the history of our constant struggles against them. Sometimes we won a bit, other times we lost, but it is a struggle which has been going on for a very long historical period. This is only another stage. It seems to me, Madam Chair, we've got to recall a moment when we clashed with them before because I believe the present political climate indicates that we are clashing with them again.

Throughout Bradford, you will find people who have been directly involved in past struggles against the political organisers of our exploitation. Bradford is an area to which people came from Dominica and Jamaica. On the Asian side, from Pakistan. It used to be India before. And I'm going to point to a particular struggle to show you how our presence here is a direct result of the constant warfare that has been going on since British capital set in motion international black labour. And I don't want to go too far back because I'm not an anthropologist. I will refer, simply, to the period just before and after the Second World War. I know that is pretty far back for some of you, but I'm 35 today and I could go back that far.

If you are living on Manningham Lane and you came from a place called Azad Kashmir, you would have been, before and after the Second World War, the owner of a piece of land, five acres in size. You and your family, your uncles and aunts etc. would be working the land for a portion of the day, selling some of the food, buying some clothes and other commodities. And then, for another portion of the day, you would be working for a landlord who owned a larger tract of land, and he would pay you nothing and give you very little. If you were in Kingston, Jamaica, you would be living among thousands of people in a sea of unemployment. If you were lucky and you had a job, the wages would be minimal. There was no welfare state in those parts. If you were ill, you couldn't go to the doctor and tell him, 'I'm registered with you.' Or, when you got a prescription, you couldn't go to the chemist and say, 'I'm only paying you 10p!' 'No way!' If you were in Dominica those were the circumstances, and apart from the economic circumstances under which you lived in those days, there was also an assassination of your spirit.

Defeat and Demoralisation

Out of those circumstances, there developed a movement which challenged the British. There was no Parliament. If you were in India there was a viceroy; in Africa and the Caribbean, a governor. He was in charge. Nobody could vote against him. Nobody could prolong a bill as they do in Parliament nowadays. Nobody could put him in the dispatch box and ask him any questions. He was in charge. And when you rebelled against his rule, as they did before and after the Second World War, he would hardly listen to you. He would call Britain and they would, in turn, decide to send some warships. That's what happened. It was not like Jack Jones who today walks into 10 Downing Street for discussions with the Prime Minister. You didn't negotiate anything in those days. Guns and no talk. You couldn't organise a trade union. Sometimes, he declared a state of emergency, and you couldn't walk in groups of more than four, so if you had a big family, who was going to church on Sunday, one walked in front, one behind and some trailed at the back. That was the arrangement.

We carried out a merciless struggle against the colonial state. That was the independence movement, the nationalist movement. We fought for political control of our own destinies. The viceroy went and the governor went, and they got some blacks from within those societies to put in their places. No white person is the prime minister of Dominica, or Jamaica, or Trinidad. But the unemployment continues, the problem with the piece of land continues – remember I talked about the man in Azad Kashmir – and, instead of calling for the warships from Britain, they have an army and some police recruited from the local population who would shoot you down.

Nothing changes, but nothing stands still. The exploitation is more murderous, it is more vicious. Instead of them declaring the state of emergency, where you had to walk in a group no more than four, today, some of them are telling you 'don't walk at all'. We lost that struggle. We were defeated. Nobody believes that I left Port of Spain, Trinidad, to come to Britain because I liked the Mother Country. Only Judge McKinnon believes that. We were defeated and demoralised. You know what demoralised means. You say, 'Oh God, ah give up, ah take too much blows.' That's why we are here. Our presence here is as a result of a demoralisation and a defeat. It is a direct consequence of our struggle for independence and against exploitation. The same conditions that we fought against persist in those territories in a worse and more vicious form. You have some measure therefore of why we came.

I want to deal with the question, to do what? In Britain, during that period when we were suffering that demoralisation and defeat, you would have heard from an employer in the Midlands, who owned a factory where he employed and exploited a lot of people, that he couldn't get a one-armed, one-legged man to work for him. Some economists called it a shortage of labour. You know what was happening in Britain? A worker walks into a factory, he works for a week. The foreman tells him something he doesn't like and he would reply, 'You get lost, piss off, here is my notice.' The worker knew that he could go to another factory further along the road and get a job. It means that right here in Britain, white workers were in a pretty strong position. Employers would offer £40 a week, the worker would say 'No, I'm going up the road, I'm going to get £60 a week.' Where do you find a body of demoralised and defeated workers and peasants to attack and undermine the position of strength that white workers had arrived at? From the Caribbean, from Azad Kashmir, from Dominica, from Kingston, Jamaica, from Port of Spain, Trinidad, and certain parts of Africa. That was the stage that was set.

I want to describe to you what it was like to come defeated. I interviewed a young man from Azad Kashmir in 1974. I asked him what was his work situation like when he first came to Britain. He said, 'Listen, I thought of my boss as a big man who could do a lot of things to people.' He likened the boss to his landlord for whom he worked for a portion of the day in Azad Kashmir, the feudal lord who had the power of life and death over him.

I worked as a postman on a big shop-floor situation in central London. And could some of you youngsters believe what I once experienced. A white man, the foremen, one day, for no reason, threw some letters on the floor and said to me, 'pick them up boy' – I bent down and picked them up. You were frightened to play. You met a policeman in the street who said, 'you come here boy' and you went running, not because you believed you were inferior, but that is a consequence of a defeat and demoralisation. You had no choice. When we came off the boats at Southampton, we didn't walk into council houses. My room was so small I couldn't even change my mind in it, and the rent I was paying was so large I couldn't change my mind in the post office. That was the situation. I want to get into some slight political theory about that. You know what that means, when you are doing anything for your employer, at any time, and at any speed? He makes a lot of wealth off of you. And where, in this society, the government raises revenue from that wealth to spend on council housing, they didn't have to spend it on you because you were living in a room. And we didn't have many children around in those days, so they didn't have to spend it on the children for education. And even if you were sick, you would drink some bush tea sent over from home, and were frightened to go to the doctor. So in that period, as a result of our defeat in the nationalist struggles at home, there was this enormous creation of wealth in Britain on the backs of blacks. That is the system of exploitation that I am talking about.

Our Recovery and Their Fight Against It

I want to go a little further. The whites you were working with, a very small minority would take your side, and the rest of them felt privileged that they got and you didn't. Every single government, during our presence here, has been able to mobilise white workers on the basis of the little petty privileges that they get over blacks. That's the position that we have been in. I began with a system of exploitation. I go a little further now and call it a system of colonial exploitation. They once colonised us in Azad Kashmir, and in some village in Africa, but they are colonising us now 15 miles from Downing Street, and 200 yards from the Town Hall. And wherever we struggled against that system, there is one distinctive position that we must maintain, that we had to come through on our own – as blacks, independent. We would have loved some help from white workers. Didn't get it. Little clubs here, social groups there, attempts at political organisation, moving from the position of running when police called to demonstrating and laying siege to police stations. Moving from picking up those letters off the floor to the editorship of *Race Today*, and one of the most serious political thorns in their side. That is how we have moved over the years, and the main vehicle for that movement is our willingness to say no, and to develop an independent movement against it. Nobody could question me on that. It is the independent struggle of blacks in this country which has eased us from that position. So I'm talking about moving from picking up the letters, from seeing my boss as someone big who could do a lot of things to people, to the Grunwick strike and the campaign to free George Lindo. That is the span of history we have created in this country. And just as we begin to see the end of the tunnel, enter Mrs Margaret Thatcher to put us back precisely where we were before.

What is that lady saying? I'm living at no. 11 and I've got a white friend who is living at no. 13. We work in the same factory. We leave to go to work in the morning, and every day we work, and so on, and holiday time comes and my white friend goes on a holiday. If he meets a senorita in Spain, or a belle in Paris, or a fraulein in Germany, he wants to bring her back here to marry her, OK, but if you are black and you want to go to Bangladesh for your bride, or Dominica, no way. That's what she's saying. They have gone a little further, others of her ilk. A ruling by this Labour government goes a little further. They are saying that my workmate has three white kids here and I've got three black kids in the Caribbean, he could claim child benefit and tax allowances for his three, as he is white, and if you're black, you can't.

I want to go into how she's advancing her position. I've lived in this country for 17 years, and I feel I know a little about British politicians. On any issue, when you see them speaking on television, they say 'this is the issue, this is my programme and policy, I have done some research, this is what I'm against, and this is what I want to do.'

When Mrs Thatcher enters, she deviates from that tradition altogether. When you are declaring war, serious war, you don't tell the enemy what your strategy is, you try to be as mysterious as ever, and what you put in its place is a political atmosphere. You have everybody jumping and nobody knows where you're coming from. And that is what that woman has done. She says, simply, I know there are too many blacks in this country. She couldn't tell you how many must go or how many must come, how many of us have children in the West Indies and what she is going to do about it. Who wants to marry whom, when and where, and how many are going to come and go. She hasn't said a single word about that. All she has done is to create a political atmosphere to challenge the black community and invent tactics and issues as she goes along. It's warfare. You have to know when someone is fighting a serious war against you or when they're playing out to win an election. I separate myself tonight from any notion that her talk is simply about winning an election. She is against a community that is no longer willing to live in the room, traipse after the police, no longer willing to do their bidding so that they could create the wealth. We are no longer that defeated, demoralised working class. That is what she wants to attack.

On Organisation

Madam Chair, I believe I could divine the political moment. She has got a fight on her hands. I told you she came with warships when she was Churchill and Baldwin. I believe, today, accompanying her is likely to be a military struggle. Ireland is not so far from Bradford, and I believe the black community should now be preoccupied with the building of disciplined political organisation to counter that threat. If I didn't believe that we could do it successfully, I would pack my clothes and go home. We have to think about these matters. I'm not asking you to go outside and form an army, but I'm posing it as a matter for thought and development.

We know now what she has got at her disposal in order to take us back to the colonial conditions of yesteryear. What have we got? I believe we have got a sentiment and an undoubted capacity to say no. I believe we are weak on organisation. And that is not a matter of colour. These are matters which are historically caused and can be historically cured. The highest form we have reached in organisation is the Campaign Against Racial Discrimination of the early sixties. There were black workers, some white trade unionists, some white professionals, some black professionals, in the organisation. We had contacts in the Caribbean, we had contacts in our places of origin. That's the furthest we have reached, and that organisation collapsed. There are two things I want to extricate from the collapse.

One, that the leadership of that organisation consisted of white and black middle-class professionals, and the working class, the ordinary people, followed. Secondly, there were whites in that organisation who believed that we didn't have any experience at all, and what experience we may have had was not valid, and that they should dictate the terms and pace of our struggle. When you are looking back into history, you have to see what were your weak points, and when you are surfacing again, you decide what you want to mend.

After that period, there emerged a lot of small Black Power groups all over the country, and I want to extract one experience from that. We talked a lot, but didn't have a measure of political direction, and historical understanding. That's our history in fighting back organisationally.

Bradford Black and *Race Today*, in approaching Political Organisation, have those extractions as central to our minds. The black working class insofar as Bradford Black and *Race Today* Collective are concerned, will always be in charge. If you are a black professional, you could join and do a lot of things, but you are going to be under the leadership of the working class or leave it alone. We are not going to make that mistake again. And in our alliance and relationships with whites, we are not going to hear any rumour even that our experiences are not valid. So that in the *Race Today* Collective and Bradford Black Collective, there are these principles by which we live: the black working class will be in charge, and that the black struggle has an independence, validity, and vitality of its own.

When we celebrate today, we celebrate the fight against colonialism and we point to what we are doing in both Collectives to be a stage in the organisational development of that fight.

Long live Bradford Black, Long live *Race Today*, and forward to an international organisation, from Bangladesh to Port of Spain, from Jamaica to Canada, and the United States where our brothers and sisters have emigrated, right throughout to Britain. Forward to an international organisation that would finally break the back of colonial exploitation forever!

Thank you Madam Chair.

'BUILDING THE MASS MOVEMENT'
Race Today, August–September 1982

In the last 18 months, the black community posed three major questions to the rulers of this society. The first was quite specific. What caused the fire which destroyed the lives of 13 young blacks at 439, New Cross Road on 18 January 1982? The question was not politely posed, nor was it raised in the formal and discreet lobbying of parliamentarians. Some 15,000 blacks marched across London in order that our concerns and genuine fears be brought before the whole society. Police investigations, the coroner's inquest into the cause of the deaths and finally judicial proceedings before the High Court failed to provide any satisfactory answers. More than that, all these investigative and judicial activities were replete with chicanery, vacillation, incompetence and coarse political manoeuvre. To date, the parents and relatives of the dead and the black community are no wiser.

The second issue was raised with equal dynamism and vigour. What is to be done about the British police who have for 25 years trampled wildly over the rights of the black community? For several weeks last summer, thousands of young blacks firebombed their way into the headlines as they attacked and fought the police in every major city in England. Our rulers called Lord Scarman to enquire. His report was lame as it was tame. Even so, 'the authorities' have vacillated over every single one of his recommendations. One year later, no one could identify any fundamental attempt on the part of the authorities to respond to the genuine grievances of the black community on this score. Again, vacillation punctuated by crude violence characterises the state's response.

Thirdly, implicit in the uprising of last summer is the question, what is to be done about the plight of young blacks? An entire generation has been consigned to wagelessness and social misery. While government ministers lie and cheat about the impending economic upturn, this vibrant social force, stimulated by all the material gloss of modern society, are offered police and more police. Thousands of black youth have grown into their teens aware of no other social force but the Special Patrol Group, the Vice Squad, the Regional Crime Squad and now the riot police.

Police apart, thousands are now dragooned into the meaningless and sterile work experience of the Manpower Services Commission. Leading economists have identified this mass unemployment as permanent. They tell us that modern technology applied to production means less labour and more advanced machinery and this trend is now evident in several industries. To young blacks, this government has offered no policy for incorporating their energies and creative capacities into the development of British society.

The situation assumes greater complexity with the sterile bankruptcy of the other parliamentary parties. Where do we go from here? Or perhaps where do we begin? We begin as we must with the mass of ordinary working people. We hold to the view that only a mass movement, sweeping all before it, can attempt to resolve these issues.

And such a movement is on the agenda in the Britain of today. The evidence is there for all to see. Blacks are in complete revolt and everyone is aware of it, as they are aware of the fact that at any moment the slightest incident could trigger off an explosion which would bring the army on to the streets of England. The Irish continue, without respite, the armed struggle against the British Army. Voices within the white working class call for a political strike to bring the government down, though not stating what will take its place. And these voices are not without significant support in the population. Then there is the militant opposition among health workers, stirrings among the miners, water workers and other proletarians.

Therein resides the beginnings of a mass movement in Britain. At this stage, it is the responsibility of political militants to assist in strengthening that movement, assist in developing it to new and more powerful stages. We in *Race Today* are dedicated to that task.

'BLACK REPRESENTATION IN THE LABOUR PARTY'
Race Today, September–October 1984

The Labour Party goes to Conference in October with much on its plate and little appetite for the tasks at hand. The leadership, whose major reason for existing is the political defeat of the Thatcher government, can hardly be said to be in the vanguard of that struggle.

The party has been completely displaced by the National Union of Mineworkers and its leadership overtaken by Arthur Scargill. It is commonplace that those of us who are either actively or otherwise hostile to the Thatcher government look to the miners and their leadership as the major force which could, at a minimum, achieve the demoralisation of the Conservative government. It is ironic that Kinnock et al. will only retain some semblance of authenticity in the current political struggle if the miners are defeated.

Another time bomb ticks slowly but surely beneath the seats of the Labour Party leadership. Among the resolutions which will be before the conference, 13 of those demand an amendment to the Party's Constitution. The amendment calls for the legitimisation of black sections in the party. Like the trades unions and women, blacks are demanding representation as blacks in the highest echelons of the party.

This is a new development and can be understood only in the context of the tremendous social explosions in the UK involving blacks in the last three years or so.

There was the mass demonstration on the New Cross issue followed by the uprising against the police in 1981. Much more lies beneath the surface, which can come to the fore with great force and power at anytime. It is on the strength of this movement that those blacks in the Labour Party are making their bid for power. The strength of the movement only explains why the blacks in the Labour Party have chosen to move at this time. It does not explain their particular reasons for their dissatisfaction.

Here goes. Blacks participate in almost every area of national life. We fight and die as members of the armed forces in the Falklands and Ireland; we produce and consume the commodities in several of the major industries in the country; we are active in most if not all the service industries in the urban centres; we are well represented in the professions. Yet, there is not a single black Member of Parliament out of 625 constituencies. Not one.

And the struggle has broken out in the Labour Party and not the Conservative Party, the Liberal or SDP because it is the Labour Party which blacks have always supported and continue to support.

It is a shame and a burning shame that after 25 years the Labour Party has not been able to find a single safe seat for one of its many black aspirants. We in *Race Today* are very reluctant to accuse others of racism, but when blacks in the Labour Party throw such an accusation at the party leadership we say that their case is strong, very strong indeed and consequently they have every right in the world to organise themselves to put that matter right.

Having said that, we now turn to the black organisation within the party. Whether they win the demand for a section is not too important; the fact is they are organised. This begs the question organised around what and for what? Merely to get a black person in Parliament? Such vulgar careerism will win little support among blacks who have already experienced in the colonies middle-class elements who have leapt to power and glory on their backs, only to turn savagely on those who they claim to represent initially.

Figure 1.2   Black People's Day of Action, 2 March 1981. Darcus Howe on a truck.

The alternative to careerism is a political approach and orientation in several areas of national policy. To date, not a single word has been spoken or written by the black sections in this regard.

How is the issue of mass structural unemployment to be resolved? Are we to demand jobs when technology is systematically displacing manpower, or are we to demand a shorter working week, a shorter working life and more leisure?

How is the Irish question to be resolved or is it that the Irish question is not the business of blacks?

Is the American military to be stationed in Europe forever either, with or without nuclear weapons?

Do Third World countries need the knowledge and discoveries of western civilisation? If they do, is this to be transferred by aid in its current form? If not, then how? These are some of the questions of our age and of the moment and pressing questions they are.

Unless the black groups in the party speak to these, they are clearly bound to be trapped within a series of racial squabbles and recriminations which take the rank and file in the black community and the population in the UK nowhere.

'THE NEW CROSS MASSACRE: WE WILL NEVER FORGET'
Linton Kwesi Johnson, January 1986

As 1985 draws to a close and Christmas and the New Year approaches, for some of us, there may be moments of sad reflection as we remember lost loved ones. The relatives of the 13 young blacks who died as a consequence of the suspected racially motivated arson attack on a birthday party at 439 New Cross Road, Deptford come to mind. For them and the survivors of the holocaust – indeed for the black population as a whole – January 18, 1986 will be a most significant date in the new year calendar, marking as it does the fifth anniversary of the New Cross Massacre.

It will be the eternal indictment of the police officers involved that, after nearly five years of 'investigation', no one has been charged. The case, as far as the police are concerned, is officially closed. On August 27, four-and-a-half years after the fire, New Scotland Yard issued a statement announcing that the Director of Public Prosecutions had 'decided there was insufficient evidence to charge anyone with any offence'. They gave as a reason for their failure the most facile of excuses: 'Police cannot force people to talk and the right to silence hampered the persistent efforts of the police to find the truth.' Anyone familiar with the facts of the fire and the way the police conducted their 'investigation' during those four-and-a-half years cannot help but conclude that the police statement was the final cherry on the cake in what the New Cross Massacre Action Committee has always maintained was an elaborate police cover-up:

To begin with, Mrs Amza Ruddock at whose house the party was held and who lost a daughter and son in the fire was told by two police officers that a firebomb caused the fire. Early press reports spoke of an arson attack. Evidence was found by the ground floor front room window of the house consistent with a firebomb attack. Moreover, eyewitness accounts pointed to a firebomb attack on the house. Before the investigation could get on the way, the police suddenly changed track, putting forward the idea that the fire could have started inside the house, ruling out the possibility of a racist attack.

The initial horror and anger of blacks up and down the country soon found organisational expression in the form of the New Cross Massacre Action Committee. The committee turned out to be the greatest mass movement of blacks Britain has ever seen. They adopted the slogans 'Thirteen Dead And Nothing Said', 'End Racist Attacks Now', 'We Demand Justice' and 'No Police Cover-Up', 'Blood Ah Go Run If Justice No Come' among others. They condemned the silence of official society on the deaths, demanded that the person or persons responsible for the fire be brought to justice and that the government and police do something about racist attacks and murders. A national mobilisation was set in motion for a Black People's Day of Action to let the government, police, racists, the nation and the world at large know that blacks were not prepared to take racist murders lying down.

The police, rather than concentrating their efforts on finding the arsonist, directed all their efforts at discrediting the New Cross Massacre Action Committee and the mass movement of blacks and began looking for a black scapegoat to charge with starting the fire. At first they arrested four black youths who were at the party and tried to frame them, arguing that the fire resulted from a fight between them. All the witnesses at the party denied that any fight took place at the party and the police were thwarted in their efforts to frame the youths by the New Cross Massacre Action Committee and the parents. In spite of the effort of the police to undermine the Black People's Day of Action, over 15,000 people from all over the country marched from 439 New Cross Road to Hyde Park on March 2, 1981, six weeks after the fire.

The inquest which followed two months later amounted to a complete travesty of justice. The coroner, a Mr Davis, took no notes throughout the hearing and made no attempt to conceal his bias towards the police line. The police for their part pursued the fight theory and completely obscured the forensic evidence of a firebomb, arguing that the seat of the fire was the centre of the room and not the front window as eyewitnesses had said. The parents and relatives of the dead and injured expressed their outrage and disbelief at the subsequent open verdict of the inquest jury. They immediately went to the High Court to get that verdict overturned and a new inquest. Chief Justice Lane was having none of it. He dismissed the police attempt at framing the youths as irrelevant.

Since the inquest in May 1981 the police, aided and abetted by their friends and agents in Fleet Street, have been engaged in a shameful campaign of disinformation, lies and innuendos in an attempt to confuse the parents of the dead and injured and public alike. They tried to vilify Mrs Ruddock and create divisions and confusion among the parents. Having failed to frame the four black youths with the fire, they then tried to implicate a man named Norman Higgins with a jealous lover motive for causing the fire. They said that they wanted Higgins for questioning but that he had absconded to the USA. Higgins returned and was not arrested, but the damage had already been done. Finally, they tried to hound to madness, Leslie Morris, a key eyewitness whose evidence contradicted the lines the police wanted to pursue.

All has not been negative. The Black People's Day of Action showed powerfully the ability of the black community to mobilise itself to take action in defence of our rights and our lives and has provided us with an organisational framework for future action. Secondly, the police were prevented from framing blacks for the fire and from making scapegoats out of us. Thirdly, the New Cross Massacre Action Committee succeeded in drawing national and international attention to the alarming increase in racist attacks and fascist murders against blacks and Asians and the police and government's indifference to them. The parents and relatives of the 13 dead and 26 seriously injured will never forget January 18, 1981. Black people in Britain will not forget the police cover-up. We will not forget the names Commander Stockwell, Sergeant Wilson and Superintendent Bell. We will never forget the New Cross Massacre.

2
Black Youth in Revolt

INTRODUCTION
Stafford Scott

I start this piece with an embarrassing confession; for as a young Black man in my teens in the mid- to late 1970s I did not read *Race Today* on a regular basis. In my defence I was born on these shores, and grew up in a time when the 'Black youth rebellion' against the 'racial prejudice' that was endemic in the UK was in full swing. As a result, I grew up following a path that my peers – those who had been educated in schools in the UK – had already begun to plough. That would be the rejection of all that was considered to be of white origins, because of the racism that came with it, in particular an education system that we believed was nothing like the '*equalizer*' in terms of the opportunities it would provide for us, that our parents' generation had been conned into believing that it would have been.

As a result, my first contact with the *Race Today* Collective was in March 1988. I recall this occasion well, for Brother Darcus Howe honoured me as I was one of the people to whom he was dedicating his latest book *From Bobby to Babylon*, a *Race Today* publication. At this point in time, I was one of the youth leaders on the Broadwater Farm estate in Tottenham and the spokesperson for the BWF Defence Campaign, an organisation set up in the aftermath of the Broadwater Farm uprising of October 1985 in which a police officer lost his life.

As a Defence Campaign, we campaigned against the overtly racist and violent nature of the police investigation into the October uprisings, arguing that self-defence was no offence; the Defence Campaign fought to provide support to those arrested, particularly to the Tottenham Six whom the state wanted to scapegoat for a cop's murder. But we were introverted and only recognised our own pain.

Meeting the *Race Today* Collective certainly helped me to better understand that the pain that Black youths were enduring in the UK was little different, if any, to the pain being suffered by millions in Africa, Asia and the Caribbean and all of the other colonies that made up the so-called 'Empire'. Although a most militant and radical group, the *Race Today* Collective were much more than rebels; they were our pioneers and renegades. Where we rejected the education system, they had already benefited from this learning in their homelands and were intent on putting it to good use now that they were in the 'belly of the beast', which some euphemistically called the 'motherland'. They had come together under the banner of socialism, in recognition of their shared history of resisting imperialism and colonialism in their homelands.

But whilst they spoke and wrote the language of Marxism they were able to deliver their messages in a style and with a voice that was distinct and politically Black in its messaging. They were able to write about the battles on the streets of the UK and link these revolts to the various insurrections happening elsewhere in the empire; thereby providing a political context and language that we could then use to understand and defend the uprisings that took place in the UK during the 1980s.

Their writings helped to ensure that the struggles of Black youths in Britain would be seen in the wider context of an oppressed people's continued fight against imperialism and colonial rule. Most importantly, for my generation, *Race Today* also gave a voice to the youth who were rebelling against the endemic racism that they found in British institutions. In the articles that follow under the headings of 'Youth in Revolt', *Race Today* shows an innate ability to not only describe to their readership the nature of the Black youth rebellion taking place on the UK's streets but they were able to give a political context in which the revolt was taking place. This was at a time when there were no Black or Brown politicians and such voices were seldom if ever heard in mainstream media. *Race Today* provided authentic voices of challenge, protest and demand!

Race Today helped us to better understand that the fight against apartheid in Soweto, South Africa was part of the same battle that we were having here in the UK. They taught us that it was 'one struggle, one fight' and that we had to be organised and strategic if we were to have a chance of winning.

They came to the locations where the uprisings/insurrections took place and reported from the very heart of the community that was under attack. But they were so much more than simply journalists and reporters; they helped to galvanize communities at a local level and built nationally by playing a leading role in bringing 20,000 Black people to London for the 1981 Black People's Day of Action. The articles that follow, on education, housing, employment and policing are as relevant and insightful today as they were when first written.

'THE BLACK EXPLOSION IN BRITISH SCHOOLS'
Farrukh Dhondy, February 1974

The presence of black children in British schools has posed a singular set of questions, the answers to which necessarily threaten the system they indict. The black child – his or her performance, behaviour and reaction to the schools – has taught the teachers and administrators a new kind of self-consciousness. That lesson is still in progress.

Black children, acting independently of the hopes and aspirations of their fathers and mothers, have caused the British state to think and rethink about how to control them. Various bodies working directly and obliquely for the state have tried to gauge the dimension and nature of the problem. The latest fact finders, the Parliamentary Select Committee on Race Relations, identify in their report their worries about the size of the problem, which they characterise as the provision of the black child's needs. They ask for more money to accelerate the socialisation of black children. The *Evening Standard*, paraphrasing the report, called the black children in schools a 'time-bomb': inaccurately, because above all British schools have recognised that the time is up and the bomb is sizzling.

State Initiatives to Black Rebellion

For a number of years, the initiative on the issue lay with the state. Successive governments felt confident that an old process of socialisation would work equally well on new material. They expected that the machine that had processed white labour power and passed it through the sieve of the meritocracy, would do the same for the blacks. It didn't. The black population, in two distinct steps, carried their opposition to the forms and functions of schooling through the cohesion of their communities into the schools.

As on other fronts, the action of the new section of the working class began with protest. Black parents complained about discrimination and lack of opportunity. The protest phase called attention to the phenomenon; the Labour government and associated agencies went into action to study it. The Select Committee had five successive briefs. The first was called 'problems of coloured school leavers'; then they tackled immigrant and police relations; the latest brief concerned schools themselves.

Why does the state see the relationship between itself and young blacks as worthy of so much attention? What does this attention focus on? Three times over the last few years the government has reviewed its policy of 'dispersal' of the black school population. In 1965, the Department of Education and Science instructed schools to keep the black influx to a maximum of a third of their intake. The directive resulted in black youth being sent to schools some distance away from their homes. In Haringey, the parents fought the decision tooth and nail and 'busing' became a British issue. The DES reversed its decision; schools were advised to extend their accommodation of black youth and find means to integrate them into the working class, to rely on the school system, with its 11+, streaming, exams, etc., to force the black section to find a level in the hierarchy of labour.

The latest report of the Select Committee recommends providing schools with enough money and powers to make the 'special' education of immigrants a priority, to teach them standard English, to teach them about 'their culture'. Why? Principally because without a renewed effort on the part of the schools' system, without tipping the balance of forces within the world of school, Britain cannot expect to contain the infectious resistance of black youth.

The black child is now classified as a special case. West Indian and Asian youth, by and large, do badly in school; they do worse in exams than the white working-class children with whom they are schooled. They are put in low streams and this produces bad behaviour.

Who rejects whom? Does the school reject black youth and give them places in low streams, fail them in tests, dissipate their interest in all forms of attainment associated with the classroom? Or does the black child reject what he or she learns of schooling through actual contact with it? The behaviour of black youth in reaction to the discipline machine can be called nothing less than a crisis of schooling.

The ESN Battleground

These questions have to be asked because they have been the centre of a controversy, the battleground for which is the high percentage of West Indian children in schools for the educationally subnormal (ESN). The ESN school is the point at which the function of schooling suffers maximum exposure. Bernard Coard, in one of the first serious exposures of this, examined the machinery by which black children find themselves classified as subnormal. The pivot of his argument was justice, and he posed it in terms of the language and culture bias of IQ testing. He was criticising the functionings of the school system rather than its actual function, so inevitably it led him to believe that the bias could be corrected by fairer testing. His conclusions are not only inconclusive, they are confused. In a later book, he offers a little nudge in the direction of correcting this by writing a 'Johnny and Jenny' book with black faces and black names, identifying the black Caribbean child as African, and in this way tackling, it must be assumed, what he saw as a crisis of identity.

Coard's contentions about cultural bias and 'middle-class' testing in no way explain the situation as it is in the schools. Undoubtedly the prejudices he exposes do exist, but they are not the root cause of the separation of working-class children, black and white, into clever and stupid, educable and ineducable. If we are to be severe, we can say that the whole question of performance is, at best, a symptom of the malaise; at worst, a red herring. Black youths' performance and behaviour in schools is not something produced merely by the content of textbooks or the alienated language of instruction, or the prejudice of the teachers. These are factors, but factors which have operated on white youth for a hundred years, if we recognise that Standard English is not in fact the mode of expression of the working class. The reaction of black youth to discipline, grading and skilling processes is substantially different and potentially more dangerous to schools. And it is precisely because the education of black youth starts and continues within the communities of which they are still a part.

Eysenck and cronies would have it that poor performance reveals what blacks are genetically capable of. Liberal educationists come closer by saying that poor performance is a product of deprivation – bad housing, hard-worked parents, and so on. They mistake strength for weakness.

The School and the Community

Recently, the Inner London Education Authority gave Tulse Hill, a comprehensive school in South London with an 80+ percentage of black students, £1,500 to convene a conference in Eastbourne to discuss the problem of black youth in the school. The most useful thing that came out of the conference was the fact that teachers, social workers, headmaster and all couldn't begin to speak about this without referring to the conditions within the community from which the pupils came. Brixton, the school's catchment area, has the largest population of black unemployed youth in the country. It also has a few labour exchanges offering varieties of jobs in London Transport. Clearly, there aren't very many takers; they refuse the work that society allocates to them.

Their rejection of work is a rejection of the level to which schools have skilled them as labour power, and when the community feeds that rejection back into the school system, it becomes a rejection of the functions of schooling. It is this rejection that causes the buyers of labour most anxiety, and it is in this context, that of labour and capital, in which we must set the black experience of schools.

Culture Means Political Identity

In this context, the commodities normally associated with 'education', such as culture, critical awareness, and so on, need to be re-examined. Education is a cultural weapon and to black people, culture means political freedom. For Asians and for Caribbeans in Britain, cultural identity has been an integrative force in their fight for democratic rights and in the extension of that fight, the assault on the way in which capital uses their labour. Language and tradition determined, to a large extent, the capability of the first generation of immigrants to respond to the organisation at their place of work, and in the meeting places and social institutions of their localities. At the lowest, but indicative level, the smell of cooking that floats into the street in black communities is banteringly referred to as 'culture'. More seriously, the Asians have carried out several successful struggles against managements, against repressive laws and against the reaction within their own unions, using only their common identity as an organisational force.

The Power of Language

The language of schools is an oppressive instrument. It does for the black what it has done for the working-class white, only more so. It is used as a basis for separating the various levels of skilled and unskilled workers that school produces. The principle is enshrined in the hierarchy of exams: the more job-worthy GCE O-level English is examined in essays, whereas the CSE works through 'multiple choice' questions in which memory and identification gain points and expression counts for less.

The culture of blacks, Asian or Caribbean, is capable of opposing this wedge of interests. To put it simply, if a large number of youth in a school speak only Punjabi or Gujarati, it becomes impossible to grade them into clever ones and thick ones. It becomes virtually impossible to treat them as anything but mass workers, produced to share a fate that they resent and defy.

There is little doubt that the second generation of Asian workers will learn more English than their parents. Life will produce the Gujarati cockney, and the school, whose function is to grade and divide, will speed up the process and use it. In one sense, this can be seen as progress. We cannot stand in its way, but must spell out its implications.

43

Forced to Fight

Teachers and teaching have attempted to assimilate the black explosion in the school, a process which has not been without pain or painstaking effort. All the jargon of the teaching world went through a sieve of redefinition. 'Motivation', 'relevance', 'pupils' needs', and even, 'intelligence', 'ability' and the other cliches demanded re-examination. In reacting against being the agents of racism, certain groups of teachers began to shake off the accusation and in order to do this had to react against the functions of schooling. It is no exaggeration to say that black youth have catalysed the creation of a forward section of teacher militants. Historically, the black influx and the move to comprehensives on a large scale came into schooling at approximately the same time. The need for cheap labour brought the first, and the need to solve the difficulties of producing all sorts of labour in one plant caused, or allowed, the second. The experience of black youth and the experience of the workers who teach them has been an exposure of the failure of the ideals that liberals act out for the comprehensive school.

The international black movement fermented a rejection of what Black Powerists referred to as white culture. The demand for Black Studies within the English school was a distillate of this ferment. At one stage, this demand became formalised and schools began introducing courses with that name. This was a change in what was dished out to black children as history and as 'relevant' material, and also a change in the attitude towards the response the black child gave. One teacher of English in a fairly mixed comprehensive (racially), talking about the stories a first-year class had written for him, said about the only Jamaican girl in his class: 'She writes in this delightful Creole, I never touch it with my red pen, it seems sacrilege to correct the vivacious flow.' He recognised her right to her language; but when he was asked if he corrected the spelling, syntax, or slang of the 29 working-class white kids in the form: 'Oh yes', he said, 'of course I do', and then: 'Hmmm yes, I see your point.'

Black Studies: A Battle for Minds

In providing Black Studies, schools hunted around for materials which were black. Studies gave rise to syllabuses and the impetus that gave rise to Black Studies drifted into the formalities of history and geography. Inevitably, this co-optation of the impulse and the demand killed the interest which black youth took in the 'subject'.

44

Schools saw Black Studies as a response to the needs of the black student, and now this very student was saying that he or she didn't need quite that. In some schools this led to interesting developments. At Tulse Hill, one of the first to introduce Black Studies, the class became a forum for a critique of problems faced by the black community, and in so doing became a potential political platform. The political answers which the discussions threw up seemed to take the blackness away from Black Studies. They became working-class studies and the potential nuclei for a battle of ideologies – cultural nationalism, Marxism, etc. Hand in hand with the metamorphosis of content, went the problem of who would contain the class, the curriculum, the organisation. Teachers handed it over to a committee of youth. The question of what was relevant passed, though not entirely, into the hands of the pupils.

Within the black population of large comprehensives, there is already the makings of a sort of black elite. The sixth forms of these schools, through the process of streaming and exams, are endowed with a breed of black pupils earmarked for this second-rate elitism. They are the good students, the tributes to the system, groomed for A-levels, perhaps, and for semi-professional destinies. Through dint of the interest they display, they become the controllers of the black programmes. Some of them will move on to university, some to train as teachers themselves, some will go on to be social workers and some will join the race relations industry proper. They aren't co-opted blacks, their socio-political interest is as yet undeclared and so still in the balance.

The curriculum of Black Studies is to an extent a fight for their minds. Clearly, the state sees them as the potential uniters of the black section of the population. But it is also from this section that the administrative articulacy of the black struggle can emerge. They are a tiny minority, potential readers of *Race Today*, potential makers of 'Open Door' programmes, and also potential activists in black revolutionary groups. A few of them will be paid to contain the rest. The state is already using their imagination to spawn projects for the vast majority who see Black Studies as just another mind-blow. This majority, by no means silent, is indicative of the failure of schooling to turn out willing workers.

Refusal to Work: A Culture of Resistance

Within the school, they are the inveterate imitators of the generation that has just left the schools and is struggling to survive in the community. Their models of ambition don't include the work ethic and this single fact enlivens their reaction to the systems within school. They challenge discipline, study and routine. Sylvanus and Suzanne in the fourth year assume as their models of behaviour Charlie and Donna, who've left school after skulking around the sixth form for two or three years and have had very little employment since, if any at all.

They are the breed most dangerous to capital as they refuse to enter the productive partnership under the terms that this society lays down. They have turned the sale of their labour into a sellers' market by refusing to do dirty jobs. Their refusal accounts for the shortage of staff on London Transport, in the hospitals, even on the assembly line. The infection of this particular brand of class defiance, the refusal to work, spreads to the schools. While the white child asks: 'Will this help me in my job?', or 'Will it get me more wages when I leave school?', the black teenager knows that it won't do either. School has not succeeded in inspiring them with ambitions they know they will not be allowed to fulfil. Their culture is a day-to-day affair, an affair of the styles and fashions they collectively generate. They educate themselves within the community, and carry their community into the school where one may see them gathered around reggae, developing the social image of their groups. It is futile for a Black Studies course to attempt to encapsulate their culture. Its only text is survival, and it is bound by a rejection of the disciplines of work that the society offers them, and will therefore be called a culture of resistance. It is a culture antithetical to the idea of schooling, and so finally unco-optable. It is possible for them to force the dissociation between being productive and having rights within school. When they leave school, they carry the dissociation with them into the life of the community. The counterpart to their material struggle is a material struggle inside the institutions of compulsory schooling. The apprentices to the refusal to work demonstrate their demand for a wage for their enforced apprenticeship.

'NO LONGER SLEEPING ROUGH'
Race Today, May 1974

Over the past three years the number of black youngsters between the ages of 15 and 21 without homes has risen to over 3,000 in London alone (Dashiki Report 1974).

Thousands of words have been written about this in newspapers as diverse as the *West Indian World* and the *Sunday Times* colour supplement, and armies of social workers and do-gooders have been drafted into black communities to 'alleviate the problem'. Home Office monies have been earmarked, under the lofty title of 'Urban Aid', to provide hostels for the homeless and the Community Relations Commission 'is presently reporting to the Home Secretary on homelessness'.

State Thrust

Never in the history of our presence here in Britain has there been such a concerted thrust by different organisations of the state on matters concerning the black population. Informing all the words and scores of community projects is the notion of the black youth as victim. Nowhere does he/she enter the issue as subject, capable of acting independently to deal with the situation, only as an object over which liberals, black and white, scramble to pursue their missionary work.

In the last year, Brixton has emerged as the main battleground on which the notion of 'liberal aid' has been challenged. Here, the problem of homelessness, which is most acute among young blacks, has spawned a vibrant movement towards dealing with their own homelessness. The victims are in the process of becoming protagonists. More than a hundred youths have occupied council-owned houses in the past few months, thereby posing the alternative to a continued existence in hostel institutions. As one housing activist says: 'I know that you have to help yourself, you can't wait for other people. Some see the setting up of hostels as a solution to homelessness: I am against this. We need homes, not hostels.'

The modern squatting movement emerged in Britain in 1968 but it has its antecedents in the squatting movement of 1919 when returning servicemen seized empty properties to live in, to the astonishment and rage of the government of the day, and in 1945 when empty houses in Blantyre, Scotland were occupied. This mushroomed into the Vigilante movement when committees, made up largely of ex-servicemen, installed homeless families in empty properties by night. By 19 October 1946, the government announced that 39,535 people were squatting in England and Wales and 4,000 in Scotland. In September the police were instructed to keep watch on all unoccupied property in order to prevent further squatting, and the Home Office instructed Scotland Yard to 'enquire into the origins of the organisation behind the squatters'. The government capitulated and many of the squatters were given alternative accommodation.

Growth of the Squatting Movement

The modern squatting movement came into being in 1968 with the formation of the London Squatters' Campaign, largely organised by professional protesters of the CND period and subsequently augmented by activists in the student movement. Their bold and dramatic activities hit the news headlines and the idea of capturing empty houses became firmly rooted in radical political activity. Everywhere groups emerged to haunt property speculators and recalcitrant local councils.

There were very few, if any, black participants in the squatting movement. Our status as immigrants, coupled with the fact that we are in the minority, understandably bred a cautious approach. This lack of confidence, however, was overcome by the resurgence of the black movement internationally. The younger generation grew to maturity in a climate of open hostility to being placed in subordinate positions in society.

That the young blacks have been informed by the white squatting movement is true, but their squatting activities are qualitatively different from it. The black squatting movement in Brixton has broken new ground. It is local council policy that the single person does not qualify for public housing and therefore the black youth seemed destined for a life of homelessness or hostel existence, but they see it as the responsibility of the council to house them – single person or not, waiting list or not. They will not tolerate the one-roomed existence offered them nor continue to sleep rough and be objects of liberal pity.

Another difference is that the radical white squatting movement tends to take over old dilapidated, short-life council houses, spending hours of their time and energy in decorating the houses, thereby (so they believe) earning the sympathy of the council. Not so the black youth. They do not accept that they have to ingratiate themselves to the authorities in order to be housed. Kathleen, 18 and born in England, says: 'When I left home all the social workers wanted to do was put me in a hostel, but I couldn't stand it. For three nights I slept on the streets and in a hostel for a few nights. I have seen some of the places that white squatters put families in. They are old and dirty. No, I don't want to live in those surroundings. I have taken this flat because it's nice and clean.' For them it is the very best or nothing. They derive this power from the cohesiveness of the black community and their knowledge that in their struggle they are likely to receive wide community support. Whereas the white squatters, who are generally London's floating bedsitter population, set up squats in areas with no organic relation to the indigenous population.

Power of the Class

The strength therefore of the black squatting movement is the fact that it is rooted in Brixton's black community and has as its base the social organisation of the youth. They visit and frequent the same youth clubs and congregate at social functions and schools. Communication is easy; every black squatter we talked to acquired information about squatting from a friend and was able to mobilise immediately others to help occupy the building.

Council Counter-attacks

It is this power that Lambeth Council seeks to confront. In a document released in the last few weeks it states: 'At present over 100 Council properties are occupied by illegal squatters and many of them are single people. The Council has received many complaints about the activities of groups of single people who are not only illegally occupying dwellings but whose noisy behaviour causes distress to neighbouring residents.' Since 1971, Lambeth has been offering property on which it would not be economical to spend large sums of money to local housing organisations, including the Lambeth Self Help Housing Association. No less than 172 properties are being occupied through these arrangements, mainly by white squatters.

It is 'Action by illegal squatters over and above these arrangements' which Lambeth is challenging. The Council's document, which reeks of racism, obviously aims to isolate the black squatting movement which consists overwhelmingly of single people who are 'noisy neighbours', which we remind them was (and still is) the slogan of the fascist attacks on black people in the 1950s.

They must know that their frontline support will come from Brixton's racist whites. Already the police have made their intentions clear: 'The night I moved in the police came round and asked me who gave me the house and I couldn't stay here because I was stopping a family of eight from moving in' (Mark, aged 22). 'The police came and asked what we were doing and we told them we had moved in and showed them that we had keys for all the doors in the flats. They threatened us with eviction but we knew they couldn't do it' (Frank, aged 18).

As we go to press, the Council is meeting to plan action against the squatters. The organised state machine is poised to attack the black squatting movement. For the black community, it is a test of strength and in the impending confrontation we have everything to gain and nothing to lose.

'CARNIVAL BELONGS TO US'
Race Today, September 1976

Two weeks before Carnival, we in *Race Today* gave an interview to the BBC about the forthcoming event. We said then, that we saw the staging of Carnival on the streets of Notting Hill as a political victory. This is true in two senses. Firstly, because we have forced the police, councillors and some freewheeling racists in Notting Hill to retreat one step. Secondly, Carnival brings sections of the West Indian community together with a particular sense of its identity and its strength. So when the police drew the battle lines, the black youth moved to the forefront. They had flocked there in their thousands, some to follow pan, some to follow dub, some for the theft and pickpocketing to which their wagelessness directly leads.

It was this section of the West Indian population, this youthful majority, that saved the community from total humiliation that weekend. Even the most antagonistic commentators didn't dare to say that it was the pickpockets who put 325 police into hospital. The *Financial Times* commented: 'Those who steal or assault must be classed as criminals. But those who crowd round to prevent the police from arresting them, must surely be seen as expressing a kind of social or political anger, however inarticulate.' In the same vein, the *Sunday Telegraph* moaned that the police could not operate without the consent of the community and that West Indians had clearly withdrawn such consent. The truth is that no one at Carnival saw Patterson and his baton boys as people who'd come to win consent for anything. The West Indian community saw a force, and saw the possibility of instantaneously generating a superior one.

The post-mortem on the event, by no means over (David Ennals at the Home Office says nobody should make any hasty judgements), has been carried out using the discredited anatomy charts that the press and politicians pull out with each expanding act of black rebellion. The hard-liners call for a ban on Carnival. Writing in *The Times*, Inspector Wilkinson of Notting Hill, one of the chief culprits says: 'The Carnival used to be an occasion of innocent entertainment. If it goes on next year, it will be an occasion of hate and violence.' The more cautious, including William Whitelaw, call for an enquiry. We say no. No enquiry can tamper with the support that Carnival has from a quarter of a million blacks who were there, and millions who were not. We move on to Carnival '77, and we say (in our open letter) what must be done in order to establish its organisation through the democratic forum of those with an interest in it.

That means, by and large, the whole West Indian community, and some besides. This battle for Carnival is no different from the battle that awaits the community over the trials of the sixty defendants or defenders of Notting Hill. After Peckham Fair '72, Brockwell Park '74, The Cricklewood Club '74, Leeds Bonfire '75, Notting Hill '76, the state is conscious that an energy which makes spontaneous battles and turns them into politically supported defences in court, is capable of generating fierce organisation in class combat. How the new Home Minister, veteran of Ireland, will counter, is not yet clear. Liberal journalists and frightened politicians have come up with the old formula: blacks are feeling their deprivation, feed them anaesthetic funds. They have even suggested a Ministry for the Inner Cities to be concerned, in the main, with blacks.

In spite of the welfare spending drought, the threat of civil disorder that the West Indian community has posed, will bring state funding – for more hostels for the black urban homeless; for the drive to recruit more blacks to the police force; to fatten the rising black class that each year finds new gimmicks to induce young blacks to accept training and humble employment. The solution has not worked in the past and will not work in the future. A bed in a hostel, a blue uniform, projects which subtly try to do what schooling has failed to do, are not what the youth want. Until and unless British society ensures that this growing section of the population gets what it needs and demands on its own terms, it will have no option but to turn up, looking for the main chance at public gatherings. Especially those gatherings which they feel are demonstrations of their community's social power.

'IS A POLICE CARNIVAL'
Darcus Howe, September 1976

Darcus Howe, editor of Race Today, *has participated in Carnival since its inception. We asked him to write a personal diary of his experiences and observations at Carnival this year, and below, we publish his account.*

This was my eleventh Carnival. I have been participating in it since its inception in 1965, sometimes as a reveller and sometimes at various levels in the organisation of the event. Once it emerged in January 1976 that police, local councillors and a few white residents were determined to have the Carnival removed from the streets of Notting Hill, the *Race Today* Collective asked me to carry out a campaign in our journal, aimed at winning the struggle to retain the festival on the streets. In the February, April and May issues of *Race Today*, we sought to demolish the frivolous objections of the opposition and we outlined what we felt to be the responsibility of the organisers of Carnival.

The opposition mobilised a petition and Chief Superintendent Patterson received it, posing, petition held high, for photographs in the local press. In his capacity as the senior police officer responsible for the Notting Hill area, he exploited the local press to the full, as well as trying to split the organising committee, threatening, cajoling and manoeuvring. Mrs Lennon, spokeswoman for the white residents, threatened a High Court injunction if she did not have her way. Alderman Methuen, deputy leader of the local council, sought the support of the Home Secretary.

Patterson, we are told, waved a copy of *Race Today* before the Carnival organisers protesting the contents. To all our accusations about his activities and manoeuvrings, we received no reply. The same cannot be said for Methuen. He wrote to *Race Today* complaining about the tone of our article and our editorial policy. We published these. The chairman of the Carnival Committee visited our offices. We outlined our strategy and won his cooperation. It was a hard-fought campaign, and by 31 April, we were the victors. It was Carnival as usual. Or was it?

The minicab turns into Pembridge Road. We are on our way to the Carnival. Along Pembridge Road, into Chepstow and left into Westbourne Park, there are policemen everywhere. This is Sunday. The minicab stops at the corner of Great Western and Westbourne Park and I make my way towards the Mangrove Restaurant.

The Mangrove is my permanent link with Notting Hill. The streets around link the terrain on which I received my first baptism in the realities of political life. I am on the alert. It is a discipline which most West Indians have learnt when in the presence of police officers. Rhythm and steel penetrate the air. I turn into Powis Terrace and I hear the Ebony Steel band jamming a Kitchener calypso. I meet Pepe, Joe and those brothers and sisters who, for weeks, could talk about nothing else but costumes and sweet-pan. Someone passes me a bottle of vodka and I oblige. I cease counting at twenty uniformed policemen. The jamming continues and then there is a sharp interruption. 'Move on! Move on!', snaps the senior police officer. 'Get moving, get moving.' I cross Westbourne Park and into All Saints Road. I am greeted by the Mangrove crowd on the corner.

'Oh God, Darcus, it's a police Carnival.'

'Boy, it look like the police have dey own band.' The flippant comments betray a feeling of shock, but Terry confirms what we all know: 'It boun' to have trouble, they take too much rass clart liberty.' The comments are now flying thick and fast as we settle down in front of the Mangrove: 'Who it is negotiate wid the police?' 'Darcus, you ent know that the police was coming out in force?' I confess ignorance. 'Why the Committee ent tell we?'

I leave with a companion and head for 'under de bridge'. It is the other focal point of Carnival. I arrive to witness the first confrontation. A group of blacks surround two police officers: 'Whey yuh take him for?' 'Wha wrong wid selling drink? Yuh ever hear 'bout a Carnival without drink?' 'All yuh dread. Ah know whey all yuh want, you know. Ah know whey all yuh looking for. Yuh go get it.' I inquire and am told that Chief Superintendent Patterson's Pale Ale Brigade is in action. They locate a vendor who is selling it. They stalk their prey and then pounce. The Pale Ale Brigade registers its first success in the military encounter. I have an image of General Patton, no, Superintendent Patterson, receiving on the radio the first report of success in his Pale Ale Campaign. Within minutes, the Brigade has whisked off a second victim. In frustration someone protests that black people are fuckries for allowing the police to get away with it. I disagree but hold my peace. The confrontation will come but it's early days yet.

Walking around, and searching out, the police operation begins to take shape. There are two central points where police are concentrated. One of them on Acklam Road, opposite the teenage disco; the other situated around the corner from the Mangrove. They sit idly in coaches, reading paperbacks, playing cards, or simply chatting to each other. If they are on hand to search for pickpockets, then Robert Mark has to explain how a police officer does that sitting all day in a bus. No. It is a reserve force ready for the confrontation that Scotland Yard has predicted.

1 make my way back to the Mangrove. Ebony is turning into Lancaster Road still chaperoned by forty-odd uniformed policemen. They are certainly not looking for pickpockets; they have come expecting a confrontation. The bands are chaperoned along a defined route, forty policemen to a band. Along that route, vanloads of policemen are strategically placed. At the first sign of trouble, the forty officers form a cordon, a long line across the street. At the other end, reinforcements are called in and the crowd is sandwiched between two lines of police officers. It is a military strategy to defeat a hostile rebellion.

I return to the Mangrove and as the hours pass by the tension mounts. Bay 57, one of the steel bands, is standing in front of the Mangrove entertaining the crowd. Further along the road there is a scuffle. About seventy police officers are disgorged from the green coaches parked around the corner. They stampede in the direction of the scuffles. I distinctly hear a police officer say to another beside him, 'This is where it starts.'

'INVASION OF THE MANGROVE'

Race Today, September 1976

The Mangrove restaurant has always been a favoured vantage point from which to see and hear the mas and steelbands of Carnival. Every year, the management runs its own private steel band competition, with two members of the steel band community as judges. All the steel bands pass by the Mangrove, which attracts many hundreds of people, particularly those with children.

So, as the festivities approached the Carnival's last lap, All Saints Road was jammed with revellers of all ages. The Melody Makers steel band, which had participated in the Mangrove competition earlier, had returned to salute the revellers. Everybody was totally unaware that a police army was on its way.

It entered All Saints Road from Lancaster Road in two groups. Police buses immediately sealed both ends of the road. They formed themselves in lines across the width of the street and swept along All Saints Road, using their truncheons to beat out a military rhythm on their riot shields. People began running hysterically in all directions, screaming. The only places of refuge were doorways and buildings. The Mangrove was packed to capacity with terrified children and horrified adults.

The invasion force approached the Mangrove, beating on its plate-glass window with truncheons. Frank Crichlow, owner of the restaurant, attempted to appeal to a sergeant to call off his troops. He was clubbed over the head from behind by a police baton. Stewards inside tried to hold the door but it was broken down. A gang of between 15 to 20 policemen charged in, beating the people inside, yelling at everybody to get out. Some people were literally pushed through the back window, which has a 14-ft drop. Basil, of Basil and the Black Patch sound-system, who has provided sounds at Carnival for years, recounts:

The first I heard was somebody shouting that the police are outside chasing people. Somebody else shouted to close the door. Next thing I knew was a charge. The window next to the door was smashed by truncheons beating on it and then they came in. They started beating everybody and telling us to get out, but we couldn't because the door was cordoned off. I was thrown across the room. Police smashed my amplifier on to the floor and tossed my records all about. There was a couple with a child near to me and I protested to the police to let them get out. It's just nonsensical to me that the police come into a place in that way, beating people and smashing property and making no arrests.

This is the story of a young white man who had spent most of the day in the area outside the Mangrove and was also badly injured:

No attempt was made to arrest anybody. In fact, the raid appeared to have no purpose whatsoever. The raid shocked everybody as the Mangrove had been considered a place of refuge and safety both from muggers and police. No one attempted to defend themselves. Eventually I was thrown into the street by the police. Blood was pouring from my head and, as it was covering my eyes, I couldn't see clearly. I was directed towards an ambulance and told to get into it. However, it contained two injured policemen who told me to get out. I tried to get out but was pushed back in by police outside. In the course of the next few minutes I was pushed in and out of the ambulance a total of three times, and I was kicked by the police outside for not getting in. Eventually the ambulance drove off. The police were still running up and down the street. A few bottles were being thrown but they did not appear to be aimed in any particular direction. As the air now seemed a bit calmer, I crossed the road and found my friend, who helped me to an ambulance. We got in together with another man who had been hit on the head. The ambulance then drove off, past the Mangrove, where a group of people begged the driver to stop and take a friend whose face was badly injured and a girl whose arm was in so much pain she could not sit still. The ambulance man gave her gas. Her arm was in fact broken in two places. The man with the injured face said that he had been thrown through the window of the restaurant from the inside by the police and glass had gone in his right eye. He may lose it. A girl whose wrists were so badly cut she couldn't move her two middle fingers on her left hand said she too had been thrown through the window. I had four stitches to my forehead. In all, some twenty people were treated for serious injuries

The savage manner of the police invasion and the fact that no arrests were made left everybody in no doubt that what took place was part of a planned attack by the police on the Carnival. Although it had been agreed, through negotiations with the CPC, that the festivities would continue until 11 p.m. on both nights, from approximately 8.30 p.m., an army of police began a military sweep to clear the streets. In some circumstances, they were met with pockets of resistance from groups of youths, who engaged them on a hit-and-miss basis, but their strategy was quite clearly to arrest the Carnival.

Figure 2.1 Darcus at Clifton Rise during the anti-National Front demonstration, 13 August 1977 (photo Syd Shelton).

'BOBBY TO BABYLON: BRIXTON BEFORE THE UPRISING'
Darcus Howe, February 1982

The Metropolitan Police, London, in a confidential report on the uprising of young blacks in Brixton, recorded these historical facts:

Between 6.10pm on Friday, 10 April, 1981, and 11.34pm on Monday, 13 April, 1981, during a very warm early spring interlude, serious disorder occurred in the immediate area of Brixton, SW9, within the Greater London Borough of Lambeth when large numbers of persons, predominantly black youths, attacked police, police vehicles (many of which were totally destroyed), attacked the Fire Brigade and damaged appliances, damaged private premises and vehicles, destroyed private premises and vehicles by fire, looted, ransacked and damaged shops, and there is one instance of a white girl being raped in her flat by a black youth whilst

56

the disorder occurred around them. During the entire period some 7,472 police officers were used to police the area, some on more than one occasion.

The report goes on to inform that there were 285 arrests, 415 police officers and 172 members of the public injured, 118 police vehicles damaged, 4 police vehicles destroyed, 61 private vehicles damaged, 30 private vehicles destroyed, 158 premises damaged and 28 premises seriously damaged by fire. Measured by any standards, this revolt assumed serious insurrectionary proportions. From Brixton, the revolt snaked its way through Peckham, Southall, Wood Green, Finsbury Park, Woolwich, Forest Gate and Notting Hill in London; to Liverpool, Birkenhead, Sheffield, Manchester, Leeds, Hull, Newcastle and Preston in the North of England, taking in the Midland areas of Coventry, Leicester, Derby, Birmingham and Nottingham. And the South was affected too. Southampton, Cirencester, High Wycombe, Gloucester, Luton, Reading, Aldershot and Cardiff, all experienced the violent revolt of young blacks and whites against the police. The number of arrests, the extent of the damage to property and person were multiplied many times as British society saw no peace until the uprising petered out at the end of July.

The period between 10 April and 23 July must be taken as a whole, distinguishable, as it was, in range and depth from previous revolts waged by blacks against the police. This general uprising stands head and shoulders above all that had gone before, and not simply in relation to the historical development of the black working class in Britain. Not since the insurrection of the 1830s – the Chartist movement – has English society experienced such extensive revolt. Of equal importance is the fact that the uprising represents a massive leap from the late 1960s and early 1970s when young blacks combined under the Black Power banner to combat police violence and corruption inside the black community. To investigate, as far as we can, what blacks did and how they did it during this period is to appraise ourselves of the stage that the black movement in Britain has reached and its impact on those sections of the society closest to us. In this way, we are able to discover what is likely to develop in the coming period. To know is to be prepared.

The revolt of Brixton's young blacks against the police did not begin when the media and the rest of British society discovered it on the weekend of 10 April 1981. In the last ten years, young blacks in Brixton have engaged the local police in minor skirmishes, organised protests, violent street confrontations and hand-to-hand fighting in youth clubs and other social haunts.

Much of this has taken place behind the backs of the rest of British society, often unrecorded except as a sensational one-off event, vulgar propaganda aimed at bolstering up the image of the British police, or at preparing public opinion for the introduction of, say, the Special Patrol Group.

22 November 1970 marked a significant turning point in the struggle. Joshua Francis worked at London Transport and lived in Brixton. On 22 November, the normal routine of this middle-aged West Indian was brutally interrupted. Four white men, one of them an off-duty police officer, stormed into his home and assaulted him; his wounds required thirty stitches. The Brixton police arrived, carted Mr Francis off to Brixton police station and charged him with assaulting three police officers.

The West Indian community had, until then, followed official practices in dealing with experiences of this kind; they sought the advice of local, voluntary organisations, or the Citizens Advice Bureau, or the local vicar. They would either engage their own High Street solicitors or one touted for in the corridors of the Magistrates' Court. The touts were mainly police officers who, it has been alleged, received 'backhanders' for their recommendations and were ensured cooperation in convicting the defendants. The radical lawyer, black or white, who would challenge police evidence, did not exist then. Convictions came thick and fast, as magistrates tended to rubber-stamp police evidence. The most extreme action undertaken by the West Indian community entailed a complaint to the local Member of Parliament or to Scotland Yard. Such complaints invariably came to nothing.

Joshua Francis broke away and followed a new course of action, assisted by members of the Black Panther Movement, which had been formed in Brixton by young blacks a couple of years earlier. The membership, which at its height numbered close to three hundred, was overwhelmingly working class with a sprinkling of intellectuals. They declared themselves opposed to police malpractice and published a newspaper which reflected a militant stance on the question. They distributed the paper door to door and in the main shopping centre, held public meetings, sold radical and revolutionary literature, and demonstrated and agitated in an effort to mobilise public vigilance and alertness with regard to the Brixton police. They demanded, too, that arrested blacks be tried by a jury of their peers. Nor was their platform that narrow. They drew up the battle lines on the education and housing fronts; they placed the struggles of Africans against Portuguese colonialism before the local community; they mobilised in support of Caribbean liberation struggles; they hoisted their banners on the Irish civil rights demonstrations and were solid, in their support for the Palestinian liberation struggles. Internally, they debated the pitfalls of nationalism and teased at Marxism and its various Chinese interpretations.

It was a movement distinguishable from previous forms by its radical vibrancy, but the central issue remained the malpractices carried out against Brixton's black community by the police. On this score, the Panthers introduced the local black community to an alternative to the barren and bankrupt approaches which characterised the preceding period. Joshua Francis placed his case in the hands of the Panthers, and they at once set about organising a campaign on his behalf. It was, perhaps, one of the first of such campaigns recorded in the history of the struggles between blacks and the Brixton police. *Freedom News*, the journal of the Black Panther Movement, recorded the events as follows: 'Since the attack on the life of Brother Joshua Francis, the Black Panther Movement has been organising a campaign to involve the community in demanding justice for Brother Joshua and an inquiry into the activities of the Brixton police, who have been allowed to mount these attacks on black people.'

Freedom News linked two similar events to illustrate the point: 'In 1967 a Brother Campbell was dragged from a bus on Brixton Road and beaten unconscious in broad daylight.' And again: 'In November 1969, three brothers and a sister were again beaten, one of them (Bro Tex) received a broken arm. Black people in the (Brixton) market were protesting against an unwarranted attack on a Nigerian diplomat.'

Later on, the journal drew our attention to the attitude of the judiciary and Joshua Francis's lawyer: 'These criminal activities of the police have again been upheld with the conviction of Bro Joshua whose defence lawyer refused to raise the political issues involved in the case. The response of one barrister to a request by Joshua to have black people on the jury was met with the question, "Are you mad?"'

The campaign involved pickets of the courts, a public demonstration, public meetings and the publication and dissemination of reams of leaflets. All Brixton knew about Joshua Francis's case. All Brixton, black and white, was being introduced to a new and radical approach to a long-standing problem.

The responses were by no means uniform. Young blacks were unreservedly for this new approach, while older West Indian workers expressed a cautious 'wait and see' attitude, while offering a reserved sympathy. Working-class whites were in the main sceptical, but by no means unalterably opposed.

Following this, in almost every black community in the country, groups emerged using the Panther organisation as a model and these organisations coalesced into a national formation at the National Conference on the Rights of Black People held in the spring of 1971 at Alexandra Palace. More than eight hundred representatives of the different organisations were present. The movement had reached its peak after a period of five to six years. A combination of a black movement in its formative stages and the rise of Powellism prompted Harold Wilson, then Prime Minister, to make the following remarks during a speech on the steps of Birmingham Town Hall on 5 May 1968: 'That tragic and intractable phenomenon which we watched with horror on the other side of the Atlantic (burning cities in the USA) … is coming upon us here by our own volition and our own neglect. Indeed, it has all but come. In numerical terms, it will be of American proportions long before the end of the century.'

Later on, in 1971, with the black movement now at its peak and with a massive youth following, Harold Wilson again intervenes: 'This century, with a loss of millions of lives, has underlined the fact that democracy survives as long as it is fought for. It is challenged today across the Atlantic. It is for us, living in the home of parliamentary democracy to decide how we respond to their challenge here in Britain.'

We cannot ignore the alarmist aspect of Wilson's speeches. There was no threat to democracy in Britain and the parallel with America was as baseless as it was vulgar. It was typical Wilsonian cynicism – a dramatic presentation of the problem to conceal a complete lack of creative social policy.

The black community in Brixton experienced two aspects of state reaction to the youth revolt. Firstly the stick. Panther members were harassed by the Brixton police at every turn. They were picked up as they sold their literature and distributed leaflets; their headquarters and fundraising functions were raided; they were arrested and charged indiscriminately as they pursued their campaigns. On the eve of the Conference on the Rights of Black People, Special Branch officers raided the Brixton headquarters and rifled the files. For months on end, the Panthers were bogged down in court cases involving their members and supporters. This period of repression, repeated wherever local groups were established, generated the most debilitating consequences. Membership dwindled, new recruits were hard to come by and enthusiastic support mellowed into passive sympathy. After all, only the most finely honed ideological maturity could withstand such an onslaught, and the Panthers were not quite there.

Then came the carrot. The government had unfurled its Urban Aid Programme in 1968 at first without much impact. Slowly, they filtered small sums of money into the black community, aimed, they said, at ameliorating the problems of young blacks. The programme was conceived in the Home Office Children's Department and its major thrust was the social control of young blacks in revolt. The funds cascaded, eventually, under the Inner City Partnership and the Community Relations Self-Help Programme. By 1973, the radical Black Power organisations, now considerably weakened by the repression, crumbled before this onslaught of government funds. Young cadres, once headed for the Panthers, now gathered around government-financed projects. Organisations which were once autonomous and politically vibrant, were now transformed into welfare agencies.

The Panthers fell into decline. But their impact on Brixton was enormous. For five years, Brixton had experienced an intense, radical politics. The militant and organised opposition to the police had percolated down to the very base of the community. The Panthers had left their mark on Brixton. The community would never be the same again.

At the same time, the rulers of British society were busily reforming the colonial mould inside which the black population's confinement had to be perpetuated. For the police who stood guard in our communities to ensure social obedience, order and discipline, first on the agenda was a technological revolution with a wide range of new gadgetry for surveillance and increased mobility. Specially constructed police stations replaced the traditional buildings.

Administrative manipulation and case law also extended police powers. The Association of Chief Constables, the feudal barons who run Britain's police forces, exercised a power and authority which bordered on the unconstitutional. Locked in committees behind closed doors in Whitehall, this body demanded and got from government literally what it wanted. Its power owed much to the fact that successive governments, lacking in policy in regard to the escalation of unemployment among young blacks, relied exclusively on the police to contain this growing section of the population. It is no exaggeration to note that huge numbers of young blacks have grown up in British society having little contact with any other section of British society but the police and courts. They have developed in the shadow of the SPG, the Vice Squad, the Flying Squad, the Starskys and Hutches of the panda car brigade, the Old Bailey, Inner London Sessions, etc. These young blacks spend a major portion of their day contemplating, plotting and scheming against the advance of police power which is devoid of the traditional constraints, because the traditional vigilance through which democratic Britain had contained police power was being exchanged for free licence. An economic recession was at hand, the blacks were stirring and the Irish had given an indication of how tensions in the United Kingdom would develop. Fearful of the impending revolt and lacking in a social and political policy which would involve young blacks in the development of British society, successive governments gave full rein to the coercive powers.

The police proceeded, confidence growing by the day, to trample wildly over the rights of the black community, all behind the backs of society at large. Judges and magistrates provided uncritical support for the most unorthodox of police methods. This unrestrained licence, along with the technological revolution, had disastrous consequences within the force itself: internal structures were undermined and the ensuing lack of control plunged the police into the most damnable corruption. Take note of these statistics: between 1969 and 1972, a score of London detectives went to gaol and hundreds more left the force in disgrace. Even the most conservative fanatic could not deny that this was the tip of the iceberg. An entire elite drug squad appeared in the dock at the Old Bailey when a drug ring comprising police officers of the Drug Squad and black drug dealers was exposed. Most of the black dealers were Brixton based.

Not a month passes without some investigation into any one of the police forces in the country. In 1980, close to seven such investigations were proceeding at the same time. And the most damnable corruption of all triggered Operation Countryman which sought, in late 1978, to investigate the complicity of London's CID officers in bank robbery, extortion and murder. The operation revealed corruption of a serious nature at the highest echelons of the police force, up to the level of Assistant Commissioner. The government panicked at the prospect of a mass revelation and wound down the investigation after spending £3,000,000 on it. Only a handful of junior officers have been prosecuted. All this in full view of the black population, for whom revelations of police corruption simply confirmed that what they were experiencing had spread like a cancer.

And yet for ten years there has been little overt, consistent, political opposition coming from the black community. It has been a veritable desert with the odd moments of political offensive. And what is the cause? We need a thorough examination here. Side by side with the increase of police power ran the development of black compromise. Out of the ashes of the Panthers, there emerged the proliferation of a whole host of state-financed projects, among them the Brixton Neighbourhood Centre, which, staffed by blacks, re-instituted the old approach of ushering defendants to solicitors and MPs. Then there was the Railton Youth Club, which was thrown into the vanguard of modernity along with the Melting Pot Foundation, the Abeng Centre, the Black Ink Collective, the Black Women's Group, the Brixton Law Centre and the local Community Relations Council, all of which appeared as the outer layer of the re-plastered colonial mould. And who are these folk who have been drawn into sustaining colonial social relations here in Brixton? Firstly, there are those who perceive themselves as a cut above the ordinary labourer. Failed businessmen and women of the older generation, they have sought social elevation by way of government grants. They are immersed in venality and ruthless in their fraudulent acquisition of government funds for personal use. What is important here is not the moral issue. It is that the police, the government and those agencies, who parcel out government funds, are fully aware of these types and what they do. But official society needs them and is willing to use them. Then there are the born-again blacks who are distinguishable from the mass of blacks by educational attainment. And here I refer to those who are unable to take five GCE O levels in their stride. Among them, a university degree conjures up expectations of the most grandiose kind. Meritocrats they all are. Plunged into the fiercely competitive world of the meritocracy, they cry racial discrimination at the slightest opportunity in order to cover up their individual inadequacies. They have retreated into the world of black projects, a terrain which they guard ferociously at the slightest sign of white encroachment. They sound radical enough, but on close inspection their hostility to the white working class disguises an even greater hostility to its black counterpart. For the past ten years, here in Brixton, they have abjured all political campaigns, all militant stances on the police question. And finally the political entryists. These projects, they hope, will provide access to rebellious blacks from which they would attempt the recruitment of members for the Labour Party, the Communist Party, the International Marxist Group, the Socialist Workers Party et al.

It is from this milieu that the police have managed to draw assistance for a propaganda coup which has succeeded in pulling the wool over the eyes of sections of the host society for ten years. The name of the game has been the police liaison committee. Gathered in this empty shell are police officers and representatives of projects, there to discuss how to improve relations between blacks and the police. It is the most vulgar whitewash. The police representatives are not representing the police and the black representatives are not representing the black community. It is merely a cloak to cover up the continuing escalation of the struggle between the police and the black community. What amazes is the fact that official society staked all and continues so to do on this meaningless exercise.

By the mid-1970s, the new social arrangement had been established. Policing had been revolutionised, police power had been afforded free licence and a section of the black community emerged from the ashes of the Panthers to give some impression that something positive was at hand. They proceeded to the 1980s arm-in-arm with the police on their liaison committees. Those who stayed away from these committees kept within those limits which ensured that next year's grant was safe. The re-plastered mould, the new social arrangement, meant that there was little possibility of a Joshua Francis campaign recurring. The projects made sure that each case was kept in its little cubicle; each experience was atomised, never to gel into an organic and vibrant organisational movement. This atomisation led to a ten-year period of organisational paralysis.

Meanwhile, several profound changes were taking place within the mould itself. The sharpening of the economic recession increased the numbers of young blacks who could not find jobs. Their presence on the streets heightened the conflict between them and the police. The very existence of these various projects teased the black community into expectations which delivered no change whatever, with the result that the most intense passions were being concentrated inside the mould itself. From time to time, those passions exploded into open violence. Who better to articulate these moments than the police themselves? In a memorandum to the Select Committee on Race Relations and Immigration, in March 1976, Scotland Yard made the following admission:

> Recently there has been a growth in the tendency for members of London's West Indian communities to combine against police by interfering with police officers who are effecting the arrest of a black person or who are in some way enforcing the law in situations which involve black people. In the last 12 months 40 such incidents have been recorded. Each carries a potential for large-scale disorder ... Experience indicates that they are more likely to occur during the summer months and that the conflict invariably is with young West Indians. They can occur anywhere in the Metropolitan Police district, but are of course more likely in those areas which have a high proportion of West Indian settlers.

The historical moment could not have been more clearly described. The demise of the Panthers meant that the black community in Brixton had been deprived of and outmanoeuvred out of an organisational framework through which they could express their revolt politically, through which they could link their experiences with others nationally and internationally.

This did not mean revolt was at an end. Revolt was alive and kicking and living in Brixton. On the evening of 19 June 1973, young blacks clashed with police at the Brockwell Park Fair. Bottles, stones, any available missile was thrown. The police called for reinforcements and so did young blacks. The battle raged for half an hour. In those circumstances, the police grab and arrest who is at hand. Whether you were fighting or not is irrelevant. Robin Sterling, a young student at Tulse Hill School, once a nursery for the Black Panther Movement, was arrested. He was innocent of the charge of assault on police, as were Horace Parkinson and Lloyd James. At the end of the day, all three were sent to prison. Tulse Hill School had retained the Panther tradition in a small organisation, the Brixton Collective. They raised a campaign for the freedom of Robin Sterling under the slogans 'Move as a Community' and 'School Today, Jail Tomorrow'. Robin was eventually freed on appeal, but not before the Brockwell Three Defence Committee, created by the Brixton Collective, had staged a successful strike of school students and a massive demonstration in the South London area. Within weeks, there followed violent clashes between young blacks and the SPG at the Railton Youth Club. Hand-to-hand fighting ensued. Then, in September 1974, young blacks again took on the police at the Swan disco and then Stockwell tube station. Again in June 1976, close to a hundred blacks spontaneously marched on Brixton police station following the wrongful arrest of a middle-aged West Indian on Railton Road.

The British government had one solitary reply to this phenomenon which reproduced itself in several black communities up and down the country. Clashes would be followed by intensive police investigations. Such investigations involved the wringing of confessions and statements from participants. Case papers would be sent to the Director of Public Prosecutions who returned charges of Riot and Affray. From Notting Hill to Wood Green, from Leeds to Bristol, the formula was the same. The projects sat on case after case ushering young blacks through a maze of judicial procedure, their friends, parents and relatives providing a passive audience for the performing circus of lawyers.

The confidence and social growth which an involvement in political campaigns brings were denied young blacks and their parents, introducing young blacks, particularly, to the violence of despair. Wherever the opposite tendency prevailed, however, it has been remarkably successful. The campaign to free North London student Cliff McDaniel, in 1975, led to the formation of the Black Parents' Movement and the Black Students' Movement. The campaign to free George Lindo established strong foundations among the West Indian community in Bradford. Similar campaigns in Leeds and Manchester generated like successes. But not until the New

Cross Fire, which claimed the lives of 13 young blacks, was political campaigning returned to the position of centrality which it occupied in the days of the Panthers and other similar groupings. The gusto and enthusiasm with which the black community gathered in their thousands on the Black People's Day of Action on 2 March 1981, indicated the extent to which they had been frustrated by the projects from expressing themselves politically. They were free at last. The mould had once more been shattered.

Black Brixtonians walked the streets of Brixton with the confidence that a new era was at hand and they were prepared for 'Operation Swamp 81', which was mounted by the 'L' (Lambeth) District of the Metropolitan Police, 6–11 April. There were ten squads (four assigned to Brixton), of between five and eleven officers in plain clothes in each squad, operating under the following written instructions:

> The purpose of this Operation is to flood identified areas on 'L' District to detect and arrest burglars and robbers. The essence of the exercise is therefore to ensure that all officers remain on the streets and success will depend on a concentrated effort of 'stops', based on powers of surveillance and suspicion proceeded by persistent and astute questioning.

'THE NINE-YEAR-OLD LEADER'
C.L.R. James, May 1982

Free For All. I love that title. Freedom is a very rare thing: it is, for example, rare in the account of great events. It was only a few years ago that a French historian really got down to it and brought out some of the greatest and most important events in the French Revolution. You may think that that is History, with a capital 'H', because it is one of the greatest events and everybody, particularly the professional historians, ought to know something about it. But enough of that. I have been exercising my freedom to say a few things about history which are not only important in general but relate directly to the riots which took place in Britain during last summer.

Darcus Howe is talking to an American about those events. He picks up a paper and reads this:

> After the uprising in Moss Side last July they appointed a local Manchester barrister called Hytner to enquire into what happened, and how it started. Here's what he writes: 'At about 10.20pm a responsible and in our view reliable mature black citizen was in Moss Lane East, and

observed a large number of black youths whom he recognised as having come from a club a mile away. At the same time a horde of white youths came up the road from the direction of Moss Side. He spoke to them and ascertained they were from Withenshawe. The two groups met and joined. There was nothing in the manner of their meeting which in any way reflected a prearranged plan. There was a sudden shout and the mob stormed off in the direction of Moss Side police station. We are given an account by another witness who saw the mob approach the station, led, so it was claimed, by a nine-year-old boy with those with Liverpool accents in the van.'

You believe that you have read this and that you understand this: pardon me if I tell you that I don't think you have. Let me select a passage and draw it to your attention:

[He] observed a large number of black youths whom he recognised as having come from a club a mile away. At the same time a horde of white youths came up the road from the direction of Moss Side. He spoke to them and ascertained that they were from Withenshawe. The two groups met and joined. There was nothing in the manner of their meeting which in any way reflected a prearranged plan. There was a sudden shout and the mob stormed off in the direction of Moss Side police station.

That my friends is the revolution. There is no highly educated party leading the backward masses. There is no outstanding leader whom the masses follow because of his great achievement in the past. There had been no prearranged plan. They met and joined, they shouted and they stormed off, (note this particularly) in the direction of Moss Side police station. The great leader? Before I deal with that, let me quote from one of the greatest historians of the 20th century. I can quote at once because I made quotations from it in *The Black Jacobins*:

It is therefore in the popular mentality, in the profound and incurable distrust which was born in the soul of the people, in regard to the aristocracy, beginning in 1789, and in regard to the king, from the time of the flight to Varennes, it is there that we must seek the explanation to what took place. The people and their unknown leaders knew what they wanted. They followed the Girondins and afterwards Robespierre, only to the degree that their advice appeared acceptable. Who then are these leaders to whom the people listened? We know some. Nevertheless, as in all the decisive days of the revolution, what we most would like to know is forever out of our reach; we would like to have the diary of the most obscure of these popular leaders; we would then be able to grasp, in the act so to speak, how one of these great revolutionary days began; we do not have it. (*G. Lefebvre, contemporary historian of French Revolution*)

So much for these great leaders. This time we know that it was a boy of nine who was leading this particular part of the revolution. I don't think I have anything more to say here. But for the greater part of my long life, I have been saying and preaching and teaching 'the two groups met and joined. There was nothing in the manner of their meeting which in any way reflected a prearranged plan. There was a sudden shout and the mob stormed off in the direction of Moss Side police station.' Work at it please.

'WHAT WE LACK'
Race Today, December 1985

Amid the public din and clamour which followed the revolts in Handsworth, Brixton and Tottenham, the one voice which loudly and clearly stated what the vast majority of young blacks think and feel was Bernie Grant's. This is a very peculiar state of affairs. Young blacks, who led and participated in the revolt, are in the main under 25, are not members of the Labour Party and hardly vote for it. Yet Bernie, well intentioned we are sure, is close to 50 and leader of the Haringey Council in his capacity as a Labour councillor. This begs the central question: what has happened to the political leadership which ought to come from within the ranks of young blacks?

It is necessary to go back in time. In the late '60s, we witnessed the first organised mass, black movement in Britain. The major issue then, as it is now, was the excesses of the British police. Organisations were formed in almost every black community in this country, newsletters and news-papers were published, demonstrations were held, the roving bookshop was started; we engaged in political education classes, spoke on platforms organised by ourselves, formed and developed international contacts and held conferences. The list is long. These organisations were financed not by Moscow, Libya, local government, or central government but by ourselves. We produced a string of leaders. There was, at the head of the movement, a woman, Althea Jones Lecointe. Add to this Leila Hassan, Barbara Beese, Mala Dhondy, George Joseph, Darcus Howe and Farrukh Dhondy. They spoke not only on black community matters but on a whole range of national and international issues; political, social, economic and literary. In short, a political foundation and tradition was established in the black community upon which future generations could build.

We have retrogressed and we have to address ourselves to the reasons why if we are to emerge from this vacuous state. We contend that the continuing development of a radical and revolutionary culture is being undermined by the entry of educated young blacks into the Labour Party and a wholesale imbibing of what we refer to as 'welfarism'. The Labour Party has almost ruined an entire generation of black activists. The pursuit of the seat in the House of Commons or in local councils has replaced genuine, black, political activity. What do they do in the Labour Party we ask? Apart from knocking on doors, attempting to explain to voters Labour's half-baked socialism, they spend all their energies in endless manoeuvring and manip-ulation which they dignify by the term 'political activity'.

This is not mere abuse. Only days ago, a black, prospective parliamentary candidate, after endorsing Hattersley's economic medicine as the cure-all for Britain's economic decline, stated her task as 'empowering the working classes, black and white'. Any A-level student of politics would know that this is the last thing the Labour Party could or would do; that is the surest way to self-destruction. But such are the trite and banal political statements that come from those who float around in a sea of political nothingness; their speeches on political economy are without content, mere babble, a far cry from the heights scaled in the past. Where are the political journals, the newsletters, the pamphlets which circulated week after week in the black community only 18 years ago? Now Labour Party activists complain about who discriminates against them, call for positive discrimination in favour of themselves and their kind, but would not be seen dead publishing a journal of their own. They bully their way into getting a few lines in left journals but that is about all.

At the same time, we are literally swamped with a sea of welfarism funded by grants from the state sector. So that the first thing that comes to the mind of a young black man or woman on the verge of political activity is the formation of projects, and that which is furthest away is the formation of a self-sufficient political organisation which advances the revolutionary and radical political traditions.

The revolutionary spirit is alive and well and lives in Handsworth, Tottenham and Brixton while the revolutionary political movement flounders. We need to rekindle and develop upon the organisational flair which characterised the '60s.

3
Sex, Race and Class

INTRODUCTION
Kennetta Hammond Perry

In recent years, there has been a growing body of work by historians aiming to understand how Black people in Britain encountered, lived and resisted the politics of race and the practice of racism. However, in revisiting the pages of *Race Today*, I am profoundly reminded of how much there is yet to be written, and how many questions we have yet to ask in order to better understand the conditions that have shaped the making of Black life in contemporary Britain. In particular, one of the areas that requires much more attention is careful consideration of the voices, experiences and intellectual contributions of Black women. One could certainly argue that two of the most well-known Black historical figures in Britain are women – Mary Seacole, the Jamaican-born nurse who provided aid to British soldiers during the Crimean War and was honoured with a statue in London in 2016, and Claudia Jones, an outspoken journalist, community organiser and political activist whom the Royal Mail recognised with a commemorative postage stamp in 2008. However, while these two Black women have managed to find some degree of visibility within British history, there is still much to know about the historical contours of Black women's lives, including the various ways in which they have laboured and critically reflected upon their status in British society.

The following articles provide an instructive set of provocations. They showcase some of the ways in which *Race Today* functioned as a platform that voiced the political concerns of Black women. In the pages of the magazine, one can find facets of an intergenerational conversation among Black women about strategies of resistance and modes of survival that were adapted over time to navigate life in Britain. Perhaps more importantly, the pages of *Race Today* present us with an under-examined archive for interrogating how Black women have made sense of the ways in which the gendered processes of racialisation have shaped dynamics within the working classes. As readers, we are taken into the lives of Black women like Patricia Mathews who arrived in England from Barbados at age 17 in 1962 and chose to train as a nurse as an alternative to factory work. Patricia arrived in the year when Parliament implemented the Commonwealth Immigration Act, a bill that marked the first in a series of immigration policies passed during the second half of the twentieth century that began to redraw the boundaries of British citizenship in ways that, to this day, continue to disenfranchise Black people and create pathways for deportation. In narratives like Patricia Mathews's, not only do we gain a glimpse of the conditions that Black women entering the nursing profession encountered as they aimed to find routes to professional opportunities and career progression in a sector of the British labour market that only made room for them at the bottom, but we also can get a sense of where Black women workers fit within the formation of the post-war Welfare State. Anticipating the groundbreaking work of Beverley Bryan, Stella Dadzie and Suzanne Scafe in *Heart of the Race* (1985), these articles prompt readers to consider the lives of Black women as narrated on their own terms as a means of gaining different perspectives on the political economy of British society during the 1970s and 1980s.

In addition to providing an archival resource to uncover the contours of working-class Black women's lived experiences in Britain, the volumes of *Race Today* also speak to the importance of considering Black women's intellectual labour. All too often, Black women's reflections on their own lives are absent from the ways in which leftist and/or Black radical thought is imagined. But the articles that follow highlight how Black women in Britain and beyond have historically used their experiences as women, as workers, as migrants, as caretakers, and as observers of their circumstances to create new frameworks for thinking about power, the distribution of resources and the various forms of labour that they performed. What does state power look like when seen from the vantage point of Black women working within the National Health Service during the 1970s, before the emergence of Thatcherism? How did Black women's struggles to provide opportunities for their children serve as a basis for making demands of the state and theorizing about the social, political and economic trans-formations needed to address the gap between their circumstances and their aspirations? *Race Today* certainly provides some insights into these questions. And yet for as much as one might turn to *Race Today* to gain new insights, as noted at the outset, it is important to think about the new research agendas that can be formulated by visiting the pages of this important resource for understanding Black life in Britain and the inter-sections between race, gender and class. To be sure, these are questions that will no doubt involve bringing much-needed attention to Black women's histories in Britain and what they can tell us about the conditions, struggle and resistance in the past and in our present.

'BLACK WOMEN AND NURSING: A JOB LIKE ANY OTHER'
Race Today, August 1974

In the present struggle, nurses for the first time have come out on strike in support of their demands for more money. They have acted in opposition to the myth that women administering to sick, young and old, should not behave in this way.

Nursing is traditionally women's work, especially black women's and in the following article, widely illustrated with interviews, we maintain that the presence of black women in the health industry has been crucial in bringing the struggle to its present stage. This is not a comprehensive statement, in that most of the nurses who participated in writing it are of Afro-Caribbean origin and work in London hospitals, and we know that the most militant action has come from outside London. We concentrate here mainly on nurses, rather than ancillary workers, not because we see them as subsidiary to the hospital structure (as the nurses' unions do), but for reasons of space. However, we point out that it was these workers, recruited from Southern Europe, Ireland, the Caribbean and Asia, who first brought the strike weapon to the hospitals in Britain.

Nursing is a 'caring profession', and traditionally the work of women – to be of service not only to their own men and children, but to other people's. No woman is more identified with service work than black women, especially the black women with a slave or colonial past. The relationship between the black woman and nursing, wet or dry, of other peoples' children and other people's husbands and wives, dates from before any National Health Service. Whether working in hospitals as auxiliaries, SENs (State Enrolled Nurse) or SRNs (State Registered Nurse), in the head of the black nurse from the Caribbean is the echo of slavery; in the head of the Asian nurse is the servitude to Sahib and Memsahib.

The colonial legacy expresses itself today in the young woman who from very early on knows she must take disciplined responsibilities in her own family, for example, for younger sisters and brothers. This legacy is alive in another sense: often the only waged jobs open to women in the ex-colonial world are in the kitchens of the middle and upper classes. From these traditions, plus the need for a huge injection of immigrants to service the

National Health Service (1948) flows the tradition of black women in hospital work, an army of workers who not expect too much in wages and would not be in a position to challenge their working conditions.

During the last twenty years, the class composition of nursing has changed. A hundred years ago, the Report of the Committee for the National Association for providing trained nurses for the sick and poor (1874), said: 'Many gentlewomen were recruited because it is the belief that this type of nursing required the highest type of women who were well educated.' This is not a picture of nurses today and certainly not a description of the recruiting policy of the National Health Service. What used to be a vocation for women of the middle class is now a job for women of the working class, and particularly for black and other immigrant women.

Overseas Nurses: Cheap Labour

The number of overseas student nurses coming into the British Health Service increases rapidly each year. In 1959, approximately 6,000 arrived; in 1970, just under 19,000. They come mainly from the Caribbean, Hong Kong, Mauritius, Malaysia (which is now the highest sending country) and Ireland. We do not know the specific conditions that exist in their own countries which force them to come to Britain for training as a way out, but a way out it certainly is. Few come with the desire to nurse. But whether the desire is there or not, the National Health Service ensures that they will work here for at least five years. Many of them are deliberately directed to take the SEN qualification which is of no use to them outside of Britain, but which guarantees a trained, low-paid workforce on the ward floor.

One way of pushing women from overseas into SEN training is by demanding educational standards which overseas students are less likely to have. During their stay here, they have to renew their permits through the hospital every six months. They have also to give an undertaking that they will stay for a certain period of time after they have trained so that Britain can benefit from 'the training she has paid for'. Yet since most of her training is spent working on the ward, the SEN pupil nurse repays for her training a million times over by the cheap labour she provides. The NHS need for unskilled as opposed to skilled labour is shown by the fact that in 1972 only 120 qualified nurses were allowed into the country.

Labour in the hospital is organised according to sex, race and age. Different jobs are done by people in different uniforms, getting different wages, and having different degrees of power. Those who work the hardest have the least status and the least wages. These divisions are further reinforced by the division between those who are 'professionals' and those who are not.

There are two types of training from the beginning: a two-year course leads to an SEN, a qualification which cannot lead to promotion. A large number of Asians, Irish and West Indians are deliberately directed to SEN: 'When you are interviewed they ask you if you want to do the course in two years or three, and all of us said we would like to do the two-year course. It's only when you get here that you realise that if you do two years, you will be an SEN.' The three-year SRN course is the only route to promotion.

Few black women see nursing as a vocation, with the intention of becoming a matron. And for those who do, it soon becomes clear that this is not what they have been recruited for. For black women, nursing is a job, nothing more, and by refusing to treat it as a vocation they are not only exposing the real nature of nursing in the health service, but are undermining the hierarchy which depends on them wanting to be a part of it.

Grace Jenkins, SEN, Trinidadian:

I came to England to train as a nurse in 1970 when I was 22. I applied to the Trinidad Health Service and they sent me a list of hospital addresses in England. I chose one in Birmingham. I went for an interview in Trinidad and took a sort of intelligence test. I was accepted by the hospital. I came direct to the hospital. I didn't really want to nurse but I wanted to leave Trinidad, I have never had a job there. I did eight weeks – training and then went straight on the ward working, that is, changing bed pans, cleaning lockers and generally fetching and carrying. At first I got £45 a month after deductions. It took me a week to realise that I didn't like England and not much longer to realise I didn't like nursing, but I have to stay five years; that is the condition under which I came. From Birmingham I went to Nottingham to do a special Theatre training – it's more money once you are trained.

I find nurses are very conscious of what position they hold – even some of the black ones. When I was in Birmingham in 1970, they told two black trainee nurses that they would have to leave because they had failed three times a test you take after your eight weeks' initial training. About fifty of us [black nurses] went on strike, some for half a day, some for two or three days, and demanded that they be reinstated. We got the help of the local West Indian Association and we got them back in. I'm doing Agency work now – during my holiday period. I need the money.

Mrs Andrews, Nursing Assistant (psychiatric hospital equivalent of an auxiliary in a general hospital):

But this is what I think was wrong from the beginning, by giving us the name of nursing assistant, this 'nursing' – it shouldn't be, it should be workers ... To me it is just a job like any other, if I was in a factory or anything like that. All of us have to do a lot of things they [nurses] do, except we don't give injections and write reports. We have to admit the patient, we have to make beds, take them to ECT treatment, we do everything they do ... only they sit in the office. We are the ones outside with the patients all the time. People ask me why I have stayed so long. Come December I will have been there for eight years. I just want them to accept me as I am and I accept them as they are and do their work.

The majority of the Nursing Assistants here are black. For example, on the children's ward, I counted that they had twelve Nursing Assistants, two sisters, a Charge nurse [male equivalent of a sister] and a staff nurse and an SRN. All the Nursing Assistants were black. It's little things like that I check up on. Some people ask me why I don't want to go further. I don't want to because I have fulfilled my goal by bringing up my two children on my own. I don't want any status behind my name because it is a whole bloody racket ... I can't see where they are going anyway, they have more heartaches than anything else. Just where I am is where I want to stay and I will be just on the outside looking in at them fighting. They don't have time for their husbands; it's just position, position. It doesn't help the patients recover, it's only themselves ... Now they have a new badge. When we were first there all they put on it was Nurse Andrews or Nurse Brown. On this new badge everybody has their status on it – T.T. Andrews, which is my name and this is causing some dispute from those who feel that their years of service mean they are more than just workers – and want recognition of it. I am pleased because once they see it they know exactly who I am and they can't ask me to do certain things and I can refuse to do a lot of things.

Agency Nurses

We believe that the Agency nurse has represented the spearhead for the force for change in the National Health Service. The attempts to victimise her are racist and anti-working class.

A significant number of black nurses are doing work for agencies which have mushroomed in the last two years, because it offers a flexible alternative, especially for those who have children. In the London area especially, the teaching hospitals rely heavily on agency supply easing their labour problems. For example, the last available figures from the DHSS show that on 30 September 1971, 'the equivalent of 2,720 agency nurses and midwives working the whole time were being employed in the area of central London and the four Metropolitan Regional Hospital Boards ... 54% were employed in the teaching hospitals, which employed only 11 % of NHS nursing and midwifery staff' (Brigg's Report on Nursing, 1972).

The Agency nurse has been singled out and made a focus for attack from within the 'profession', from the union executive of COHSE, and from so-called 'revolutionary' organisations. All have said that NHS nurses should refuse to work with Agency nurses. At the time of writing, COHSE has withdrawn use of the strike weapon by its members, pending the Halsbury Committee Report, but their ban on working with Agency nurses remains and is to become permanent. The National Rank & File Organising Committee, who produce *Hospital Worker*, have also called for a complete end to the use of Agency nurses, and a recent report in *Women's Voice*, paper of International Socialists Women, said:

> At our first meeting we decided that the best action would be to ban working with agency nurses. There's 300 in King's [Hospital] and £12,500 a week is spent on them – the hospital would collapse without them. Of course it's hard on them, but if they're bothered about the state of nursing they should be in the NHS fighting with us.

The reality is that the National Health Service wage rises with seniority, from grade to grade. If a nurse breaks her service, for example to have children, she loses all seniority and the wage that goes with it, and when she rejoins must begin over again, working her way up the pay ladder. This kind of penalisation excludes almost all black nurses who are mothers from rejoining, because whether or not there is a man in the house, the woman must work. Also, the lack of child care which the black nurse can afford means that she must do the night shift and look after her children by day. So they do Agency work because that is their only choice.

Patricia Mathews, SRN, Barbados:

> I came to this country in 1962 when I was 17. I went to look for a job and the Youth Employment Officers suggested that I go for a job in the factory. I didn't want to work in a factory – but I didn't know what I

wanted to do – I didn't really want to do nursing but I went to a London Teaching Hospital to train as a nurse. They said I would have to work as an auxiliary first because of my age. I now know this isn't true; they could have taken me on as a cadet. So I worked as an auxiliary doing bed pans, washing babies' woollies, cleaning lockers, etc. When I first started it was so depressing, I was one of the only black girls there. Then more and more black girls came into London and it wasn't so bad. I remember one incident. I was living at the nurses' home and at that time I was wearing clothes I had brought with me from home. As I was going out while living at the nursing home the matron said to me, 'Where are you going dressed like a tart ?' They used to do things like going through your clothes and then ask you how you could afford certain things. I remember that the first pay I got was £9 a week.

In 1963, I started training for an SRN, and I felt so isolated; there would be times when I would sit in the canteen all by myself with no one to talk to. I was unhappy but I didn't want to work in a factory and my family and friends all felt nursing was better than that, so I stayed. It was during that period of my life that I saw I was being victimised. When I finished training and was on the wards, the doctors especially wouldn't recognise black nurses. Many is the time I was asked to fetch a nurse.

But this has changed; they can't do without black nurses at all now. In 1964, I qualified and left the Health Service immediately, and went to work for an Agency. I will never work for the Health Service because of what I went through during my training. The patients are not being looked after properly – and the nurses have no say in the way the patients are looked after and the money is disgusting. Everyone on the ward is divided by what status they are. In the NHS, you have to put up with things that as an Agency nurse you don't have to. Matron doesn't rule you any more. When I first started Agency work there were not many agencies around and in those days it was mostly private nursing that they catered for. I don't particularly like working for an Agency either but you get more money and more freedom. If my daughter is sick, I just ring up and say I am not going in. Whereas in the Health Service they would try and persuade you to come in saying how short-staffed they were, and if you didn't you would lose a night's pay. But I do feel that they are making a big business out of us. You get different rates from different agencies and some take up to 12½% commission. I work nights all the time because I have a child. I chop and change agencies to get more money. I work four nights a week from 8.30 p.m. to 7.30 a.m. at a London hospital where the majority of nurses are from overseas. I find that whenever people talk about Agency nurses they mean black nurses, but there are nurses from all over the world working for Agencies. I feel very sorry now for the girls, say, from Philippines and Malaysia who don't speak English very well and who are being exploited. They remind me of when I first started training.

The question of how much money the Agency nurse earns is wildly exaggerated and some Agencies operate a pay scale for white nurses and a lower one for black nurses. We were told: 'At the Agency they said you were never to discuss your wages'. I did and I discovered that Australian nurses were getting more.'

At critical points in struggle, when the interests of two different sets of workers seem to clash, the stronger often win their case temporarily by excluding the weaker. The trade unions were formed in Britain to exclude women from skilled trades. The trade unions in the US were formed to exclude white women, all 'foreigners' and blacks from skilled trades. The nursing workforce appears to be divided by different unions and professional bodies, but they are not. In this case, the divisions between unions need not divide workers, and may even be helpful since nurses are getting together across trade union barriers. Non-trade union workers (and that includes Agency nurses) are therefore not excluded by the workers' own way of organising. The divisions that are dangerous are between hospital workers – nursing and non-nursing staff, NHS and Agency nurses. They must come together and refuse these divisions that the government, unions and the Left are trying to deepen. Racism and sexism are not about abstract moral attitudes, but about whether you take position with black women, Agency or non-Agency, auxiliary, SRN or SEN.

The Agency nurse is the first to refuse to be tied to the hospital hierarchy, thereby confronting the blackmail that faces all nurses, that they are caring 'professionals' and not workers. The issues which have created the Agency nurse are fundamental to all nurses and in fact to all women, but the unity necessary to make a fight will come only when NHS nurses join with Agency nurses to raise these issues.

Mrs D., who comes from Jamaica, started off as a nursing auxiliary and after some years trained as an SEN. She is now doing Agency work and explains why:

Well, I wanted to go home on a holiday. I hadn't seen my mother for over ten years. I went to the matron and asked her if I could have my five weeks' holiday, plus three weeks without pay. She said 'No', I would have to resign and then rejoin . So I resigned ... It's not that you have to start training again, but after you're qualified, each year you're a year up, and when you get to three years you're a Senior Enrolled Nurse and you get a higher pay than when you are first or second year. If you break your time before your three years are up, you have to start back at Grade 1, which is what happened to me. I tried to rejoin but I couldn't get in, so I decided to go to the Agency ... I don't know why I couldn't get back in – they're supposed to be short of nurses. I work the night shifts ... It's not more money. You may get £2 or £3 more than on days, but for me it's much more convenient because ... it suits me and fits in with my housework ... I'm working now in Battersea. Most of the night staff are black. Night nurses are black because they have children and it's more convenient for them to be at home in the days to see after the children. If you work days you're not there to send them off to school, you're not there to receive them when they come back, and you have to get somebody to look after them. With nights, you can actually put them off to bed before going to work.

I support the strike wholeheartedly. Nurses are saying they won't work with Agency nurses and I think they're being silly, because they should find out why nurses have to go on the Agency, because in my case it's not because I wanted to but because I was forced to – I can't do without working. If I could have got back into the hospital, I would have because there is more security and there are periods with the Agency when I can't get work at all, like in the winter when the nurses are not on holidays. If you are ill on the Agency, you get no pay and no looking after.

'CARIBBEAN WOMEN AND THE BLACK COMMUNITY'
Race Today Women, April 1975

Five black women hospital ancillary workers were elected by their fellow workers as part of the negotiating team to represent them in government talks in the recent pay beds dispute at Westminster Hospital, London. Their presence confounded many. From a hostile white public came a racist backlash in the form of hundreds of abusive letters, and a bomb. More importantly, their presence shows that a new stage has been reached in the struggle of West Indian women in Britain and smashes the myth that this generation of West Indian women do not participate in militant action. The following is part of an interview with one of those women. It is clear from her confident manner that she feels an equal to those government representatives, and is in no way intimidated by them. In short, it is the expression of a woman who, for centuries, has had to be subservient because she has always had to evaluate the needs of others before she could consider her own:

The dispute arose when, because of a shortage of staff, management decided to close 48 beds in NHS wards while all the private wards remained open. We auxiliaries went on a work-to-rule in protest against that decision. Eight of us met with government representatives, five of us were West Indian women. I went to negotiate and sat and heard what the other side had to say. I had to tell one of them that I was not fighting for money but for my people out there. I asked him how he would feel if he fell ill and could not get a bed at the hospital because none was available. He mumbled something and I warned him not to talk to me at the back of his teeth. 'Speak up and say what you have to say', I said to him. I give as much as I get. They were forced to compromise and 14 NHS beds were kept open.

My first experience of strike action was in 1972. We did not stay out very long. We wanted more money. At that time we worked in the hospital scrubbing and cleaning. You came to work at 7.00 a.m. and went home at midday, back again at 2.00 p.m. and left at 7.00 p.m. and at the end of the week you had £10 in your hand. It was a wonderful experience striking. We marched and shouted. From 1972 to today, we have had to fight for everything we have since won. Now we no longer work the split shift but we work harder than before because after 1974, they introduced the bonus system – where before there were four of us to a ward, now there are only two. We have problems with patients and doctors alike. I had to threaten to throw water over a doctor the other day. She said to me, 'You don't talk to doctors like that.' I told her she was only a woman and she must learn some manners.

The nurses were all against us in 1972, but when they came out in 1974, they wanted us to support them. We didn't bother about them. Now they see that we are getting what we want, some of them are trying to join our union, NUPE. They come to our meetings and say what they have to say and if we think it's all right then we tell them they can join. If it's not all right then we tell them they can't join. There are spies, because a lot of them go off and tell their union, (RCN) what we have to say and then the trouble starts. To me, the nurses feel that they are with the government and nothing can touch them, while we can be kicked out or kicked around at any time. I know NUPE are against agency nurses but the way I look at it, if in my job I could get more money by joining an Agency, I would do it? It's not the work I want. I am only lending my labour for the money. So if I can lend my labour to something to get more money, I would. I think it's useful to be in the union now, especially in this hospital, 'cause if it was not for the union then a lot of us would suffer. Although we have this union, with the chair, the secretary, stewards and so on, we have to be on our toes all the while, 'cause the management tries to cut you in every way they can. But once they find out that we are not stupid then they don't bother.

These black women are representatives of that section of West Indian people who came to Britain during the early years of immigration. They came as part of a defeated and demoralised section of the Caribbean working class, to a hostile country, to do the worst jobs with the lowest wage. Beginning in this country with little but themselves, these women have been crucial in laying the foundations of the black community as we know it today. Their capacity to fight is not a phenomenon new to their presence in Britain, but is a continuation of their struggle in the Caribbean. Their rebellion in the workforce in Britain has not always been seen, although it has been central to the trends of rebellion currently being shown in all areas of the health service.

Anti-colonial Struggle

Under colonialism in the Caribbean, those women in the lower middle class and the working class who could get employment worked as teachers, nurses, in the sugar industry, as domestic servants and seamstresses, and washing and ironing for white colonials and the black middle class. A large number of women were employed in agricultural work and 'petty trading' – selling whatever surplus produce they could glean from the land at the markets. Male unemployment was extensive and in many cases the money earned by the women was the only source of income for a family.

The population saw the presence of the British as the central cause of their condition and in the hope of a brighter future, women threw themselves into the independence movements whose leaders promised a better deal if they were put in power. Their activities were instrumental in defeating British colonialism and in bringing to power the working-class leaders of these movements, e.g., Bustamante in Jamaica and Eric Gairy in Grenada.

Women were the organisational backbone of the political parties. They formed their own sections within them. All the administrative work fell on their shoulders. They organised meetings, rallies, went on demonstrations, and entered into physical fights if anyone spoke against their particular leaders. They were used also as leading spokeswomen to win over support from other sections. In Trinidad in the early '50s, the women's auxiliary of the Oil Field Workers' Trades Union was formed. Women were leading speakers because they were free to speak out against employers where the workers themselves could not. Daisy Crick, a founder member of this organisation, later became a leading spokeswoman for the People's National Movement, Trinidad.

In Grenada, Gairy was able to find out the views and plans of the British colonial administration by using the network of domestic workers who worked in their homes. These white men and women were so contemptuous of black women that they would discuss political affairs in front of them, never believing that they were capable of comprehending the significance of what was being said.

In Guyana, in 1953 (pre-independence). the party manifesto of the PPP demanded that the position of domestic workers be addressed. They did so not because they were sympathetic, but because the struggle of the domestic workers haunted every single political formation. Support was essential if woman's votes were to be won. A committee was appointed under Jesse Burnham to look into the conditions of employment of domestic workers who were getting a very low wage and no time off. Women particularly in Georgetown were active on the issue of rents. They staged a demonstration demanding that the Governor look into the malpractices of landlords, high rents and security of tenure. They were met by mounted police, tear-gassed and beaten. At the same time, women's groups were formed in both the rural areas and towns; they raised issues particular to themselves and discussed the position and political activities of women all over the world.

Pitfalls of Nationalism

After the British had been driven out and these leaders came to power, the real political complexion of the leadership became clear as the leaders compromised with Britain and America to further exploit the national resources of their countries – bauxite, oil, sugar, asphalt and also people. Large-scale unemployment was the order of the day; all the hopes and aspirations of the people betrayed.

None felt this betrayal as much as the women. The little that was gained by the population did not include them. The administrative jobs that became vacant with the departure of the British were filled by middle-class men and a minority of women. Those industries that came were primarily assembly industries and clothing industries, but never on a scale large enough to absorb the mass of women. They were the chief source of labour for this work, but the intense competition for the few jobs available kept wages very low.

The Flight to Britain

The migration of working-class men and women began in the early 1950s. During the years following the Second World War, the British economy developed two distinct features. There was a shortage of indigenous labour, and an expanding economy meant that the native workforce could begin to bargain more successfully for the terms of their employment and where that employment might be. It meant also that a huge injection of labour was needed to fill these areas and thus undermine the fight of British workers. In other words, capital's plan aimed at killing two birds with one stone: to use the defeat of the West Indian working class to undermine the gains of workers in the metropolis, and to get some cheap labour at the same time.

Black workers were recruited into those sections of industry requiring cheap unskilled labour, and in service industries. Their arrival in Britain was greeted with extreme hostility by white workers and in the late '50s the two fought running battles in Nottingham and London. West Indian women were especially suited to fill these two areas because of their experience in their countries of origin. Service work was something that every black woman was familiar with, from slavery to colonialism and they had constantly rebelled against it. The factories which employed them were food factories (Lyons had its own recruiting facilities in the Caribbean), shoe factories, garment factories and unskilled assembly lines. Because the wages they received were so desperately low, they supplemented it by taking home 'out-work' – machining at home for which they were paid on a piece-work basis.

Many of them came as independent workers leaving their families behind. Some were recruited directly in the West Indies, some heard of jobs through friends who had gone before them, some found jobs for themselves on arrival. They came to Britain with nothing but themselves, no material goods – but brought the tradition of rebellion and resistance they had fashioned in the womb of colonial society. For the majority of them, it was the first time they had engaged in wage labour in a modern industrial economy. They worked long hours for little pay. The average wage was around £6 per week, compared to white women who during the same period were receiving an average wage of £8 a week. They not only maintained themselves and the children they might have with them, in food, rent and clothing, but maintained also their children and relatives in the Caribbean.

Ninety-eight per cent of the children of Jamaican women were left behind when they came to England, and between 1961 and 1963 some £22 million was sent back to Jamaica. A survey taken in Nottingham in 1965 showed that 85 per cent of West Indian women were sending money back home. They lived a one-room existence in houses often shared by several other immigrant men and women. To find accommodation as a black person was no easy task and most houses carried signs saying 'No blacks here'. Facilities such as irons and radios were shared and women cooked not only for themselves but for those men in the houses who were single. Their major preoccupation was to earn enough money to provide a stable situation into which they could bring their children.

What follows are some of the experiences of Jamaican families who were interviewed in 1962 about their lives in Britain.

Mr and Mrs Davis

When the money for the fare to England arrived from Mrs Davis's husband, she was sick, desperate, and she spent it on other things. He refused to send her any more. Although she had six children, and a mother to care for, she worked in Jamaica until she had saved up the remainder. She had been working for 15 years as a maid and felt that if only she could go to England for six years or so and then return she could make good. The six children were left with their grandmother in Jamaica and Mrs Davis joined her husband in England. Her first experience of work here was in a button factory 'It's a button factory, drilling and wrapping parcels. I knew someone working there; she told me about a vacancy and I went and asked. They pay me £4.17 less tax. I went to many places before I got this. I saw one job in a paper, when I got there they said the vacancy had gone and the next day I saw it in the paper. There were no coloured there, pure white. That is why they wouldn't take me, pure white.'

Mr Davis earns £12 a week and their weekly expenditure reads like this:

£3. 15s. On rent
£1 1s. 6d gas and oil
£4. 0s. 0d. to Jamaica
£3. 0s. 0d. Food
£1. 7s. 6d. transport £1. 0s. 0d. clothing
£2. 6s. 0d. baby things, etc.
£16. 0s. 0d.

Mr Davis said, 'We have no furniture at all. We stay at home, don't jump around much, we don't even have the money at weekend to start anything. Just once in a while we go to church, nothing, no show, nowhere. Can't afford to lose a shilling. I would like to go back to Ja. but not save a halfpenny, that's what troubling me now. You see as far as I am concerned I really like Ja. very much, but you know, you see the politician run Ja. into a wreck'.

Mrs Sylvester

Mrs Sylvester left her four children aged six, five, four and three in Jamaica with her husband. In London she lives in a small room just large enough to hold a bed, dressing table and wardrobe. She works as a 'spotter' in a dry cleaning establishment. She rises at 5.45 every morning to go to work. Working overtime most nights, to earn more money, means she doesn't get home until 6.30 or 7.00 p.m. The long hours Mrs. Sylvester work earn her £7 a week, but some weeks up to £8 with overtime.

Cynthia

Cynthia is 34. In Jamaica she would do any work that came to hand – a little cooking, dressmaking, or helping in the local shop; but it was difficult to obtain regular employment so she decided to come to England. At first she worked washing dishes in a railway cafeteria for less than £5 a week. She then worked inking shoes in a shoe factory earning nearly £7 until finally she found employment as a domestic help in a hospital earning nearly £8 a week with overtime. She lived in Stoke Newington in a house shared by about eight families. She had met a lot of hostility from white people.: 'Today, if only I could take a bus home to Ja. I would go. It is because you haven't got much money, then to make yourself better you have to come, and because people here feel that they have a little whiter skin, that they can take liberties with you.' She often works three hours overtime to bring her salary up to £7.12 and she puts aside £1 for Ja. each week but saves it

85

for a few weeks as: 'I can't send £1 to Ja. looks too cheap.' She is still paying back the fare she borrowed to get to England in the first place.

The Making of a Community

In one way or another, the vibrancy of the black community today is traceable to the social activities of those black women who arrived here first. Organisations and clubs emerged to give a scattered community a sense of identity here. As in the West Indies, the Church became an important vehicle for looking after the welfare of the community. Women not only formed the majority of its congregation but organised social activities such as outings, dances, meetings. In those early years, these activities provided the only means whereby working-class black people could come together for relaxation and entertainment in what was otherwise an intolerably isolated existence.

Later these clubs were to form the basis for the first national organisation of black people in Britain: CARD (Campaign Against Racial Discrimination). The women were never mentioned, for it was primarily the men who did the talking, but they carried out the essential administrative donkey work necessary to keep the organisation alive and intact, as they had done in political and social organisations in the Caribbean.

Since the British government did not increase expenditure on its social services to deal with this new addition to the workforce – i.e., provision of housing, nurseries, adequate schooling, etc. – the entire burden of servicing black labour rested with the women. In the absence of child-care facilities, the women had to create their own. Many West Indian mothers who were unable to work because they had young children, undertook the burden of childminding. In the late '60s when the community mobilised against the large numbers of their children being channelled into ESN schools, educationalists and social workers avoided responsibility by putting the blame on the mothers for working and using childminders. The racism of the social services meant that only direct action from the black community would result in changes of policy. This is clearly shown in the area of council housing, where the policy of the authorities was either to give no house at all or to allocate those houses which were in the worst conditions.

In 1970, Merle Major from Trinidad, after a number of years waiting to be re-housed by the council, was the first black woman to squat with her children in council property in Notting Hill. Within days, the council made her an offer. Today, squatting is widespread in the black community.

In the home, the mothers constantly impressed upon their children that they had to get something better for themselves, that they should not go through what their parents had to. Education was seen by parents as a way of guaranteeing a better future for their children and much of the militant activity by women has been around ensuring this. When they saw that the schools their children were attending were 'dustbin' schools, they were instrumental in setting up supplementary schools in black communities up and down the country – Birmingham, Nottingham, London and Leeds. (In London, one such school has been named after a black mother, Albertina Sylvester, who was crucial in its organisation.) They also campaigned against the racist policies and practices of the education authorities. In 1968 in Haringey, they stopped the banding scheme which was an attempt to channel black children into 'special' schools under the pretext of attending to their disadvantages. In Chapeltown Leeds in 1973, black mothers sustained the campaign against conditions in Cowper Street school and its racist headmaster. As part of the campaign, they withdrew their children from the school. Faced with this, the authorities promised better conditions and removed its headmaster.

New Development

By the late '60s and early '70s, the immigrant workforce here began to feel strong enough to confront their employers openly. The strength to do so came from the strong communities they had established and from the rebellion of black people that was taking place internationally, particularly in the United States and Africa. For immigrant women employed by the NHS, it meant that they could qualitatively change their form of rebellion and we see them now at the vanguard of bringing the strike weapon to the NHS.

Immigrant Workers – The Unions

Whenever immigrant workers in this country have moved in their own interest they have not only had to fight management but also the unions, which have often not only refused to support them but have actively opposed collective action taken by groups of black workers. It is only when workers have organised themselves independently that the unions have rushed in, eager to recruit and to control that action.

West Indian women have not only had to face the racism of the unions but have also had their interests as women ignored. In the auxiliary strike of 1972 and again in the nurses' strike of 1974, the unions gained thousands of new members, mostly women in whom they previously had no interest. Their opportunism was clear for all to see. However, when black women tried to raise issues specific to them they were told that this was not what the union was for:

> We haven't raised the question of discrimination because at our first meeting it was said it wasn't a meeting for that. I joined the union COHSE since the strike for protection. I have been to two meetings, one at the Maudsley and the other at Bethlem, and the things Mr Spanswick told us were different from what he said on the television. 'STRIKE', he said to us, and when 1 saw him on the television he said that he thinks that nurses are dedicated and that if they walk out on patients they would lose their reputation. (Nursing assistant in a psychiatric hospital)

The Second Generation

Young black women are today continuing the traditions of rebellion handed down from their mothers and grandmothers. Not only do they draw on the experience of their mothers but also of those hundreds of young women who participated in the Black Power organisations in Britain during the late '60s. This rebellion is characterised by open confrontation with the police, against school authorities and employers, and indeed within their own families, all of whom have been unable to contain them. Their boldness stems from their never having experienced the bitterness of defeat as their mothers once had. Violent clashes between mother and daughter often ensue, as the push for independence from one conflicts with the aspirations of the other. As a result, hundreds of young black women are in hostels provided by the state.

Sociologists, psychologists, police and community relations workers are eager to blame this on black mothers 'not caring' enough, and advance spurious arguments about the breakdown of the black family. This is an attack on the black woman who as we have shown has always had to carry the burden of the black family. What distinguishes this rebellion of young black women from their mothers is that they know what is available now in Britain and want it without having to be wage slaves. The seeds of this rebellion were sown in the homes where they have witnessed at first hand what the lives of their mothers have been and what they themselves have had to say about it: 'My mother is a ticket collector for London Transport. She's in a lift all day just collecting tickets. When she comes home she is always tired, saying I won't encourage anyone to work at London Transport' (18–year-old West Indian woman).

But for the parents, the activities of the young refusers of work seem to be in opposition to everything they have fought so hard to achieve:

If I had my daughter here and I told her to go out and work for honest bread, and she refused, I would ask her, 'Which is better – to go on the street or work for her honest bread?' Don't get me wrong, if she has the education and she can find a job, then that's all right with me. But suppose she can't find a job – what would you do? I would prefer to do what I am doing now than going on the street and robbing, and I don't want social security cause they have to go into too much of my private life and my private life is my private life.

Sometimes it makes me mad to go on the street and see the young people, the things that they are carrying on 'cause it makes me ashamed to be in England. Young people if they have the education, and came out of school and can't find a job, should not let the police manhandle them on the street, because don't forget, the way they handle the white youth they are not going to handle a black youth. They bash them about. Before they come into conflict with the police, if it's even to sweep the street just for the money, then they should accept. I am truly sorry for the young people of today. Some of them turn around and don't appreciate what their parents have done for them. They abuse the parents and it makes me mad because it's my own colour. The way the police treat them is disgusting. I take my own eyes and see. They walk down the street and the first black one they can see they pick on. (Member of the Westminster Hospital negotiating team)

It is not that they are against young people refusing to do the work that their parents were forced to do. They oppose the alternative activity practised by the youth because it makes them vulnerable to attacks by the police. The weakness of their situation stems from the lack of a regular wage and the discipline that goes with getting one. The fact that a number of them have young children means that they suffer also the powerlessness of being a housewife.

Mugging, shoplifting, and other such activities are all manifestations of powerlessness. We do not believe that as an alternative these young sisters should be told to work in a factory, for London Transport, or to clean hospital floors. Rather they should receive a social wage. What the state has so far been forced to give in the form of urban aid in response to the rebellion of blacks shows that the money is available and the demand a possibility.

From receiving either no wage at all in the West Indies, or at best an irregular one, to receiving a regular wage under the discipline of a modern industrial economy in the metropolis has given older West Indian women an access to power previously denied to them. Although the West Indian community here is relatively new (25 years old) those women on the NUPE negotiating team have shown that they are now ready to begin to exercise that power. If any event is to be celebrated in this so-called International Women's Year, then surely this must be it.

'BLACK WOMEN AND THE WAGE'
Race Today, April 1975

As black women, we are a substantial section of the workforce of this country. In the West Indian community, women comprise the largest section (130,300 women to 127,300 men; 1971 census), yet so far little has been said about either the quality of our lives under the rule of capital or our resistance to it. The article, 'Caribbean Women and the Black Community', begins to look at who these women are and what they are in the process of becoming. This article looks at Asian women from the same perspective.

In contrast to West Indian women, the majority of Asian women came to Britain as the dependants of male workers. Their arrival into the cities of Britain put them into contact with both white society and wage labour for the first time. Up until the late '60s, few Asian women worked outside the home but with the end of male immigration in the '70s, thousands were suddenly recruited into factory production.

The London Council of Social Services (LCSS), in its recently published report, 'The Inner City', confirms that there is a growing tendency of black and Asian women towards wage labour. A working man's pay packet will no longer of itself support a family in London and it asserts that Asian families may find themselves the most vulnerable in this situation. Many Asian men suffer from underemployment. They have qualifications which are not recognised or accepted here and find themselves therefore typically in low-paid employment. The normal pattern would be for the wife to work to supplement the family income, but this runs contrary to the whole Asian pattern of female domesticity. Either they adhere to tradition, the wife does not work and the result is a significant degree of poverty ... or the wife breaks the normal cultural patterns and goes out to work, either as a second wage earner or even, in some cases, where there are vacancies only for female workers, as the sole breadwinner. The result of this on the stability of the family within this community can only be guessed.

In the early '70s, the state intervened with a series of 'socialisation programmes' – language teaching classes, child-care education, health education, etc. – all geared to teaching Asian women English habits, to give them an 'alternative' culture and generally to integrate them into British society. The programmes were, underneath all these liberal-sounding sentiments, a comprehensive preparation for the entry of Asian women into production. New to the labour market, they needed to be both trained and disciplined. The failure of many of these programmes indicate the women's resistance to them. They learnt only what was in their interest and disregarded the rest.

However, this is not to say that Asian women, and generally speaking black women, have not been transformed by the process. The opposite is true. Ever since their arrival in Britain, they have experienced a fast-changing relationship to production, to reproduction (housework), to men and to each other, because capital sets up relationships between people and production, and between people themselves. For instance, if a woman does shift work at a factory and is away from home between 2 p.m. and 10 p.m., she is not available that week to cook and serve the evening meal at home. The consequence is that the division of labour within the family has to undergo some change. Housework has to be reallocated and someone else – either husband or child – has to do it. It is a process which alters the power relations within the family itself. And if white men traditionally do the washing-up, it is because white women have been in contact with wage labour for several generations and not, as some sections of the white women's movement would have it, because as men they are less chauvinistic than their black counterparts.

For the Asian woman who comes from a tradition of the joint family, and the West Indian woman who comes from a tradition of the extended family, both the roles of housewife in the nuclear family and 'factory worker' are in some senses new. The two experiences interact – one informs the other – and by receiving a wage for her labour outside the home, she is able to evaluate her labour in the home. When one job is waged, it provides an index with which to measure the value of that which is still unwaged; in order to demand a price for ones labour power, one must be aware of its value. And black and Asian women are showing that they are very aware.

As one woman in Southall puts it: 'Equal pay with men? We do twice as much work – we should get double pay.'

'THE FEMINIST BOOK FAIR'
Sarah White, October 1984

The First International Feminist Book Fair took place in London on June 7, 8 and 9 this year, with an accompanying programme of associated events, spread over a two-week period and taking place throughout the country. The Book Fair was a trade success, a media success, a social success, possibly a literary success – but it was not a radical political success. Why? Should one ever have expected it to be in the first place?

Book fairs are not automatically radical and neither is feminism. The women's movement is like the black movement. To understand any feminist organisation, you have to see where it is coming from, where it is going to and whose interests it represents. The First International Feminist Book Fair did project itself as part of the tradition of radical book fairs in Britain, the tradition of the Socialist Book Fair and the International Book Fair of Radical Black and Third World Books. But if you look carefully at the pre-publicity put out by the organisers then you find a heavy emphasis on the trade and commercial aspects of works by women writers rather than any particular concern with the way forward in the women's movement.

On the form that went out to publishers seeking their participation in the book fair, the major quote used was from a Mr Poultney of W.H. Smith's: 'We are supporting this promotion because the demand for feminist books is a demand for more books – a real growth.' Then the preamble to the 'List of Recommended Books' published by the Feminist Book Fair Group states: 'To celebrate the quantity, quality and diversity of women's writing internationally and to focus attention on one of the healthiest *growth areas* of the book trade, we are happy to announce this major trade and cultural event' (my italics).

So you got special displays in W.H. Smith's and other bookshops during the two-week event. Up and down the country, books by Alice Walker, Maya Angelou, Toni Cade Bambara and other women writers were being promoted to the British public. There were signing sessions with visiting writers and point-of-sales promotional material. But this was not because W.H. Smith's had suddenly decided that Alice Walker, Maya Angelou, Toni Cade Bambara and others were good writers; nor had W.H. Smith's turned into a supporter of women's rights. W.H. Smith's was just doing its job of selling books – and at the moment books by women, in particular Afro-American women, do sell. That was one message that came out of the First International Feminist Book Fair very loud and clear.

The organisers were equally successful in getting extensive media coverage for the book fair. There were interviews with many of the women writers visiting Britain on the radio and TV, write-ups in many of the national newspapers, and numerous articles in the more radical alternative press. The *New Statesman* for example devoted three pages to the event, something it has certainly never done for the International Book Fair of Radical Black and Third World Books.

The First International Feminist Book Fair brought over a large number of women writers from many different countries, courtesy of UNESCO, who footed the fares bill. These included such writers as Toni Cade Bambara, Rosa Guy, Audre Lorde and Adrienne Rich (the US), Suniti Namjoshi, Madhu Kishwar and Urvashi Butalia (India), Maureen Watson and Faith Bandler (Australia), and Jester Tshuma (Zimbabwe). They spoke in numerous forums ranging from 'An International Lesbian Writers' Celebration' and 'A Black and Third World Women Writers' Evening', to individual presentations of works from the different countries involved.

But what was the purpose of all this activity? Apart from selling books and generally having a useful and enjoyable social encounter among women writers and publishers? Was there a solid political core to the book fair and to the events that 'tried to show the way forward in the women's movement today' or 'tried to raise and discuss key issues facing the women's movement today'?

I went to what I presumed would be the keynote forum in Kensington Town Hall: '"Different" Concepts of Women's Liberation Internationally'. I could not believe my ears when the chairperson, Robyn Archer, introduced the evening by saying that her brief from the organisers had been to find four non-controversial readings representing different aspects of the women's movement internationally. And she had clearly been prepared to accept such a brief. Well, I thought, perhaps this will work as a cultural experience, a prose reading that will give the audience the same lift, excitement and inspiration that a good poetry reading does. Unfortunately it didn't. Toni Cade Bambara came closest with her brilliantly funny reading of her short story 'Gorilla my Love'. Faith Bandier (an Aboriginal writer from Australia) and Dorothy Nelson (Ireland) had the difficult task of making something out of short extracts from long novels. Petra Kelly (from the Green Movement in Germany) did not even try. After disowning the recent publication in English of her book (because it was full of sexist mistranslations), she then treated the audience to some words of wisdom from her mentor Emma Goldman, again too short and disjointed to make much sense or impact. And none of this gave any idea of the women's movement internationally (which is how the forum had been billed), nor what are or were the particular problems and concerns of women in the four areas represented: black Australia, black America, Ireland and West Germany.

That forum certainly did not come to grips with any issues and from what I could see looking at the programme, neither did any other of the forums. Interestingly, I could not find any mention on the programme of what have been two major developments in Britain: the Greenham Common Women's protest, and the vital solidarity shown by working-class women, miners' wives and others, to the National Union of Mineworkers in the current miners' strike.

The First International Feminist Book Fair succeeded in putting on a good book fair (in the sense of a good representative selection of books) and a wide number of events, primarily because at the moment books by women sell and it was that aspect that the organisers took as their starting point. So what happens when the boom in women's publishing passes, as all fashions come and go? There will be no guarantee then of W.H. Smith's promotion, UNESCO's fare money, wide media interest or even GLC support. When the fairy godmothers have gone, what core will remain?

'TALKING TO TWO BLACK AMERICAN WOMEN WRITERS'
Race Today Review, 1985

Novelist Toni Morrison and poet, playwright and novelist Ntozake Shange are among the most notable writers of this decade. In the following interviews, Toni Morrison discusses feminism, publishing and writing. Ntozake Shange describes her personal and social background.

Toni Morrison

Publishing opportunities for blacks in America have been limited, and as whites select black literature, it would appear to indicate that most blacks who are being published are found to be acceptable only to the white-dominated publishing industry. Has this changed in any way?

The white publishing industry is still interested in books that make a stir and sell extremely well. That means that they are quite willing to take books by blacks, provided they do make a stir. So they don't have to be acceptable in the sense of being supportive of the system of the country. They will publish quite sensational, revolutionary things, or they used to. As a matter of fact, it was very fashionable at one time to do so because it was easy to promote and people were interested in it. What is difficult to acquire in a publishing house such as this one [i.e., a commercial publisher], is a book that has some literary element to it, rather than political or polemical. But that's true of everybody, and I think it is difficult only because the market is difficult. I can't really say that there is this gate that is closed to blacks. I'd like to say it, but I know that first novelists, fiction writers, poetry writers – all over – can't get published either. I'm inclined to think that the reading public prefers diet books and sex books and spy stories, the kind of things that are easy to solve. So that it's harder to get any fiction, let alone black fiction through.

In the task of reconstructing the literary history of black women, do you think it important that the black woman writer should not negate her gender, but leave a clear imprint in her writings?

Oh yes, she shouldn't negate her gender, ever.

We make men and women, we give birth to boys and girls, and that makes us much more egalitarian in our outlook than men. So I think it should be easier for a woman to write convincingly about a man, much more easy than it is for a man to write convincingly about a woman. The normal concept of women writers is that they are in a nest, or some closed-up place, and that women should only write about women, or be able to do that. But I think that simply puts us in a position of doing precisely what we've accused men of doing, which is only to write about their own games and to write about us in a very insensitive manner. We ought to be able to do much better than that, because of our gender.

What do you see as the responsibilities of the black woman writer?

To bear witness to a history that is unrecorded, untaught in mainstream education and to enlighten our people. If it happens in so doing that one sheds light to anybody else, then that's fine, that's great, but that's not its purpose.

Do you see the need and justification for a black feminist perspective?

I don't really know what that is. I sort of know, but every time I read some criticism written from a black feminist perspective, I don't know what's making it black feminist. I can't follow; it's elusive. I'm attracted by the phrase 'black feminism', but it sounds so contemporary and so new. It suggests that there was nothing like that in the past. Sojourner Truth and Harriet Tubman were enough black feminism for me, but they were women, and they were nurturers and they did not need to stand tall only when men were on their knees. My brother, my sons are men. I will not betray them, and if black feminism requires me to, then I won't. But there are other black feminists who don't find that a problem at all. You know the phrase is not clear to me – that's what I'm saying.

I find it interesting that you say 'betray'. That leads on to my next question. In Black Macho & the Myth of the Superwoman, *do you feel that Michele Wallace presented too harsh a picture of the black man?*

Her picture was inaccurate, because she either didn't do her homework, or she was caught up in headline language. Her research was questionable, her logic was fallible. So that the subject was an important one, and I was disappointed in the superficial way in which it was treated.

In your first novel, The Bluest Eye, *your anger was more apparent, perhaps than your later works. If you confronted it, do you think it would seriously change the direction of your writing?*

I never felt that way, ever, in any of them.

You didn't? In an interview with Melvyn Bragg, on the South Bank Show in London, I believe he asked you a question: were you ever seriously tempted to let loose, like Baldwin has? Do you try to shelve it?

Absolutely. Anger is not an artistic feeling, that's not what my writing is for. I think it is inappropriate in my work, really inappropriate, because it subjugates the work to one single emotion, an emotion that is sometimes blinding. I resent the need for anger in art. It's very much like the books of the '60s when they only wanted black books to show it, the kind of flag-ellation that white people enjoy – Tell me how terrible it was for you, tell me what we did to you, show me your anger. You know? And if it's there and it's honest, and it informs the sensibility, then it should be there. My anger is much more direct in my life, but I don't need a way to show it. Art is not therapeutic for me, I don't need to express it in that way. It's bigger than that, much bigger than that. The characters in the book can show whatever they are: some of them are furious; some of them are not; some are rather sweet and abiding and some of them are not. But I try to make them whoever they are. I could never write out of that place. James Baldwin can because he is very cold, his mode is very cold. He can control his anger and convert it into an art form so that it looks extremely passionate, but it's very well controlled. He feeds it to you, and there's this coolness about it; it's never harangue in that sense. But I think that's because he writes a lot of non-fiction. In his fiction sometimes it's harder to control, when the characters are jumping up and down, you know they are slippery. But when he writes non-fiction he has to appear along that line. I wouldn't trust anger as a motivating force for any book I wrote. I wouldn't trust it.

A question mark hangs over Sula's ten-year absence from Medallion yet we glean she has been to college, which seems even more mysterious when we ponder the economics of the black woman's situation in the late 1920s and 1930s. Is this in keeping with the idea that the person who leaves the community is capable of doing anything?

She had a lot of money, Sula. She lived better than every black person in the community, and in the '20s and '30s it was a very inexpensive proposition to go to college. It must have cost all of 30 dollars a semester. But she didn't stay very long. I wrote a section in *Sula* about those ten years when she was gone, only a small part of which was her on the campus, but I didn't like it; it moved the book from the town in a way I didn't wish it to be moved. Nel goes away as a little girl to New Orleans with her mother that one time, and I wanted Sula to go away, and then both to return; so I had written that part, but it wasn't right and the life of those ten years disjointed it somehow, so that I only had to allude to it, so that she is, in those ten years only, what she is when she comes back. And I threw all that away.

Do you think that black men and women will ever regain the comradeship which you remember as a child?

Yes. I'm not sure that in some ways it was entirely lost. Certainly it has a new form. Black women, historically, had the same expectations as far as work was concerned: they were always in competition with men; white women generally were not, so that there was an interesting if oppressed kind of egalitarianism between men and women. There was not the little babydoll.

97

Then economics changed and there was some desire on the part of the men to have their women stay at home, which was viewed as progress. The ability to take care. Now the situation is in a crisis state again, so that everybody's working, the men encouraging their wives to work, all men, because money is so hard to find. So that may restore the comradeship, two people working. Years ago, both of them had to get to the end of the field at the same time, and carry as much cotton as the other. Black women were the first labourers in this country in slavery, and they had to produce as much as the men. Then there was a period when that wasn't true. Now, even though it may not be field work, it is still very necessary. I would imagine that with young couples that get married now, it's not so necessary for the man to pretend that his wife doesn't have to work, so therefore they can have a hand-in-hand relationship – the younger ones. People of my generation may have more trouble with it; you would hear men in my generation speak of 'my wife doesn't have to work', as though that were a plus, an advantage, and some mark of their abilities. She may want to, but his boast is that she doesn't have to, to show how far along he has come. But for the young people now, that may not be such a big deal.

So what it comes down to is the economics of the situation?

Of course.

Have you any major aims to fulfil?

I have an important book I'd like to write, but I haven't begun to think coherently about it. What I really want to do is what we were always taught to do, which is to make it possible for somebody else to do the same thing, so that young black writers who don't even know they're writers yet, will think about it seriously, or that young black people would work in the publishing world. If one does that, it's like an open door, so that it is a communal effort ... one tomorrow, two, then three ... then you know ... the Jackie Robinson syndrome. It only needs one to open the door.

Who are your favourite black women writers?

Toni Cade Bambara, Gayle Jones, Alice Walker. I haven't read much of Zora Neale Hurston, just the short stories, but what I know is enough.

Nikki Giovanni?

Some. I like her. But a lot of her poetry I don't like.

I recently bought two of her books: one was My House *and some I really like, but others I couldn't unravel.*

Yes, some of it was so hoary, I'm not sure out of which place it came. But I think I can recognize the value of a genuine emotion in her writing – what is really there, and in some irrevocable way you get it. In some of her poems it seemed less honest, although the craft sometimes is there. The poems are deft but I don't trust it. There's a black man writer, who is dead now, named Henri Dumas, who is my favourite black American writer of all time, and it was quite extraordinary because he could write out of so many places. He wrote about women in a quite extraordinary way, like Jean Toomer was able to in *Cane*, write about men and women in this most incredible, sensitive way. So that a list for me of black writers must include those two, in spite of the fact that they are men!

Ntozake Shange

What is your family background. Where and how did you spend your childhood?

I was born in New Jersey. My father was a physician, my mother is a sociologist. I have two sisters and a brother. We stayed in New Jersey until it was time for me to go to kindergarten. My father was inducted into the army and we moved to upstate New York. From there we moved to St Louis and then back to New Jersey.

How did you spend your schooldays?

In St Louis. I was sent to a Magnet School for gifted children. In a certain area, they would pick out the children they decided were gifted. You had to take an IQ test at about the age of eight or nine. My particular school was all-white. It was predominantly German-American. It was very difficult for me, not because they had never seen black people before, but they'd never thought they'd have to associate with them. And it was just rather bleak in a sense that the kids who were in the gifted class with me didn't seem to mind my presence but the other children in the school seemed to resent us very much. My sister came to the same school and except for one other girl, we were the only black children there for years.

You have said about your childhood that sometimes a poem was the only safe place you could find.

I think I was very sensitive to being isolated. I was very sensitive to the fact that I thought people weren't treating me what I would call ordinary, normal. There was always the possibility that some white person, some white kid would make some snide remark to me. I felt very uncomfortable about that. So it made the few moments I could spend by myself, usually, reading, very important to me. It wasn't that anybody was in any way jeopardising my person, but I think I was an isolated child. I had friends on the streets in the neighbourhood I lived in but I could only see my black friends at the weekends and after school. On the other hand, they went to all-black schools and I sort of envied them because they didn't have the disruption of their lives the way I did. They saw each other all day so their sense of unity, of being free with one another was stronger than mine. Also, at that time, the mid-1950s, there was still a lot of places that would only serve black people at certain times. I wasn't unaware that it was peculiar for me to be going to this white school. It was peculiar for everybody.

What are your earliest memories of being interested in the arts?

My mother always wanted to be an actress. And she was, and still is, a great elocutionist. To entertain us, I guess to give us some kind of cultural background, she would sometimes recite poems by Paul Dunbar, Countee Cullen and Langston Hughes. She genuinely liked this poetry and these poets and had seen some in her lifetime at poetry readings in New York. She would share with us what she knew and liked. She was a great friend of Paul Robeson and Marion Anderson, so these names were familiar to us. My father was a real jazz buff. He knew about the Kansas City Si, Lester Young, Coleman Hawkins, Bobby Timmons, Dizzy Gillespie and a lot of Latin artists. Some were friends of my father's, who he would go to see or invite to the house after they finished work.

Were you able to pursue your interest in the arts at school?

In New Jersey, when I was about 13 or 14, I played in the school orchestra and in the band. I was in this gifted programme again where I was the only black person. You know there were thousands of black children in the school, but I didn't see them. I was in this class for so-called gifted children.

What form did this special programme take?

We concentrated on the classics. You were really lucky if you got to read an American novel. Most of the time we spent studying Greek classics, the English novel and very few American writers, which was unfortunate.

You have to remember that it was in the 1960s that students began to demand that attention be paid to contemporary art forms and contemporary artists, as opposed to moulding us in the tradition of an Oxford Fellow. I was also part of that movement when I went to college finally. I went to Barnard College which is the female part of Columbia University from 1966–1970. In 1970/71 I went to graduate school in California. I studied American Studies which had been my major in undergraduate studies. It is an interdisciplinary approach to American culture and allowed me to have a very strong background in literature, history and art history.

So at one time you were specifically interested in the fine arts?

In a scholarly way, I was interested in the fine arts.

Were there many blacks at Barnard?

Barnard is one of the elite schools in the US. It's part of a group called the 'Seven Sisters': Vassar, Bryn Mawr, Mount Holyoke, Wellesley, Pembroke, Radcliffe. They are very elite schools, although they have programmes to recruit so-called minority students. I was one of the first blacks to go.

How did you feel about being part of that elite?

In a way black students were part of an elite, but we also took part in the student rebellions of that period. We shut down the university for two weeks.

What prompted this action?

Racism, and also because we wanted courses that pertained to our lives. The term was 'relevant' as opposed to being steeped in classics that did us no good. We wanted to study North American culture. It was to protest about that – also to demonstrate against the Vietnam War and to make sure the universities divested their interests in South Africa. Barnard students were very active in the Afro-American movement, at that point called the Black Power Movement, and also in the movement against the war.

At graduate school, in the University of Southern California, I studied American Studies with a concentration on vernacular arts and fine arts in Afro-American culture. When I left graduate school, I went to Boston to do a PhD in American Studies, but dropped that. I didn't want to be a secondary source. I thought, why should I do this? We don't have enough artists yet for me to spend all this money and time trying to study the black artists who have lived. There were still a lot of things, artistically, I thought were missing.

When did you start your career as a writer?

I started writing when I was 19, during my junior year at Barnard. I read poetry with a bunch of other poets who were supporters of the Young Lords Party and the Black Panther Party at the time. There was a very strong allegiance and alliance that I think most of us, the people in my group, felt towards both of them. I went to all the Black Power conferences and saw Ron Karenga, Stokely Carmichael, H. Rap Brown, Ralph Featherstone and Kathleen Cleaver. All these people were spotlighting the struggle for the right to vote and reaching out for a broader aspect in the black community in terms of school, in terms of being self-helpers for our communities across the country.

And then of course there were the riots in 1968/69 which made everything very urgent. I was with a group of political activists. The poems we read at rallies helped to arouse the emotions and the spirits of the masses of people. We were the cultural arm of the organisations we served. We weren't organised as a separate body of artists holding exclusive workshops for artists to attend and discuss their work among each other. We served hopefully to inform the public about the issues that the party we were associated with were fighting for. Our readings were a voluntary commitment that we made. It certainly wasn't like a writers' workshop situation, because we might be reading in the middle of a tenement or on street corners.

After your involvement with political groups, did you then work exclusively with other artists?

The CIA and the FBI saw to it that the momentum that the Black Panther Party and the Young Lords Party had gained was severed. There were a lot of murders, a lot of people going to jail, a lot of frustration, and a great sense of dismantlement of a lot of the black political movements and of the Latin movement in the early 1970s.

There were all sorts of covert actions by the FBI to create chaos in the black political movements of the time. So it became important to publish because there were no longer rallies so to speak of, no more black political parties. Half the people were dead. The outlets for us changed. As opposed to being an arm of a political party, those of us who were writers joined together as writers. The more important of the groups I belonged to was a group in Boston called the Collective of Black Artists. We ran a coffee house on Newton Street that featured poetry and music. I left there and moved to California. I joined a group called Third World Writers' Collective and there was a group there – the Third World Women's Collective. We thought we should publish our own poetry and we had a visual arts arm and a printing arm, so we did all the work ourselves. That was called the *Third World Poetry Anthology* and was one of the first to be published in the US. After we did a book called *Time Degrees*. At that time, in San Francisco, there was a large and very powerful women's movement that had books published and printers to publish things that we wrote. All these things were working together, so that we became a voice on our own as opposed to being attached to a political party. There were lots of people who were concerned about the Vietnam War, and oppression in Latin America.

How did you start to write For Colored Girls, *which led to your becoming internationally known?*

When I did poetry readings in California I wanted to bring something to them so they wouldn't be quite so static. I worked with a lot of dancers in the Bay area. There were a number of poetry bars in San Francisco where poets read poetry. You don't get paid for it, you just do it. We would go from one to another, and once a month we would do a performance up to a point where I realised that I had some audience and that I could count on a certain number of people showing up. I had developed an audience. I could keep people listening to me for at least an hour. Because I was doing it such a lot, I just thought that to give some credit to the people I was working with it would be better to form a group.

The group I worked with was called 'For Colored Girls Who Have Considered Suicide When the Rainbow is Enuf'. That is what we called ourselves. It wasn't the name of any particular show, or a piece of literature. We changed it every night. There was a lot of improvisation. We were invited to be part of an alternative jazz festival in New York at the same time as the Newport Jazz Festival. We did a performance which some people who were involved in theatre saw. They asked me, 'Wouldn't you like to see some actresses do this?' It wasn't that I was against actresses doing my work. But it never occurred to me because I thought my work was poetry and I should do it. I said I would try it, and then we started working at a bar called The Old Reliable every Monday night. Several dancers I had worked with had also moved to New York unbeknownst to me. They'd show up at The Old Reliable and we'd do different poems. It was still called 'For Colored Girls' at that point.

I moved to another bar up the street and some producers of theatre came to see us, amongst them Joseph Papp and Woody King. They asked us if we would like to be in a theatre. The piece moved to Henry Street, Solomon House and then to off-Broadway and then Broadway. What was different from what I had done myself was that the pieces were 'set', they didn't change any more. I had to work very hard to find the twenty pieces that would make up the play.

Was For Colored Girls *the first time a production by a black writer has been such a hit on Broadway?*

A Raisin in the Sun was on Broadway and was a great success. During the Harlem Renaissance there were a lot of shows, a lot of reviews by black people which were very successful. But it was the first time, I think in a long time that there had been a show by a black person that ran for so long. It ran 18 months.

What do you see as the responsibilities of an artist?

My responsibility as an artist is to explore and document culture through the means which are available to me, which are fiction, non-fiction and the theatre. Art is truly a tool for one to shape one's life with and, in terms of a large number of artists, to give order and form to a community.

4

Asian Communities, Asian Workers and *Race Today*

INTRODUCTION
Farrukh Dhondy

The end of the Second World War and subsequent dissolution of the British Empire upon which the sun rapidly set, changed the society of Britain in a historically significant way. The British working classes who had laid down life and limb for King and Country were unwilling to live with the class divisions of the past. They voted out Churchill, the icon of victory, and voted in the Labour Party which promised them education, a health service and the march to meritocracy.

The newfound independence of India, Pakistan and the African and Caribbean colonies, in subsequent decades, worked in concert with the new mood of Britain to create a push-pull effect.

The British working class abandoned low-paid and sweated jobs, leaving vast vacancies in the industrial and service sectors of the British economy. The condition in which the British Raj had left their former colonies compelled significant numbers of people from rural India and Pakistan to look across the seas and continents for employment.

The trickle of Asian immigration to Britain of the 1950s turned, in the 1960s, into a current – never, as some claimed, a torrent. Liberal Britain legislated variously both to let immigrants in, for their labour, and also, through xenophobia, to keep them out; to allow their families in, and to keep their families out; to acknowledge their debt to the vast populations they had transferred as indentured labour from one continent to another; to deny those same populations, whom they had enlisted as British subjects, citizenship of the UK. One could go on.

These were decades of British pragmatism, liberal and racist as economic necessity seemed to demand.

What this historically renowned pragmatism didn't include was any social or integrative plan for the immigrant or the new communities which arrived from the ex-colonies and soon-to-be independent Caribbean islands.

The immigrants went where the jobs were. The Mirpuris and Punjabi ex-peasantry from Pakistan were welcome at first on the night shifts, and soon on most shifts of the Yorkshire and Lancashire dark, not-quite-satanic, textile mills. They populated the working-class housing terraces of Bradford, Burnley, Huddersfield and twenty others which rapidly turned, through the denials of prejudice, the magnetism of shared culture, the narrowness of employment and even through sheer differential poverty, from Mill to Mosque towns.

Other industries attracted, through low wages and the flight of their traditional workers, different Asian communities. The Bengalis of East Pakistan, later citizens of independent Bangladesh, mostly the rural dwellers of the eastern district of Sylhet, occupied the poorer streets of the East End of London, employed in the sweated leather and clothing trades which immigrant Jews, and before them the Huguenots, had manned and womanned.

The more prosperous Gujaratis, with clan connections and petty business acumen settled in Wembley in North West London, 15 miles away from the Indian Punjabis, mostly Sikhs, who settled in West London's Southall.

The first organisations the immigrant workers of these settlements formed were several regional and politically divided Indian Workers' Associations and Pakistani Workers' Associations. They uniformly and universally defined their *raison d'être* as supporting, with funds and rhetoric, one or other political party in India or Pakistan. Their members, first-generation immigrants, probably saw their personal suns setting on the horizons of their 'motherlands'. They were guest workers. They'd make their money and go home.

It was not to be. Necessity, institutional racism, the activity of right-wing groups amounting to assault and murder – and the walls, metaphorically barbed-wire, sheltering the gated communities of British privilege and even the much-vaunted British meritocracy, turned immigrant communities to self-organisation.

A hundred flowers bloomed, though some withered and died. Some were dedicated to single issues. In 1976, a 17-year-old Sikh lad called Gurdip Singh Chaggar was fatally stabbed on the streets of Southall. In 1978, Altab Ali, a young sweatshop worker was killed by a random white gang on the streets of the East End. Numerous assaults, motivated by some pre-rational xenophobia, took place in the East End of London and were popularly labelled 'Paki-bashing'.

On the industrial front, the Asian workers of Mansfield Hosiery Mills, a flourishing enterprise in Loughborough in 1972, walked out of their factory on strike, initiated by the self-organisation of the Asians in the mills rather than by any British trade union.

In 1974, Asian workers in the Imperial Typewriters' factory in Leicester, went on strike against the discriminatory practices of their white supervisors.

Between 1976 and '78, the two-year-struggle by Asian, and almost uniformly Gujarati workers, to be recognised as unionised labour at their Grunwick factory became universal news.

In the East End of London, singularly for the sweatshop workers of Bangladeshi origin, there was a severe crisis of housing. People were crammed together with sometimes two families sharing a single room, with six beds installed.

That things in the 1970s were not good is a fact. For things to once and for all change, someone – no! ourselves! – had to act.

Race Today was conceived and constructed not as a magazine, a recorder of events. We saw ourselves as instrumental in the strategic self-organisation of the new communities of Britain. We called ourselves a 'collective' and not an editorial team. We were not reporters – we were humble, if conceited, activists.

All the members and supporters of *Race Today* had history, stretching into the first inklings of Black and Asian protest, analysis and ethnic self-organisation. We unquestioningly rejected any divisions of race, religion, colour – and of course gender.

Self-organisation, the animus, the activity, the strategies and the support (OK, and applause!) we sought through writing up what we had done and publishing it was what *Race Today* did.

As the following texts will testify, the Asian communities and workers of Britain were on the move, determined to get what their strength could win. Through extracts from what we published and publicised at the time, the reader may discern that in the case of industrial workers fighting a cause we could lend solidarity, reportage of the justice of their cause and afford them our publication's international reach.

In the case of racist attacks in London's East End, where we encountered a passion without a plan, we initiated the organization of a mass anti-racist rally and the establishment, from the commitment it generated, of a force of Bangladeshi youth who went out as monitors on streets and housing estates to put an instant end to 'Paki-bashing'. Parts of the national press and the area's police labelled us 'vigilantes'. Vigilance is in the eye of the discouraged.

In one article, we tell the story of *Race Today*'s intervention in the problem of housing for the Bangladeshi community of the East End. Together with other activists, principally Terry Fitzpatrick, we founded the Bengali Housing Action Group (BHAG), the acknowledged self-organising movement which pioneered the solution to the housing crisis and to the settlement of what is now one of the most prosperous boroughs of London.

The following pages are a testimony to *Race Today*'s contributions, involvements, reservations and the Collective's dedication to those in the firing line ready to fire back.

Figure 4.1   Race Today, 6 June 1976.

I: THE ASIAN SELF-DEFENCE MOVEMENT

'A SHOW OF STRENGTH'
Race Today, June 1976

The Asian community in Britain is presently being tested in 'blood and fire'. Three members of the community have been murdered by whites. Hundreds more have been physically attacked in their homes and on the streets by small groups of white males. White housewives have in some communities banded together to make the lives of their Asian female neighbours intolerable.

These attacks have been concentrated on the Asian community, for whom Britain at this moment is, in one sense, divided between those who attack them and those who don't. West Indians fall in the middle of this divide. A small minority of them, young males and housewives, have been involved in the attacks. The vast majority stand aloof, stating guardedly the dying myths and prejudices they have fostered towards the Asian community.

The mass of Asians in the East End work mainly in the clothing industry. The elders speak little English, but the younger generation is bilingual, and these experiences have brought to the surface those tensions and divisions which have been present in the community as it has grown and developed here in Britain.

The Asian middle class speak two languages and are businessmen, lower-order civil servants and professionals. For this group, Britain is experienced as quite a different place from those who have nothing to sell but their labour power, but it is this class which has gained the leadership which involves representing to the British state what they believe to be the interests of the mass of Bengali workers and housewives.

The middle-class Asians do not want to fight. They prefer appealing to government ministers and the police to calm things down. Pressing on them are the mass of Asian families who have been facing the attacks on the ground. The latter stand for the mobilisation of the strength and power of the community – mass meetings, mass demonstrations, vigilante groups.

Wherever the leadership has been forced to call demonstrations, they have, in most cases, avoided a community show of strength. In order to get around this, they call demonstrations in the name of racial harmony. They manage to muster groups of left-wing demonstrators who are in London today, Bradford tomorrow and Sheffield on the following day. Perhaps the odd bishop from the locality is present. In this way, they hope to calm the Asian workers by pretending that the bishop and the left-wing groups reflect the white working class.

Every Asian worker knows the opposite is true. A fierce struggle has emerged in the Asian community on this question. In Southall, the very existence of the demonstration was threatened at the last minute by young workers who wanted a show of strength. In the East End, we had to fight off the left and the middle class in order to carry out a mobilisation of community power. In all of this, the West Indian community has been absent as a force.

Appeals to racial harmony, however well-meaning and noble, have in no way affected that force which has been consistently attacking the Asian community in the last few weeks. A gathering of white left-wing and liberal forces cannot be mistaken for a mobilisation of the white working class. To make such a mistake at this time is to attempt to lure the Asian working-class community into a false state of security.

There is an alternative. *Race Today* offers the line along which we have been proceeding in the East End of London. Only a mobilisation of the strength and power of the Asian community in itself and for itself could deter those who have, to date, viewed the community as an easy pushover – a target for those frustrations and energies that are better spent against the state.

'NO RETREAT FROM THE EAST END'
Race Today, June 1976

Monday night, 31 May 1976. Two gangs of white motorcyclists rumble west on their well-tuned machines. Sixty strong, they park their bikes in Hanbury Street, E1. This is just short of Brick Lane, the social and commercial artery of the Asian community of East London. Helmeted and leather-jacketed, the bikers stroll down Brick Lane in a mob. They are enforcing the unofficial curfew, from twilight to midnight, that keeps Asian families behind closed doors.

Half a mile down Whitechapel Road on the same night, at approximately the same time, a kerb-crawling car follows a lone Bengali. He is, unheedful of the curfew, walking to visit a friend. As he reaches the door and begins to knock on it, the gang from the car emerges. One of the watchers produces a knife and attempts to stab him in the back. The door opens in the nick of time. The knife sticks in the door as the rest of the Asians on the street come to their windows, summoned by the sudden scream. The gang get into their car and noisily drive away.

Monday, 7 June 1976, 9:30 p.m. Sujlu Miahand and Nuruz Zaman, two young factory workers are leaving their work place on Richard Street, E1. As they turn the corner, 20–25 whites descend on both Bengalis, stabbing, kicking and punching. Both are taken to hospital, one seriously injured. It is midnight before the police begin their investigations. They ask a few questions:

'Do you know any of their names?'

'Would you recognise any of them again?'

They take a few notes. Within twenty minutes their 'investigation' is over.

Meanwhile, we are informed by another Asian at the hospital that an hour after the incident, six Asian youths were arrested. They are being held at Bethnal Green police station. Down at the station, the police claim that they are holding an Asian vigilante squad. In the early hours of the morning, the youths are finally released on bail, but not before the policeman in charge has seen their passports.

'There are a lot of illegal immigrants in the area', he says, and sends their friends at 3 a.m. to fetch their passports from five different addresses. All of them are charged with possessing offensive weapons. Four 'weapons' between the six of them, consisting of two milk bottles, a wooden stick and an iron lever. They have pleaded 'Not Guilty' to the charge.

It is in this atmosphere of increasing racial and police intimidation that the Bangladesh Welfare Association initiated a meeting of representatives from local organisations to discuss ways in which the Asian community of East London can best protect itself. Over a hundred people attended this first meeting in the last week of May. A few days later, there was another, attended by close to two hundred people. Neither meeting had been announced publicly; the news had travelled on the internal ghetto grapevine mostly by word of mouth.

Official invitees made up only about one-tenth of the entire gathering. By the end of the second meeting, a steering committee of eleven Asians had been elected to represent a cross section of the community. On the committee are a factory owner, two restaurant owners, a barrister, a member of the Pakistani community, a member of the Indian community, two unemployed youths, two members of the BHAG (Bengali Housing Action Group) and *Race Today*, and a worker from a tailoring factory. The new organisation was named the Anti-Racist Committee for the Defence of Asians in East London.

From the outset the meetings attempted to come to grips with a new situation. The Bengali youth of the area were in the majority at both meetings. They had called themselves together, using the cafes and meeting places of the community to set up an emergency grapevine capable of mobilising a few hundred people at an hour's notice. The assembly was faced with the task of disciplining this energy in the directions it proposed.

The assembly made two proposals. First, that there had to be a massive show of strength from the Asian community. Second, there had to be a continuous, disciplined self-defence organisation which would effectively stop white gangs, National Front hooligans, or anyone else from picking on Asian individuals and homes. A few voices were raised in dissent. A couple of activists from the International Socialists (IS), who have been looking for a base in the area for years, were shouted down when they tried to dish out sermons. More serious, and more seriously rejected, were the voices from the Bangladeshi community who saw negotiation, through the contacts that individuals had with prominent figures of the state apparatus, as the machinery of Asian self-defence.

The meetings overwhelmingly rejected this view. And with it, they rejected those personalities in the East End who have operated as a mafia on the backs of the community for years. Who are they? They are those immigrants who live off the labour of other immigrants, making contacts on the way with state power and the labour movement, with MPs, with councillors, with organised business, with the political hustlers who pose as representatives of the white community.

Instead, a coalition of the young activists of the Bangladesh Welfare Association, the activists of BHAG and the hitherto unorganised young resistance in the community came together to undertake the tasks our meetings had agreed.

During the final week before the demonstration, we became aware of forces attempting to sabotage the work of the new alliance. On the one hand, there were the police and their contacts in the Bengali community who spread the story that our march would inevitably lead to violence. On the other hand, there were those whose traditional interests in the Asian community were threatened – the CRC hacks who saw their mediating services falling into disuse, threatening their jobs and threatening the illegal money-making activities that arise from their position as 'elders'. Two days before the demonstration, the story was circulated that the committee to whom the mass meetings had given their trust were National Front infiltrators.

The meeting and demonstration of 12 June put paid to this trade in political manoeuvring; three thousand people from the community responded to the call from the committee. The Naz Cinema, the venue for the meeting, was besieged by crowds who couldn't get in. All along Brick Lane, supporters waited patiently for the meeting to finish so that they could join the march.

To the organisations called on to support the meeting (the organisational task *Race Today* had been given), it was made clear that the demonstration had been called for the specific purpose of uniting and displaying the strength of the Asian community. They were welcome to participate if their position was one of support; banners and publications purely for party propaganda would not be welcome.

The demonstration went without incident, though not without hostility from the police of the area. The Commander told the stewards that it was the last time the Asian community would be allowed to walk the streets of Whitechapel collectively, a challenge we on the organising committee readily accept. The lessons of the present mobilisation have marked our friends and our enemies. It has isolated the turbulence created by the interests of the middle class. It has stamped the mediators as irrelevant. It has brought about an unquestioning unity between the various Asian and black communities of the area. And it has confirmed our belief that our strength is our only weapon.

'ON PATROL, EAST LONDON – ANY NIGHT IN JUNE 1976. TIME: TWILIGHT TO MIDNIGHT'

Race Today, June 1976

Two cars are to set out from our base. Eleven of the volunteers who have turned up are chosen mainly for their determination and trustworthiness. Everybody knows everybody else. Ten of the eleven have been out on previous nights. There's an orderly discussion on how to deal with the situations we may encounter. The routes are decided. Each car is to meet the other at hourly intervals. Both drivers know the area like the backs of their hands. One car is to check on the other bases from which other patrols will be setting out.

Nothing in the first two hours. We drive almost in silence. It's worrying that so many Asians, standing in groups on street corners or leaning out of the cafes and doorways, recognise and acknowledge our mission. They wave and one or two give clenched fist salutes. Down the Commercial Road to the East India Dock Road and then into Corbin House off Bromley High Street. We've been told that a white gang gathers there around pub closing time. The Asian tenant who brings the information has had his windows smashed, his house robbed, his children assaulted the previous day. The buildings around there have a long history of shameful racist intimidation, abuse and assault. We talk to the Asian families on our rounds. Two of the families tell us, standing in their doorways (which we do deliberately to inform the neighbours of our presence), that the police have been called each time there is an assault, and each time they have carried away the Asian who complained and charged him. We suggest practical ways of collective self-defence. We leave them two phone numbers.

Several police cars pass us on the Mile End Road. As we turn down Toynbee Street, our driver spots trouble. Two young Asians are being followed by four young white men. The doors of our car fly open before anyone has a chance to say a word. The car screeches to a halt alongside one of the Asians who is about six yards ahead of the now-running gang. We jump out through all four doors. The gang is obviously unprepared for an attack on more than two unarmed Asians. They shout to each other, 'Pakis', turn tail and run. Our driver tries to get back into the car and chase them. They run down the pavement and disappear into Brune House. We pick the Asians up, and piling into the car, drop them a few hundred yards down the Commercial Road.

Back to Brick Lane to keep an appointment at the corner of Brick Lane and Hanbury Street, where a small crowd of young men has gathered. On the opposite pavement, two young policemen in shirt sleeves, their walkie-talkies to their faces, are bullying a young Asian. He has his arms above his head and one of the police officers is thrusting a lit torch right up his nose, Nazi style. We get out of the car and approach. 'Fuck off or we'll have you for obstruction', the policeman says. He is asking the man they've stopped whether he's an illegal immigrant. They are radioing for a car. We cross the street and shout to the detainee in Bengali to tell us his name and address. He begins to reply and one of the policemen clamps a hand over his mouth to stop him. The police car arrives and they bundle him into it. We're back in the car. One of us phones to a solicitor who is on call; the others follow the police car to Bethnal Green police station.

Before the car gets to the station, the solicitor has the particulars of the arrested man. The patrol goes back to one of the bases and we call a member of the Anti-Racist Committee for Asians in East London (ARC-AEL) to deal with the police. The committee man sets out to find the relatives and the passport of the arrested man. From the experience of a previous night, we know that the police won't give bail without having the passport on hand.

The other car reports back. They've been stopped by police in Commercial Road. The Inspector tells one of the group, 'We're picking you lot up, because the whites are smarter – they can't be caught with offensive weapons on them.'

From our experience of other nights on patrol, we know different.

II: THE TIGER STRIKES:
BHAG AND THE BATTLE FOR HOUSING

'EAST END HOUSING CAMPAIGN'
Race Today, December 1975

More than forty Bengalis picketed the head office of the Greater London Council on the morning of 18 November and handed in a series of demands to GLC officials. Their demands are:

1. That all eviction notices be stayed until you are able to offer us alternative accommodation.
2. That we be re-housed within the E1 area.
3. That when offered alternative accommodation we be given sufficient notice so that we can exercise our statutory right of viewing before acceptance.

It was the opening shot fired in the campaign, assisted by *Race Today* and the Tower Hamlets Squatters Union, to win decent housing for Bengali workers in the East End. Central to the campaign are the actions of the Bengalis themselves, in this instance, eleven Bengali families who housed themselves in Montague Street, E1, in properties owned by the GLC. More than two hundred families have taken the same action in GLC and Tower Hamlets Council properties in that area.

These families carry the clothing industry on their backs. The men toil for 80 hours weekly in the local sweatshops for low wages. Their wives work at piece-work rates for half the men's wages or less, on sewing machines that the family has had to borrow money to buy. Their labour provides clothing for both the home market and for export.

Ask any official where the mass of Bengali workers are supposed to live, and nine out of ten times he has never considered it. The officials will have to begin now, for there is developing a mass movement of Bengalis who are determined to house themselves in council property. Nor will they remain content with the slums they occupy. These houses, kept deliberately vacant for years, to fit in with the area redevelopment plan, provide the bare minimum. Often, they are old decaying buildings with toilets smashed, electric wiring ripped out and no gas or electricity supply. On several streets, even the water has been cut off. The family must find money to make the building habitable and the money is borrowed from moneylenders at high interest rates.

The Montague Street tenants have been served with summonses calling them to court and issuing possession orders. Assisted by *Race Today* and the Tower Hamlets Squatters Union, they have organised themselves and confronted the GLC with the demands outlined above.

Their demand to be re-housed in the E1 area is an important one. It is to avoid being isolated and subjected to physical attacks from racist whites. As they informed the GLC: 'By sending Bengalis into places like the Canada Estate in Poplar, you have exposed us to racial attacks and our children to isolation in schools, where the local children have not yet been taught that people who do not speak English are not culturally backward.'

The delegation taking the demands to the GLC that morning comprised two members of the *Race Today* Collective, three heads of Bengali families and a member of the Tower Hamlets Squatters Union. The GLC officials, drawn from their housing department included a Mr Green, representing the absent Head of the Housing Department, Richard Balfe, a Mr Snosill and another official.

Snosill said that the GLC is not responsible: 'It is the responsibility of the Tower Hamlets Council with whom we have nothing more than an arrangement.' They could not, Snosill claimed, entertain re-housing even though his boss, Richard Balfe, had said in the *Sunday Times* on 3 March 1975: 'Squatting is a symptom of the housing crisis not the cause ... the practice of squatter "bashing", therefore, will not resolve the problem. It is merely an unthinking reaction to it.'

Two days after the meeting, 20 November, eight families appeared at the Shoreditch County Court represented by a solicitor. Possession orders were granted to the GLC. Outside the court, the GLC's solicitor, Mr Rose, told us that his clients wanted to be 'reasonable' and 'fair' in this case and offered the following concessions:

1) All families involved would be allowed to stay where they are for at least four months, and the time would be extended depending on how long it took before redevelopment plans were set in motion.
2) That at the time of eviction, 28 days' notice will be given in writing to each family.

This provided time, we were told, for us to appeal to Tower Hamlets Council to persuade them to re-house the families. So, in two days, a vague date in the New Year is changed to a definite period of at least four months and the possibility of an extension.

A few days later, the families received a formal reply from Mr Balfe, answering all three demands. On the first demand of staying the eviction order:

> I cannot accept this. So many possession orders have been obtained and others are being fought so that the council can proceed on time with providing homes on this site. [homes for whom?] ... Low demand accommodation will be made available [he means slums] for families with children or any aged or disabled people occupying the old Montague Street properties at the time of the court hearing.

On the second demand of re-housing in the E1 area, Balfe says: 'This cannot be accepted. Whilst every effort will be made to do so, there are bound to be occasions when suitable low demand accommodation is just not available in that area.'

Finally, Balfe contradicts the undertaking given by his solicitor, Mr Rose, that 28 days' notice will be given before eviction. 'It must be clearly understood', he said, 'that such offers [of re-housing] on the day of the eviction are the only ones that will be made.'

Take it or leave it.

What we have acquired is the knowledge of precisely where the battle lines are drawn. We are sure that Mr Balfe knows that he has not yet heard the last of us. The campaign is only in its first gear. We do not promise a bloody revolution, as in Clydeside, only a good fight.

'HOUSING STRUGGLE: THE TIGER IS ON THE LOOSE'
Race Today, March 1976

Out of the struggles of Bengali families for decent housing in the East End of London, which *Race Today* has reported and assisted in the last 18 months, an organisation has been born.

On Friday, 6 February, at the Montefiore Centre in Deal Street, E1, seventy heads of Bengali families gathered to form the Bengali Housing Action Group (BHAG – the acronym in Bengali means 'tiger' and in Urdu and Hindi it means 'share'). The meeting defined the perspective of the group to fight for a permanent policy on housing for black people. It approved a constitution and elected an executive committee which included a member of the Tower Hamlets Squatting Association and two members of the *Race Today* Collective.

The formation of BHAG is a formidable step in the East End housing struggle. It is a direct challenge to the housing authorities and elected representatives of the London Borough of Tower Hamlets, and the Greater London Council. And it is a challenge not only to the methods and perspectives of the Community Relations Commission in the area, but to its very reason for existence.

The Bengali Housing Action Group is at once an organisation and a campaign. The campaigns that individual families and whole streets of squatters have carried out – around the elimination of squat-selling by officials and others, around the harassment of squatters by the Gas and Electricity Boards, around the promises and prospects of re-housing – have defined the perspectives of the autonomous organisation and the further campaign.

Letters from BHAG have been sent out to the GLC, to Tower Hamlets Council, to the Gas and Electricity Boards demanding that they meet and discuss several demands with the executive and membership of the organisation.

The majority of the members of BHAG, which is open to all black people in the area, are Bangladeshi workers and their families. A large number of the members, with families about to join them from Bangladesh, are classified by the housing authority as 'single' men. As such, they have no priority on the housing lists of the local council or the GLC, and have therefore exercised their option to squat. So also have other members with families in London who have had their names on the housing lists since the 1960s.

From the Electricity and Gas Boards, BHAG is demanding a constant and legal supply of amenities, no more and no less than is given to any person willing to pay deposits and bills. Their letter to the Gas and Electricity Boards points out that the Minister for Energy, Anthony Wedgwood Benn, recently answered a question in the House of Commons saying that squatters must not be discriminated against in the supply of electricity and fuel to their homes.

From the GLC and the London Borough of Tower Hamlets, BHAG is demanding a housing policy for black people, which would entail re-housing in decent as opposed to 'low-demand' accommodation and in an area of which the family in question approves.

In itself, BHAG is a rejection of the solution to housing problems that the state has posed in other communities, providing, through the CRC and other race agencies, a restricted and restricting amount of hostel accommodation – a solution which reduces the black worker, as in Germany and other parts of Europe, to a wage labourer with no rights in the society and no claims on decent housing. The black workers of Britain have consistently refused to accommodate to this battery-chicken model of a labour force. For years, the British state has bought immigrant labour on the cheap, dodging the necessity to house, to skill and to reproduce the black labour force. The presence of organisations such as the Bengali Housing Action Group, begins to put an end to this evasion.

Several BHAG members have been, in the years past, members of squatting organisations such as the East London Squatters and the Stepney Squatters groups. While representing their day-to-day difficulties and placing them before the authorities, these groups failed to generate a perspective and policy for black workers' housing needs and, inevitably, failed to grasp the strength that the Bengali workers as a community have in that area.

Though statistics of population are not up to date, it is clear that the Bengali community of the East End can elect and dismiss councillors on the Tower Hamlets Council through organisation around the polls. The existence of BHAG means that the Labour Party and others, to win votes, will have to address a militant population of black workers directly, rather than using the discredited buffers of Race Relations legislation or the CRC.

Having been called upon to inspire and assist BHAG, *Race Today* pledged, at the first general meeting, our continuing willingness to use the magazine as a forum and voice of the group and to place our organisational machinery at their disposal. For us, BHAG is one of the clearest manifestations of the collective power of black workers fighting the state in their own material interest, seeking to use their community's cohesiveness and their particular position in the working class of Britain as a bargaining strength. BHAG is on the loose.

'A VICTORY FOR BHAG'
Race Today, November–December 1977

Squatters in Greater London Council (GLC)-owned properties have been granted an amnesty. If they register with the GLC before 28 November, they will be offered rented accommodation and become legal tenants. Otherwise, the GLC will use all measures which the law allows against anyone who moved into one of its properties as a squatter after 25 October 1977, or who remains as a squatter after November 1977.

Whatever the implications of this 'amnesty' are, certain important concessions have been wrung from the GLC which, if honoured, constitute a victory for immigrant Asian families in London's East End who, for the last two years, have waged a relentless, organised fight for their right to decent housing in an area of their choosing, and for BHAG, the vehicle through which several hundred Bengali families launched their fight.

The high point of this campaign was the squatting of fifty Asian families in the summer of 1976, in Pelham Buildings in an empty GLC building. Through the pages of *Race Today*, through mass demonstrations and pickets, we carried the fight right to the top, to those responsible in the corridors of power for housing and energy policies. Tony Judge, at that time Britain's largest landlord, in his position as Chairman of the Greater London Council's Housing Management Committee, found himself forced to sit at a negotiating table with Bengali workers.

We took on the Home Secretary too, and demanded he take action on the miserable record of the local police in responding to violent racist attacks on individuals and families, a record which revealed where their sympathies lay. We said, 'No Retreat from the East End' and supported the organisation of Asian vigilante patrols.

So now, the GLC who so recently were sticking to their guns of not speaking to squatters, have put out the white flag. At best, it is the recognition of a political reality which stems from a two-year organised assault by Asian immigrants, on their racist housing policy and a recognition too of the power of the organised squatting movement generally in London, which has resulted in the occupation of 1,438 GLC properties by homeless people. At worst, however, it covers a multitude of sins and hides another reality.

The amnesty is no solution to homelessness. Behind the facade of the 'amnesty' is the GLC's counter-attack, aimed at breaking up and dispersing the organised pockets of resistance which squatters have built up over the years. The GLC hopes that, after 28 November, it will never have to confront this force again, and its intention this time will have the backing of legislation from on high. The Criminal Trespass Bill, now in its final stages in Parliament, allows both private and state landlords to use 'reasonable force' to evict squatters. Even more iniquitous is a Private Member's Bill, currently being floated in Parliament by Tory MP Hugh Rossi which states that landlords should make only one offer of a tenancy to a family (at the moment, you can have three more if you are prepared to fight). Should the family refuse the offer, then they will have rendered themselves homeless and Social Services has no further responsibility for them. If incorporated into housing policy, it will hit directly families such as those who rallied to BHAG, who are presently being terrorised out of their tenancies by whites who don't want them there.

There is also the reality that the housing allocation policy will remain unchanged. It will remain racist and will favour only those capable of a show of strength. Thus, the allocation of families to 'sink' estates, which white families refuse, will continue, as will the forcing out of black families from their homes, by racist whites – the very condition which brought BHAG into being.

Clearly, the amnesty points to a new direction of organisation for BHAG. The concessions it has won from the GLC has thwarted, at least temporarily, the GLC's intention to disperse the families it had organised. It must, therefore, continue to provide the focus around which other families, as yet not organised, can make their fight. BHAG's membership, who presently occupy several houses in Vardon Street and Nelson Street, provides a nucleus around which a wider movement must be built.

The London Borough of Tower Hamlets, as a body, has proved to be more stubborn than the GLC in their opposition to BHAG. They have not, so far, conceded to either the demand for re-housing or shown any support for BHAG's position for housing in the E1 area. Our demand that we be housed where we are many, arises out of our own realisation that 'ghettos' are our source of protection and strength, in the present racial climate of Britain and provides the base which we can launch our attack for decent housing.

III ASIAN WORKERS: THE FIGHT FOR JUSTICE

'THE ASIAN WORKER'
Darcus Howe, April 1974

In a short document called *A Workers' Enquiry*, Karl Marx set down a hundred questions to be asked of every worker. He saw the significance of workers directly relating their experiences in the following light:

We hope to meet in this work with the support of all workers in town and country who understand *that they alone can describe with full knowledge* the misfortunes from which they suffer and that they and not saviours sent by providence can energetically apply the healing remedies for the social ills to which they are prey ... We also rely upon socialists of all schools who, being wishful for social reform must wish for an *exact and positive* knowledge of the conditions in which the working class – the class to whom the future belongs – works and moves. [our italics]

This 'exact and positive knowledge' we have sought to record in a series of interviews with Asian workers in manufacturing industries throughout Britain. This section of the working class has been involved in successive strike actions in the past five years which now threaten to develop into a cohesive and powerful mass movement of Asian workers. The value of these interviews lies in the fact that they chart with a precision and clarity the historical process involved in the span – from peasant to industrial worker. They reveal the day-to-day struggles of the Asians on their introduction (in most cases for the first time) to factory life, their customs, their values, their ideas, hopes, aspirations and fears. We can derive from them how the Asians have attempted to overcome tremendous barriers placed in their way, have sought to deal with the hostility of the indigenous population and how they have used the accumulated history of the Asian peasantry as a weapon in their struggles against capital. Introduced to factory life from the small farm in Asia, we are told that the Pakistani worker saw his employer 'as someone big who could do a lot of things to people'; that the wages of white workers were kept a secret from them, that £9.10 for 60 hours was viewed as a reasonable wage. The Asians had to find their way in the vast political organisation that is the factory floor, arriving at new conceptions of themselves and their relations with others – in short, discovering their own power.

This process cannot be viewed as taking place in isolation from all that was going on around them. For instance, they would surely experience and note the power exercised by the white workers against management in relation to which they could assess their own actual and potential power. From the interviews, it emerges that they had drawn from the fact that they (the white workers) were organised into trade unions. A movement of Asian workers into trade unions was a direct consequence of this. The trade unions proved to be the opposite of what they expected, which has been the experience of white workers as well.

The dilemma of the Asian workers is how they preserve their interest in the face of opposition from white workers, management and the unions. What kind of organisation do they put in the place of the trade union? The main issues are two: the struggle to work less (the shortening of the working week), and the reduction of the intensity of the actual work. One of the workers interviewed points to a solution. He sees as possible an organisation of workers wherever there are more than fifty Asians working, linked to other Asian workers by a central body of representatives and linking the factory with the community. It is unfortunate, perhaps, that the revolutionary implications of his suggestion – and consequently the revolutionary actuality and potential of the Asian working class – was first identified by Lord Rothschild, the architect of the counter-revolution against blacks in Britain.

Figure 4.2 Mural in tribute to *Race Today* Collective Member Mala Sen by artist Jasmin Sehra, unveiled in Brick Lane in October 2018. Commissioned by City Hall and Tate Collective, it formed part of a series of public art works to mark 100 years since women won the vote. Sehra has woven the Bengali words for 'powerful, fearless, courageous' into the image.

'THE STRIKE AT IMPERIAL TYPEWRITERS'
Mala Sen, July 1974

The workers have not followed the proper disputes procedure. They have
no legitimate grievances and it's difficult to know what they want. I think
there are racial tensions, but they are not between the whites and the
coloureds. The tensions are between those Asians from the sub-conti-
nent and those from Africa ...

This is not an isolated incident, these things will continue for many
years to come. But in a civilised society, the majority view will prevail.
Some people must learn how things are done.
(George Bromley, thirty years a Transport and General Workers' Union
negotiator, JP and stalwart of the Leicester Labour Party)

Leicester, so we are told, is one of the richest cities in Europe. Isolated
from the industrial turmoil associated with declining heavy industries, its
economic base is built on solid foundations in footwear, textiles and light
engineering. Despite its Labour council, it is a deeply conservative town,
valuing the old-fashioned virtues of hard work and thrift, self-interest and
parochialism. It has little tradition of industrial struggle; it's the kind of city
where the 'social contract' might have been invented. It's a National Front
stronghold – 9,000 votes polled in the last election – and at the height of
the Ugandan Asian exodus in 1972, the City Council took out a full-page
advert in the Ugandan press to stress the city's 'Red Area' status and warn
off the East African refugees from settling in the city with its 'overbur-
dened schools and inadequate housing'.

Towards the end of the 1960s and throughout the 1970s, the original
Asian immigrant workers were joined by refugees from East Africa. Some
of the more astute arrivals brought with them enough capital to set themselves up with a house and a stake in distributive trades. Most of them
had been clerks and storemen, small shopkeepers and petty servants of the
state. They arrived with little more than they stood up in and the name and
address of a friend or relative. With no tradition of industrial organisation,
and often with a minimal grasp of English, they appeared ideal material for
capitalist discipline in the factories of Leicester.

Huddled together in the Highfield area are many of the city's new inhab-
itants, mainly Asian, but with a scattering of West Indian families among
them. Move on past Spinney Hill Park, drop down onto East Park Road
and you find yourself at the main gate of Imperial Typewriters factory. This

is the old building, and together with the new plant, a quarter of a mile away at Copdale Road, 1,600 people work here normally producing manual and electric typewriters for the European market. Of the 1,600 people, approximately 1,100 are Asians.

On Wednesday, 1 May – International Workers' Day – four firms in the city were hit by walk-outs: 300 from British United Shoe Machinery; 300 from the Bentley Group; 200 from the GEC factory at Whetstone and 39 Asian workers from Section 61 of the Imperial Typewriters factory. All the other workers were soon back inside, but the handful from Imperial stayed out and later managed to bring out a further 500. Within a fortnight production was down 50 per cent, and by the end of May, as the strike dragged into its fifth week, very few typewriters were coming off the lines at all.

The picket line has been manned constantly since the day of the walk-out. But it's not like a normal English workers' picket line with a couple of placards and half a dozen men turning back the lorries. This is a major industrial dispute, and the picket line, manned constantly by 50–200 workers, has a vivacity and style that makes it unique. Whenever a scab or management representative appears, a fearful yowling and hollering is set up, led invariably by the women who have been stalwarts on the line since the day the strike started. The noise is tremendous as it echoes across the street and between the high buildings. Sheltering in nearby cafes and the launderette when it rains, constantly moved on by the police when it's fine, the pickets stand there undaunted by the immovable position of the union – who refuse to make the strike official – and the hostility of the indigenous working-class population. A new element has emerged amongst the strikers: young, long-haired, golden-earringed, bedenimed and brown-skinned, they are fearless and energetic. They have no qualms about attacking the National Front, cheeking the police (in particular, an East African Asian who is used to control the picket line and interpret for the other policemen) and they are powerfully hostile towards blacklegs.

The 27 women and 12 men who walked out on 1 May all came from Section 61. Their task was to assemble parts manufactured in Japan, Germany and Holland into complete typewriters: for this the women were paid £18 per week on piecework and the men £25. In addition to this basic wage, there was a bonus for completing the daily target of two hundred machines per day.

For some months, there had been discontent throughout the factory at the fact that, despite the number of Asian workers employed, the shop stewards' committee, with the exception of one Asian, was overwhelmingly white. So they demanded their own shop steward, to be elected to negotiate not only on production and bonuses, but also on all the important restrictions that made up their daily working lives – washing time, tea breaks, lunch breaks, toilet breaks and so on. In the course of making their demands to Reg Weaver, the T&GWU factory convenor, they discovered that although they were being paid bonus on a target of 200, they were in fact entitled to bonus on 168 (an agreement dating back to 1972, which would have meant an extra £4 per week). It was this discovery, heaped on top of management's oppressive organisation of production, that triggered their walkout.

By 3 May, the small nucleus of mainly women workers from Section 61, whose unofficial leaders were 21-year-old Hasmukh Khetani and N.C. Patel, had leafleted and picketed the factory so successfully that 500 other workers joined them. This realisation of their collective power led to demands other than the bonus issue: an end to the use of racialism by management to divide workers and democratic elections in the trade union. The company's response was to issue notice to the original 40 that if they didn't return to work, they would all be sacked.

That first weekend, the local MP, Tom Bradley, who is himself president of the Transport Salaried Staff's Association, intervened and tried to negotiate the workers back, saying, 'I told the strike leaders they were getting nowhere by walking the streets and urged them to adopt the proper procedure by returning to work and resuming discussions under an independent chairman.' He was supported by Reg Weaver, the T&GWU local convenor. The workers rejected it 100 per cent and stood by their demands. They also called for support from all workers at the factory, black and white. 'Rebalancing the line will mean harder work for less money', they said. 'Therefore our fight is for all workers, men and women, black and white, for all who work at Imperial.'

Free from the bureaucratic rules and regulations of the union organisation, the workers have been inventing new ways of furthering their struggle. They have come up with 'the grievance meeting', a mass meeting of the strikers in which they all voice their individual grievances. These grievances are translated into a coherent series of demands. In this way, the leadership is continually in a close relationship with the mass of the strikers. Among the streams of grievances to come forward are bonus disputes, clocking-on fiddles, waiting-time arguments and dozens of similar issues.

Nine days after the walkout, the company sacked 75 of the original strikers, but the workers refused to accept their cards and sent them back. Imperial claimed they were willing to talk about their demands, but Reg Weaver blocked the process, saying he was ready to talk to anyone except

Khetani and Patel. Mr Bromley 'discovered' a T&GWU rule that people could not be elected as shop stewards until they had been at the factory for two years – something Jack Jones repudiated as nonsense.

In this state of deadlock, the level of demonstrations moved up. Mass picketing and a strike meeting were broken up by police. As they realised the enormity of the task they had undertaken, the strikers sent out an appeal to several other factories belonging to the same branch of the T&GWU. Four factories with a large Asian membership responded with donations to the strike fund and a pledge of a 24-hour stoppage at their workplace if and when needed. On Sunday, 19 May, more than two thousand turned up to a mass meeting in Highfield.

As the strike dragged into its third week, with production slowed to a trickle, and with six of the workers facing fines of £315 for obstruction and assault on the police, the Race Relations Board intervened and stated its intention to carry out a preliminary investigation. The union officials welcomed it; the factory welcomed it. The workers were not so sure: they felt that it was slow and tardy and towards the end of the month, they rejected the intervention. 'It's a toothless Bulldog', they said. Having dispensed with the mediators, the local MP and the RRB, David Stephen of the Runnymede Trust proposed another investigator: Michael Foot, Minister of Employment. This has so far been ignored.

We attended one of the grievance meetings and listened to several men and women describing life at Imperial. This woman is a widow and the mother of three children. She joined Imperial three years ago at a base wage of £13.50:

I assemble motors in the store department. When I first started work here I had to make 14 motors per hour. But then they raised the target to 16 and then to 18 and so on. Now it's 22. To work at that speed we can't even drink a cup of tea. We have no official tea break but sometimes one of us goes out and gets tea for the others. But then if the foreman sees us he starts complaining about us in front of all the other workers, and even the supervisor, saying we always waste time and talk too much. Anyway, we didn't complain about that. We complained to them about the target – we all said 22 is too high. However hard we work we can never make more than that – and unless we make more we don't get any bonus. But on top of that if we make less than 22 – say 20 or 21 – they cut some money from our basic pay ... We are mostly all Asian in our section but our shop steward is a white woman. She doesn't care and the union doesn't care. I pay 11p a week to be a member of the union but I really think it's a waste of hard-earned money. Don't get me wrong. I'm not against unions – but our union is no different from management. And our shop steward, she hardly ever talks to us. Yet she is with the union and he is with management. She didn't come out on strike with us – she didn't even want to hear about it.

I'll give you an example. I went to our shop steward one day and told her that the supervisor had asked us to oil our own machines that morning. Normally the machines are oiled before we come in. I told her that oiling was not our job and that management was always trying to make us do more work for the same pay. She told me not to make a fuss over such a small thing. That's the kind of shop steward she is. This is why we must have our own shop stewards. In this factory, there are 1,100 of us and yet we only have one Asian shop steward. It doesn't make sense, does it? I'm not saying that all Asians will make good shop stewards – some of our people are also like the white people – they take management's side against us. But this way we are not represented at all …

The other day I went to the toilet. Someone was already inside so I had to wait. I must have been there not more than ten minutes when the foreman started banging on the door. He had come to find me in the toilet to tell me to go back to work. I was very angry and shouted some rude things to him. Wouldn't you? There's a limit to everything. When I came out he asked me what I had been doing there. I told him to go home and ask his wife what she did in the toilet. He complained about me to the supervisor … I have many grievances like this. Small things but they all add up. The other thing is that every morning when we come to work at 8 o'clock we have to stand in a long queue to clock in. I try and come at 5 to 8 because we are paid according to time. Many of us have noticed that the white women push past us and clock in first. The foreman at the gate never tells them to stand in the queue.

Another female worker outlines her working day from 6 a.m. to 9 p.m. As a woman in a Southall factory says: 'Equal pay? We do twice as much work, we should get double pay.'

In February 1968, I came to this country with my daughter and my husband. We used to live in Mombasa. We came to Leicester where my sister used to live. My husband found a job at Imperials. It was assembly-line work – making some kind or screws to fit on tripods. Now he's working as a repairman but they don't give him a repairman's wages.

For this reason he came out on strike. I had never worked before. I was a housewife in Mombasa. I have four children now ...

I started working in February 1970. Imperials used to put up a notice on the notice board saying that if any of the workers had wives who wanted to work there, they could work from 6 to 10 – after the day shift. My husband heard about it and came and told me. Since he was at home in the evenings I took the job. It was piecework and I earned £6.50 a week. Four hours a day for five days – that makes 20 hours. That's how I started.

About thirty women work in our shop, mostly Asian, but also some whites and West Indians. None of us have ever got a promotion, but the white women get the better jobs. I heard from someone that in our section they pay different rates. They don't have a fixed rate for everybody – but I don't know what other people get. I only know what I get. But now we know that this is happening. Ever since I've been there I have seen that the whites give their women just one machine to work on while they give us ten or eleven different machines in a day. You see their job is better. They have just one machine but we have to move around like gypsies. The West Indian women are treated just like us. Another thing is that the setters (we have all white setters) set the white women's machines first and take more trouble over them. Ours they do last and they don't even do them properly. Before our machines are set, we have to wait. So we asked for waiting time but they wouldn't give that to us. White women also get jobs of their choice – they can choose their jobs. But we have to do what the setter gives us to do. The West Indian women work like us but they go with the white women. Not a single West Indian in our section came out with us on strike. I don't know how they are in other sections. Even some of our own women – Asian women – who didn't support our strike have this same attitude.

After the strike, I don't know. Perhaps I will have to look for another job. If they try and change my job there – give me a worse job – I'm going to leave.

As we go to press, management has sent out notices sacking the majority of the striking workers. On the picket line, nine people were arrested in scuffles with the police, and the next day, more than two hundred of the workers came to London on a mass lobby of Transport House to try and get the strike made official. Jack Jones and Moss Evans at Head Office promised an enquiry, but the strikers are still effectively on their own.

The strike at Imperial Typewriters has, apart from anything else, put paid to certain myths. It has also confirmed that sections of British industry depend almost exclusively on cheap black labour and generally on new waves of immigrant wage labourers. It has shown that these wage labourers are not, as many predicted, a class of potential businessmen with petit-bourgeois aspirations. More than this, their actions indicate certain consequences. Over the company hangs the threat of labourlessness. The strikers predict that either Imperial must give way or collapse. It is the same choice that faces London Transport and the service industries, both run, by and large, on black labour.

We have seen how the Imperial Typewriters factory at Leicester is merely one facility in a multinational corporation whose business is composed of moving its production around the globe to obtain the most profitable combination of cheap labour and access to markets. We have seen how the prevailing rate of pay for men is £14 below the national average, while that for women is £6 below. We have also examined how the factory consistently turned to new and cheaper sources of labour – from white male workers to Asians from the subcontinent, to Asians from East Africa to women, and so on. We have also seen how the union has collaborated in this international scheme of things: the lieutenants of capital, more concerned with people 'learning how things are done in a civilised society', than mobilising sections of the class for political change.

The move away from trade union directives must be seen not only as a practical disadvantage for the strikers but also as a source of political strength. Their new forms of organisation seem to ensure a control of the action by the rank and file. The grievance meetings of the entire strike force became the organisational focus. And the Committee's demands are forced to come from there.

The power of the women comes not only from their being half of the strike force but also from their position as mothers and housewives in the community. Not only do they see capital giving them a low wage, they see it raked back by inflation. In the past, Asian women have largely come out in support of the demands of their men. They had no choice. The alternative was scabbing. This strike is unique in that the women have had the collective power to make their demand for equal pay a priority. They are the latest section of the working class to fall into factory production. They are aware of the score and less willing to take the horrors. Their militancy on the picket lines, their forcefulness at the grievance meetings and their determination to fight till the end are all proof of this.

'GRUNWICK GATES: THE ENTRY TO UNIONISATION'

Race Today, June–July 1977

In August 1976, 250 Asian workers walked out of Grunwick's film-process-ing and mail order firm in North West London and joined the Association of Professional, Executive, Clerical and Computer Staffs (APEX), a union to which they were directed by the local Citizens Advice Bureau. The subsequent struggle of APEX, for recognition in Grunwick and the reinstatement of the strikers, escalated this month into a national issue.

On Thursday, 23 June, a member of the Race Today *Collective was arrested by police while reporting the mass picketing of Grunwick. On his release from Wembley police station, he filed this report.*

At the corner of Chapter Road, sandwiched between a row of terraced houses and Dollis Hill Underground station in North West London, are the blue and white metal gates of the Grunwick photo-processing labora-tories. In themselves the gates look insignificant, the sort of garage entrance that the eye would pass over but for these last two weeks in June, the eye of British television and the gaze of the newspapers have been focused on these gates. They have become the totems of a war between two factions of the labour movement of Britain: the government, with its whole state apparatus, together with sections of the trades unions, on the one hand, and the militants of the trades unions, supported by some Labour-left MPs, on the other. They have become the scene of pitched battles between a well-deployed police force of up to a thousand men a day, and the support of mass pickets gathered from all corners of the country.

In the last two weeks, at least three hundred people have been arrested outside the gates. A few policemen have been put in hospital. Parliamentary rows have raged over the arrest of Audrey Wise MP, who joined the pickets with six of her colleagues. The TUC has officially called for financial and positive support for the strike. The Employment Secretary, Albert Booth, has called for an independent enquiry. The Prime Minister has declared that he will investigate ways of ending the confrontation.

From 7.30 in the morning each day five, sometimes six, Asian women take up their positions outside the gates. They carry placards with simple slogans urging support for the Grunwick strike. One of their posters, yellow and blue, shows the profile of a London bobby with the caption 'Meet Your New Personnel Manager'. They tell us that the poster was made by one of their well-wishers from National Society of Operative Printers and Assistants (NATSOPA): 'He has a lot of facilities, so he helps us in any way he can.'

Behind the Asian women, formed up in a tight cordon stand 15 policemen. On either side of symbolic space occupied by official pickets, stand the rest of the two hundred or so police. Around the L-shaped bend of the road, leaving open only the access to Dollis Hill Underground, are deployed the green trucks of London's police force, packed with reserves. In every side street, the rest of the force cools its heels. Behind the lines of the police stand the supporting crowds, on some mornings larger than the police force, on others, looking pitifully inadequate before the walkie-talkie militia.

A battery of reporters, television cameras, photographers, is ever-present, waiting for the promised and recurrent confrontations of 8 o'clock.

Two streets away, on the first floor of the Apollo Club, are the head-quarters of the strike committee. On Thursday, 23 June, the crowded office has been manned all night by young Asian men, the nucleus of the strike committee. The promised contingent of mineworkers is definitely arriving. Yes, Jack Dromey, secretary of the local Brent Trades Council, and chief advisor of the strike committee, has had phone calls from Yorkshire and Kent and Wales. The Scottish miners may not arrive until after the hour when the management's double-decker blue-and-white bus is escorted, by police, through the gates of the factory.

As the hour approaches – opening time for the class war – the tension in Chapter Road mounts. A couple of officials from APEX, the union which the owner of Grunwick, George Ward, refuses to recognise, are handing out 'official picket' banners to the five people who are to go round to the back gate of the factory in Cooper Road. The women on the picket line have followed the same routine of confrontation for the last ten days. The bus will rush down Chapter Road, carrying the scab workforce who have been picked up some distance away. The police lines will close in on it as the chant of 'Scabs, scabs, scabs' breaks out from the supporters and, immediately, the official picket will be pushed aside by the wheeling police cordon, the gates opened, and the bus allowed to enter.

'Today we'll stop them', says Jayaben Desai, treasurer of the strike committee. 'Today Ward will be shivering in his boots.'

'Do you think the miners will stop the bus?' we ask them.

'We'll definitely stop Ward now', they reply.

'Are most of the strike breakers Asians?' we ask.

'All sorts now', Jayaben replies. 'The people who worked there ten months ago when the strike began have mostly gone. Very few are still left, but Ward has recruited other people – whites, West Indians, Chinese, Asians and some students who need money badly.'

'So the picketing has persuaded some people to leave?'

'Oh yes, but Ward is paying everybody higher wages now. The strike has increased the pay to £30 a week and we are told that the management has stopped treating workers like slaves. They speak so politely now.'

'Did any of the workers who stayed behind when you first came out join you?'

'Last week eight West Indian ladies who were working with us came out and joined the union. Mr Ward was holding meetings inside the factory and he said, "We are going to win against the strikers", so the West Indian women said, "Who is *we? You* are fighting the strikers, *we* have no fight against them", and they left the work and joined us.'

As we talk, one of the strike committee members arrives on the line with the information that three more coachloads of miners have arrived and they are forming up outside the headquarters. Two strike organisers, both from the Brent Trades Council, are now making speeches from the middle of the road. There is a constant traffic of supporters, some of whom have come day in and day out and are aware that this Thursday is special. Someone hands Jack Dromey a poster in Chinese which she translates for him. It asks the twelve Chinese students who have recently joined the blacklegs, to join the picket-line. Dromey announces this to cheers, making some bantering remarks about 'sweet and sour and pancake rolls' in front of the corralled crowd. The policemen shift their weight from boot to boot, like horses ready for a race.

A massive cheer greets the banners which turn the corner. The Yorkshire miners arrive in formation with the Kent delegation and the coachload from Wales. Brave speeches are made as the mass picket forms up in front of the official pickets. Then someone dampens the euphoria by remembering the back gate. The Yorkshire pickets are sent post-haste to Cooper Road. They march there in formation, led by the president of the Yorkshire National Union of Miners (NUM), Arthur Scargill.

The door to the factory in Cooper Road is too small to admit the bus. The three hundred pickets in the road are flanked by five hundred policemen. Scargill addresses the pickets through the loudhailer. He talks about the right to picket and to persuade people who cross picket lines to respect them. He talks about the right of access to the scabs. In his voice there is a note of warning to the police who are also aware that, in the miners' pickets, they face a force they haven't encountered outside Grunwick before.

The bus arrives, as though out of nowhere, and is greeted by howls. The police have decided on a new tactic. The bus turns into Cooper Road and confronts a hundred pickets, who bar the door. The blackleg labour is unloaded within a ring of policemen three deep. The loudhailers begin. The police try to force a path through the pickets to the back gate. At the neck of Cooper Road, all traffic has stopped. A linked cordon of police bottles the conflict into this one street. At a signal, when there are twice as many police inside the enclosed arena as there are pickets, they fall on them. 'Arthur's nicked.' The cry goes on down the street, round the corner and into Chapter Road. Scargill is dragged by six policemen to the waiting vans.

As the police pour into Cooper Road from the main street, the miners coming round from the front gate charge the cordon and break through it. The broken cordon of police grab anyone they can lay their hands on. Pickets are dragged to the vans and the forty people arrested in the course of five minutes' scuffling are whisked away.

The scabs are through the gate and into the factory for the tenth time. One of the Asian strikers says, 'If this is to work we need ten thousand people every day.'

At Wembley police station, the forty prisoners are unloaded in the prisoners' pen. They queue up to pass through the charge room and are dumped in four cells, ten or twelve to a cell designed for one. 'The black hole of Wembley', someone says. Fags that have been smuggled into the cells are passed round. The miners, most of them from different coalfields, most of them shop stewards of the NUM, exchange notes and solidarity with other prisoners: 'We are going to bring down 64,000 miners the next day or the next. We'll turn Grunwick into another Saltley.'

On Friday, 25 June, the day after Scargill's arrest, the Scottish miners are on the line. Their leader Mick McGahey calls on Callaghan to join the picketing. His speech spells out the determination of the labour movement to force the government to force employers to recognise the union that their workers choose to join. In Yorkshire, Scargill tells the press that the miners will declare a day of action on Grunwick and seal off the factory with twenty thousand pickets.

Back in London, APEX leader Roy Grantham talks to Albert Booth, the Employment Minister, and agrees to limit the number of official pickets to five hundred. Outside the factory, the Asian strike committee rejects this negotiation as a stab in the back.

Earlier, the day before the battle of Cooper Road, the strike committee seemed sure of eventual victory: 'If Ward doesn't take us back, he will have to close the factory.'

'Would you go back to work for him after all this?'

'If he recognises the union, then we will go back and fight for better wages and everything. Also we are getting a lot of Asians from this area and other parts of the country who say that they are waiting for us to win and they will then unionise their factories too. We know that when we win this struggle and go back to the factory, Ward will try and get rid of us, make us fed-up so we will voluntarily leave the factory. But we are willing to take that. Behind us we will leave our victory.'

'WANT A LIFT TO GRUNWICK? ...'
Farrukh Dhondy, November–December 1977

Farrukh Dhondy, a member of the Race Today *Collective, was one of the many hundreds of people arrested on the picket lines at Grunwick Laboratories since mass picketing began in June this year. A special magistrates' court at Barnet has been set aside to deal with these cases, most of which have resulted in guilty verdicts. Farrukh went to court on 17 October, defended himself and had the case against him dismissed. Below, he has written his account of how his case was won.*

'Oh, you're here Farrukh', two cops who were giving evidence against him said to Dhondy. He muttered a clumsy greeting, not being sure whether to allow their chumminess to infiltrate between him and his determination to expose them for the liars they were. His case was called, amid some negotiations from the previous case, about time to pay the fine. Holding his carrier bag of exhibits, Dhondy took the defendant's chair. Saffin was called in. A surly man in his forties, he was, even in civvies, clearly in the flat-foot trade. The smiles with which he had greeted Dhondy seemed to have melted away. As he listened to his testimony, Dhondy recalled the first time he came across PC Saffin: as the miners on the Grunwick picket, three hundred strong, stormed the single police cordon thrown at the mouth of Chapter Road, this man had grabbed Dhondy by the shirt. The weight of his body was a live memory. It had been a clumsy arrest. Three coppers had fallen to the ground with Dhondy on the pavement.

'I've got you now', Saffin had shouted, amid the stomp of feet that seemed to be going over their bodies, as the miners breached the police order and stormed to the support of Arthur Scargill at the bottom of the street where supporters stood in puddles of disarray. Saffin had marched Dhondy to the police van with the assistance of two other arm-twisting constables. The other demonstrators didn't look like coming to the rescue. Telling the coppers who had him by the neck, shoulders and arms that he was a journalist and should be released forthwith, seemed futile.

'So what's your name? So what do you do? So why do you bother coming up here? So don't you know you can't win, and don't you think trade unions are taking over this country, and don't you know that Barbara Castle and Harold Wilson have … feathered their little nests, haven't they? And what about this bloke Solzhenitsyn?' said PC Saffin, adopting an all-boys-together tone. For three hours, Dhondy had had to endure Saffin's attempts to enlist him to the anti-socialist cause. He was much relieved to be thrown into a cell at Willesden with six Yorkshire miners who banged on the steel doors and yelled for room service. They talked hours about mining and the shop steward structure and said, 'Arthur better not be getting any better treatment' than them.

In the box, Saffin was a changed man. Dhondy could see he'd prepared his lines. His story was that Dhondy had confronted the police cordon. A single line of demonstrators shouted, 'We are trade unionists, we've got to get through' and charged the police cordon and managed to break it. 'No pressure from the back?' Dhondy asked.

'No … , Sir.'

Did he mean to say that other strike supporters hadn't come up from behind and exerted pressure to break the cordon? 'Yes, that's what he meant to say.' Other strike supporters were there, hovering somewhere behind Dhondy with trade union cries but not actually making bodily contact with that valiant line that broke the Special Patrol Group cordon.

'Do you mean to say, officer, that a trained Metropolitan police cordon of right men and burly was breached by a single line of the likes of me?'

The ten or so other policemen in the courtroom laughed. The magistrate couldn't restrain a smile. Saffin frowned. The prosecutor ran his tongue over his lips. Dhondy pulled out a shirt from his bag of exhibits and demanded to know if Saffin recognised it.

'No', he said.

'Would you recall it better if I said that you wrenched the buttons and eight inches of the shirt off it by pulling one way while I was pulling the other in that encounter at the cordon?'

'I don't know.'

'Could you rip the buttons off shirts if a man had his chest tightly pressed to your own?'

'I don't know.' There was a smell of defeat about Saffin's answers.

Then came Sergeant Galpin. He had arrested a man that day too and had, apparently, been in the bundle on the pavement. Yes, he remembered Dhondy. No, there wasn't any pressure from the back. No, he couldn't recall whether Dhondy was with a woman companion, neither could he recognise the shirt as having been worn and torn that day ... and so on. Other little tell-tale 'facts' fell out of his testimony. The magistrate was following the dialogue avidly.

Dhondy's own testimony described how he had risen early that fateful day and worn his school clothes (for he's a schoolteacher) and gone to Grunwick with Leila Hassan as *Race Today* representatives. He told of how he'd first talked to the strikers in Gujarati and then tried to get an earful of Mr Scargill's rhetoric. He told how, apart from *Race Today*, he had been asked by the *Times of India* to do a piece on Grunwick and had since written for the *Economic and Political Weekly* and *Debonair* on the strike.

The prosecutor asked him if it wasn't true that he had gone as a reporter and then got carried away and assaulted the police cordon.

'No', Dhondy said. It wasn't his habit to attack police cordons with people he didn't know. Nor would he contemplate militant action without being part of a viable force of people who had considered the meaning and consequence of such action. As the prosecutor ducked to the back of the court to consult with Saffin and Galpin, Dhondy, a trifle unfamiliar with the sequence of the trial, volunteered the presentation of his witness and exhibits.

'No', said the magistrate, sending Dhondy back to the defendant's seat. He knew that the charge of obstruction and threatening behaviour didn't hold water. He didn't want to see any exhibits or to hear Miss Hassan's testimony. 'And, by the way, Mr Dhondy', he added, 'on your way home, *don't* go past Chapter Road.'

PCs Saffin and Galpin walked out of court a little sheepishly. 'Don't take it like that, Farrukh', Saffin said, as Dhondy related events to Leila. Then again, crossing paths in the street, 'I expected to see you at the Hackney demonstration, Farrukh, on Saturday. Why weren't you there? It was your Marxist lot.'

'Want a lift to Grunwick, Farrukh?' Galpin asked.

'GRUNWICK REVISITED: ARTHUR SCARGILL AND JAYABEN DESAI'

Race Today, June–July 1987

In August 1976, 250 Asian workers walked out of Grunwick's film-processing and mail order firm in North West London and joined the Association of

Professional, Executive, Clerical and Computer Staff (APEX), a union to which they were directed by the local Citizens Advice Bureau. The subsequent struggle for union recognition in Grunwick and the reinstatement of the strikers became a national issue in the summer of 1977.

The dispute was the culmination of a long series of strikes by Asian workers in industries as diverse as textiles, plastics, engineering, foundries and car assembly, which had begun in the late 1960s and continued into the 1970s. In disputes ranging from the Midland Motor Cylinder Company, to Mansfield Hosiery Mills, to Perivale Guterman and to Imperial Typewriters, Asians had displayed not only increasing militancy but had also developed and sustained forms of collective organisation which had not been seen in modern Britain before. But Grunwick was particularly notable in being a strike that was led by women and in which, for the first time, black workers received widespread support on the picket line from many thousands of white trade unionists. At the time of the Grunwick strike, there was a Labour government in power, employment laws were more favourable to workers and trade unions than they are now, and the strength and militancy of the trade union movement far exceeded their current levels, yet the strikers failed to achieve their objective. The lessons of that dispute, the light it sheds on the role of the Labour Party and the trade union leadership in industrial disputes and the attitudes of that leadership to black workers, are still relevant ten years after the streets of North West London were filled with thousands of picketing and demonstrating trade unionists.

Earlier this year [1987], Jayaben Desai, the leader of the Grunwick strikers and Arthur Scargill, who led the National Union of Mineworkers pickets at Grunwick and was at the time of the dispute president of the Yorkshire area of the NUM, met to discuss their experiences of the strike.

Jayaben Desai and Arthur Scargill in Conversation

Scargill: Looking back a lot of people would say Grunwick was a failure. I certainly wouldn't say that, but a lot of people would. What would you say?

Desai: I say it's not a failure. There's a lot of achievement behind it. First, people realised how much power we have. They got confidence. Asian people especially learned a lot of things. They realised what their rights were in this country – what they can do, what they can't do.

Scargill: There were thousands of workers out there, including thousands of miners, who for the first time began to identify with Asian workers, something that had never happened before ... and I'm firmly convinced that as a result of what happened at Grunwick, the trade union movement, and particularly my union, gained a tremendous amount of experience and knowledge that inevitably led them to taking decisions to defend their jobs in 1984 and '85 in the miners' strike ... I was called to the TUC headquarters, this is something I've not revealed before ... I was asked by both TUC leaders, including the General Secretary, and also by the leaders of APEX, not to go to the picket, nor to send Yorkshire miners down to the demonstration. It was when I refused that the TUC decided that they were going to organise a counter-demonstration, and the effect was to take people away from the picket line.

Desai: I think APEX kept everything secret. They didn't tell us what was going on in their minds and what they planned.

Scargill: So you didn't even know that APEX had told us that we mustn't attend any more mass pickets?

Desai: Not at all. not at all. The first mass picket was organised with their approval. But behind the curtain they made a decision to turn all the mass picket into a demonstration. We had no idea about it, and even the strike committee had no idea ... Mr Arthur, I don't understand one thing. In Grunwick, why did the trade union leadership decide not to support?

Scargill: I wish I knew the answer off pat, but of course I don't. I only wish other trade union leaders had taken the same stand that I took. But if you look back right the way to 1926, the same question can be asked – why did the trade union leaders decide not to support the miners? Why did trade union leaders not support other workers who were in dispute? I think it's connected with the formation of the trade union movement in Britain. There's always an approach from the trade union movement which in a sense wants the status quo. It doesn't want to be associated with any dispute that looks in any sense revolutionary. And I say that in the nicest possible way, but they're terrified, quite frankly, of becoming associated with something that hits the public headlines and brings about what's described as conflict. Now, I don't agree with that; I think it is important to support things like this.

Desai: By not supporting, the same situation has been created now ... when the leadership is doing all these things to avoid conflicts, it is the people who are working and paying money to the unions, they are the sufferers.

Their families are suffering, and they are losing sympathy from the public … Nobody likes conflict, although we have to take that decision.

Scargill: I agree absolutely, and of course the important thing to remember is that if Grunwick had been supported and if the miners had been supported, then what's happening at Wapping wouldn't be taking place.

Desai: I have no faith in the law. There is no law in this land that can bring George Ward to accept the union and accept the people back inside. But I have faith in the strength of workers in this country … they can win. Not the law … the strength will win.

5
Challenging British (In)Justice

INTRODUCTION
Adam Elliott-Cooper

The campaigns for justice reported by *Race Today* reveal, for most readers, the shockingly familiar. Those reading these articles when they were hot off the press were most likely appalled and angered, but unsurprised, by the stitch-ups, brutalities and deaths at the hands of police, aided by a racist judicial process and a compliant press. Indeed, many of the issues detailed in the articles in this section ring true in twenty-first-century Britain. They resonate in more recent high-profile cases in which the public were misled by both police and press: a shoot-out between Mark Duggan and police that never happened, or the fabrication that Jean Charles de Menezes was wearing a suspiciously bulky jacket and jumping train-station barriers before he was shot dead by anti-terror police. The grass-roots campaigns to clear the names of those killed, brutalised, or framed endure in the decades following *Race Today*'s closure, but re-reading these articles shines light on the scale and militancy of Black struggle which the writers lived through. Organised, armed resistance to street fascism, a three-month occupation of a youth club threatened with closure, and a radical alliance between Black parents and student groups were as urgent in the 1970s when these struggles were at their height, as they are today when they are all but absent.

Within the militancy of the *Race Today* years, there was still fierce debate about whether more Blacks should be encouraged into the ranks of the police, and about the role of legal professionals in campaigns against racial injustice. These deliberations saw readers, regular contributors and members of the *Race Today* Collective disagreeing at different points. These arguments are, by now, well-rehearsed, with both the politics of integration and prison abolition gaining ground among liberal and radical circles respectively. It is clear that the radical Black movements that dominated *Race Today*'s pages saw the police as the primary barrier to Black liberation, and their voices dominate the news coverage, investigations and editorials in this collection.

Detailing Black movements across the country, the Collective's writers are able to aid the reader in making connections between corrupt institutions and the rebellions and campaigns that both responded to injustice and made bold demands for radical alternatives. Connecting the courtroom to the street corner, the articles express an urgency which remains grounded in the ever-present dangers of policing for Blacks in Britain.

The thread which binds these articles isn't simply the struggle for justice, but the necessity of self-defence for Black communities in Britain. The battles against racist attacks in areas such as Southall and Bradford, saw the slogan 'Self-defence is no offence' reaffirm a commitment to radical action by Asian youths. As these and many other campaigns testify, self-defence wasn't limited to the streets. Defending Black community spaces through grass-roots campaigns and civil disobedience further cemented the assertion that Blacks were 'Here to stay, here to fight'. Vitally, Britain's Black political movement defended itself in the courts. In its campaigns against state crimes, *Race Today* played a pivotal role in detailing lies, falsified evidence and key arguments. Critically analysing the radical potential of lawyers, satirising reactionary judges and championing the movement-building which galvanised these campaigns illustrate how *Race Today* was as much an integral part of popular struggles at the time, as it is an essential archive of Black history in Britain.

'BROCKWELL THREE: MOVE AS A COMMUNITY'
Race Today, June 1974

In March, three black youths from South London were sentenced at the Old Bailey to three years' imprisonment on charges which stemmed from the Brockwell Park incident last summer. Such is the importance of this trial that we have devoted these pages to an investigation and analysis of the event and the developments that followed.

Every year, the Showmen's Guild of Great Britain brings a fair to Brockwell Park, a major event in the local calendar. Situated a half-mile south of the centre of Brixton, it's a short three-penny bus ride down Railton Road from the concrete and iron of the city to the comparative quiet of the acres of grassland which constitute the nearest thing many of the area's children will ever get to the countryside. Lambeth local authority planned a spectacular finale for last year's fair: at 9.30 in the evening of Saturday, 9 June 1973, an enormous firework display rent the warm midsummer air with light and colour and sound.

Horace Parkinson, a 19-year-old youth worker at the Saint Matthews' youth club, lives with his parents and brother, Linton, in a small, neat, terraced house in Haycroft Road in Brixton. The house is that of typical hard-working, respectable first-generation West Indians. In the hall, an illustrated notice proclaims that Jesus watches over the household. The living room is a warm and cosy area which bustles with life. 'The house was always full of boys', recalls his father. In the backyard there is a weight-lifting set: Horace was nearly strong enough to beat his father, a London Transport Inspector.

As the firework display was getting under way at the fair, Horace Parkinson was setting off for his evening out with his friends, Hubert Simpson and Alec Carty. The plan was to drive round in the Humber Sceptre to meet some girls, and then go on to a party in North London. Horace, known for his smart dressing, was wearing a new white jacket. They decided to stop and check out the fair, parking along Dulwich Road. Horace was going to look for a girlfriend.

Robin Sterling had left for the fair much earlier. The 14-year-old from Tulse Hill School finished his paper round that morning and picked up his weekly wages with eager anticipation. He was a small, quiet boy, keen on running and skating. His employer trusted him absolutely; he received an extra £1 each week for helping him to mark up the papers. That night he left the house in Norbury with his two younger sisters, Carol and Maureen. The three of them spent the evening at the fair, and when the fireworks were over, they joined the crush heading for the Dulwich Road exit.

At the same time, a local white lad who had been drinking in the pub left to walk the few yards up the road to the fish-and-chip shop. It was full of people leaving the fair, so he leaned on the counter while he waited to place his order. Behind him, a group of black youths on their way to a blues, waited. Shoving and jostling broke out. The proprietor tried to hustle them out of his shop but in the melee a knife was drawn and the youth went down. Pandemonium broke out; the crowd pressed around, curious and bewildered at the sudden flash of violence, while the stabbed boy's mate ran over to the fair to fetch help. Police Constable Derek Castle, who was on duty that night at the fair went into the crowd and saw the stabbed youth lying on the ground. He was joined by Detective Harry Tucker and Temporary Detective Constable Harper.

Lloyd James was also at the fair that night. Wearing his characteristic snap-brimmed hat and his smart clothes, he saw the crowd outside the fish-and-chip shop and went to see what was happening.

Lloyd is 18 years old. He is in some ways typical of Brixton youths. He was born in Jamaica and came over to live with his mother when he was 9. He attended a local primary school but teachers couldn't deal with him so he was transferred to the ILEA Special School in North Kent. For two years, he only saw his mother every fortnight. Then he was transferred back to an ESN school in Dulwich. He left school at 15 and his first job was in a factory making dummies for tailors' shop windows. He didn't like it, nor his second job in a canteen, and left both. His next job, loading four large machines with laundry for £14.00 a week left him, his mother says, totally exhausted.

In the evenings, Lloyd would get around Brixton with his friends, and he was soon known to the police, who constantly picked him up. In three years, he had half a dozen convictions, ranging from suspicious behaviour, through theft, to assaulting a police officer. Lloyd had already done three months in a remand home. He didn't want to go inside again.

As the curious crowd pressed around the scene of the tragedy, the police felt themselves losing their grip of the situation. As they saw it, they were outnumbered by a 'threatening and hostile group of black youths', eager for confrontation. Castle called for help. Harper and Tucker drew their truncheons and attempted to force the crowd back. But the more they pushed at the front, the more people joined the throng behind as they poured out of the gates at the south end of Brockwell Park, curious to see what was happening. Castle joined his colleagues, by now thoroughly rattled.

Though he tried to stand his ground, Lloyd James was pushed from the back to the front, where the injured youth lay. Suddenly, he felt a hand in his face, told its owner to take it out, and found himself face-to-face with his old adversary, Detective Constable Harper. 'How would you like to be nicked for assaulting a police officer in the course of his duty?' asked Harper. 'Leave it alone, Lloyd,' said his mate who was standing next to him. 'He's looking for trouble.'

Temporary Detective Harper heard this exchange, grabbed hold of Lloyd James by his lapels and kneed him in the genitals. James, knowing what was at stake if he got pulled in again, banged Harper a good one and turned to run. But the crowd hemmed him in and he had no chance of making it out. Harper continued to kick him in the groin. Castle had now joined the fight and together they pushed him against the wall, punched him in the face and threw him to the floor. By now, there were two officers sitting on his legs and body, while the other one banged his head repeatedly on the pavement. He was well and truly subdued.

In the meantime, every patrol car within three miles and Scotland Yard's emergency room operators had heard Castle's call for back-up and very soon over a hundred policemen were speeding towards Brockwell Park, sirens blazing.

Horace Parkinson wasn't happy about the situation he found himself in. He was leaving the fair on his way back to the car when he saw the scuffles outside the chip shop. He too was carried by the crowd, though he shouted at the people to stop pushing him. He saw Lloyd James, who he knew, being punched and choked by the police. He didn't want any trouble; he had a future as a youth worker to consider. But he was unable to get out of the crowd and into the car. He tried to go around to the other door, but as he reached the back of the motor, Castle waved his truncheon and lunged at him. Parkinson did not retaliate, but walked around the other side of the car and tried to get in. 'Hold that one. Hold him,' shouted Castle and Parkinson felt himself being dragged by his white jacket back through the crowd and face-to-face with Constable Castle. 'If you struggle, you'll get it,' he said, crashing down on his left arm with the truncheon. Parkinson stood still and made no attempt to struggle, shielding himself from the blows and awaited his fate.

Within minutes of Horace Parkinson's arrest, word had spread through the crowd and that, together with the rumours spreading through the milling thong, created an impression of panic. As the first extra police cars arrived some of the youths started fighting back: bottles began to fly through the air; stones, pennies and clods of earth were hurled. A small group ran back into Brockwell Park and onto the flat roofs of the toilets, and it was from here that a bottle felled Detective Harry Tucker with a blow to his head that was later to put him into hospital, for stitching.

Robin Sterling, his sisters and three friends came out of the fair as the fight was getting under way. Bottles flew over their heads from the toilet roof, so he sat down on a wall to watch. Carol and Maureen started to walk away, but before Robin could join them, two police officers came over. 'That's one of them,' said the younger one. 'No, he isn't,' said the other. 'But he'll do.' Without a struggle or word of protest, Sterling went meekly down to the van with the two officers.

Lloyd James ended up in the van, with DC Harper still beating him. Then Horace Parkinson was thrown in and kept quiet by a simple threat of force. Outside he could hear the people shouting that he hadn't done anything. Robin Sterling was thrown into the van, by now protesting that he hadn't done anything.

By the minute, more police arrived and joined the small knot of those who were in the middle of the crowd. Some drew truncheons and pitched in with a will: eyewitnesses recall parents shielding their youngsters from the sticks, boys dodging blows, at least three girls receiving hits on the arms and shoulders. Some managed to escape through the crowd, while others stood petrified, unable to believe their eyes.

When the police van arrived at Brixton police station, the door opened and Sterling was dragged out by his hair into the police station. James followed, ducking to prevent himself from being hit by a truncheon. Parkinson wasn't so lucky and as he left the van, he was hit forcefully on the head. They were all taken into the general office which was by now full of policemen. Harper started to punch and kick Lloyd James who fell to the ground. Sterling was sobbing. 'I never did anything. I never did anything.' Castle shouted, 'Nigger, did you throw bottles?' Sterling replied: 'No', and Castle hit him with a truncheon until Sterling sobbed yes, he had done it. Parkinson, who was semi-conscious, was kicked and beaten on the floor. Castle threatened that he would make sure they got a long time. At this point, a uniformed officer said: 'That's enough.' They emptied their pockets, gave their names and addresses and were taken to separate cells. Horace Parkinson was visited by the police doctor who stitched the wound in his head. He didn't administer a local anaesthetic or shave the wound. None gave statements.

When Mrs Parkinson arrived there, at about 11.30 p.m., there was no one on duty at the front desk. Instead, she could hear screaming coming from the corridor to the side of the desk. With a shock of horror, she realized it was her boy and, throwing caution aside, she burst through the door and ran down the corridor. As she got near to the room, an officer came out and prevented her from going any further. 'No one's being beaten', he reassured her, but she had recognized Horace's screams and will remember the sound until she dies.

A few minutes later, Mrs Sterling arrived and was eventually allowed to see Robin, who was in a terrible state. 'If you're not for us, then you're against us', philosophised the policeman who accompanied her.

Next morning, Mrs and Mr Parkinson, with a neighbour who worked with the Brixton Neighbourhood Association, contacted Courteney Laws, the association's director, who took it from there, calling in Rudy Narayan to defend the boys in court the next morning. Mrs Parkinson then went to the police station, where she saw Horace. She was horrified. His head was still covered in blood, he was in great pain from the kicking in his stomach and groin, his clothes were filthy and his head was throbbing with pain.

'Don't worry about it', he told her. 'I've done nothing. I'm innocent, there's nothing to worry about.'

Lloyd's mother, Mrs James, was equally shocked when she saw Lloyd. She says: 'When I finally saw him, his mouth was swollen. I could see dried blood in his nose and he was holding a hanky that was covered in blood. He said he had been beaten both at the park and at the station, and my heart was too full to say anything.'

The three youths appeared at Camberwell Magistrates' Court on Monday, 11 June 1973, represented by Rudy Narayan. The charges were:

- Horace Parkinson – Grievous bodily harm to Derek Castle and assaulting a policeman in the execution of his duty; having in a public place an offensive weapon (a car jack).
- Lloyd James – Grievous bodily harm to Christopher Harper and assault on a police officer in execution of his duty.
- Robin Sterling – Unlawful wounding of Christopher Harper; assault causing grievous bodily harm to Tucker and Castle; possession of an offensive weapon (a milk bottle).

At the hearing, Parkinson and Sterling were granted bail totalling £610 and were placed under curfew from 8 p.m. to 7 a.m. Lloyd James was remanded in custody until 20 June when, at their second hearing, he was released on bail of £250, and also put under curfew. At this hearing, Parkinson and Sterling's curfews were reduced. The police case was not ready.

At the committal hearings at Wells Street Magistrates' Court, the more serious charge of affray was added by the magistrate and the charge against Robin Sterling of the unlawful wounding of Harper was dropped. The defence's request for trial at the Old Bailey was agreed.

During the following fortnight, an atmosphere of fear and hostility developed in Brixton. Youths were pulled off buses and asked if they had been at Brockwell Park and what they had seen; Special Patrol Groups toured the area; youth leader Ivan Madray was arrested; there was a rumoured armed entry into Shepherd's Youth Club. Rudy Narayan, wearing his South London West Indian Association hat, said that there were five CID officers going around the area 'mugging black youths'. This was hotly denied by the police, but it seemed likely to many.

Life returned to a semblance of normality for the three defendants. Lloyd James was re-employed by the firm making tailors' dummies but was sacked for taking time off to see his solicitors. Horace Parkinson continued to work at St. Matthew's Youth Club and study for his course. Robin went back to school and continued to study for his O levels.

Between June and their hearing at the Old Bailey, the defendants and their parents put their faith in their legal team to prepare the case. Courteney Laws and Zac Harazi interviewed witnesses, but out of 21 only 6 would sign, for fear of victimisation. Hard evidence was difficult to come by. There were persistent rumours that a group of youths, completely uninvolved with the fair, had in fact arrived in a car, jumped out and battled with the police with sticks and a car jack and then jumped back in their car when the police arrived in force. Eyewitnesses would not come forward for fear of being implicated.

The police were better prepared, readying witnesses and obtaining photographs of police injuries. Their attempt at remodelling their community relations programmes, including a new Community Liaison Officer, was applauded by the press and the local black elite, including Rudy Narayan. On the other hand, the students at Tulse Hill began agitating on behalf of the youths. The black community was polarized.

Quietly and ironically, the black youth who had done the original stabbing pleaded guilty and was fined £5.00.

On 4 March 1974, the trial began before an all-white jury. It lasted nine days. The defending barristers were Arnold Rose for Horace Parkinson, Ron Rose for Lloyd James and Rudy Narayan for Robin Sterling. The line pursued by the defence was left to the barristers' discretion. On the first day, Arnold Rose failed to appear and was replaced by a substitute who wasn't briefed on the case.

The prosecution case was put effectively. Eighteen policemen gave evidence to the effect that: a riot had broken out; Lloyd James had attacked Harper; Horace Parkinson, in going to James' assistance, had hit Castle with a car jack, and that Robin Sterling was on the wall throwing bottles, two of which wounded Castle and Tucker. Vivid photographs of the wounds inflicted were exhibited. Castle told the jury he was so affected that he had had to be prematurely retired from the police force. In fact, he had done 25 years' service and was due for retirement anyway.

The defence for Lloyd James was self-defence – that he had been attacked first by Harper and that the police were lying. He gave details of the beating at the police station.

Sterling and Parkinson's defence was a denial of all charges and was low key. The treatment they had received at the police station was not brought up, and photographs of injuries were not submitted. The defence relied on the characters of the boys, with friends, families and community members being called as witness. In Horace Parkinson's case, the owner of the car said that Parkinson couldn't have taken the jack from the boot because it was locked.

It took the jury just over two hours to find the three guilty and Judge Abdela passed judgments which stunned the defendants and their families.

On 20 March, a campaign committee was formed at a meeting at Brixton Town Hall attended by seventy people. A fund was started to raise the £1,000 needed to launch an appeal. Four people came forward to stand as sureties for bail: £338 was raised.

On Wednesday, 27 March, the school population came onto the stage. A meeting called by the Tulse Hill Students' Collective attracted over seventy schoolchildren aged from 9 to 17.

The meeting was tense. One speaker accused the police of escalating the incident and called upon the community to mobilise, to raise money in their schools and to attend the demonstration being called for the following Saturday. A Black Students' Action Committee was formed.

On Saturday, 30 March, some five hundred people, half of them white, assembled at Brockwell Park and marched around Brixton. At the rally, a school strike was called for.

On 3 April, nearly a thousand students came out on strike in schools across London. After a rally in Kennington Park, the march went past Camberwell Green Magistrates' Court, Tulse Hill School, Brixton police station and on to Brockwell Park. As they passed schools, students chanted: 'Come and join us', and about a hundred climbed over the fence and joined the demonstration.

After the rally, representatives from the Black Students' Action Committee handed in a letter of protest at Downing Street.

As we go to press, the three boys have done six weeks in prison – Sterling in Ashford Remand Home, Parkinson and James in Wormwood Scrubs. On the streets of Brixton, students and activists hand out leaflets and appeal for witnesses. The people who run community relations are busy organising the campaign to get Rudy Narayan onto the local council and then Parliament.

Some fundamental questions have been posed. First, there can be no doubt that the three people convicted are not guilty as charged and that that night's activities represented a collective response to years of police harassment. Second, the whole conduct of the defence requires examination. Third, there are political issues raised. Although the social work activists, the youth leaders, the community liaison pleaders and the Black People's Defence Committee were involved from the first, they had no effect.

Instead, new forces have emerged. The Black Students' Action Collective have mobilized for all three boys, aware of the dangers of excluding Lloyd James even though some youth workers have intimated that Lloyd, the street boy and hustler, is a block to the release of their friends.

And Lloyd James? His section does not trust the leadership that has thrust itself forward, nor did they believe that the social compact would protect Lloyd's interest in the trial. Not for them demonstrations and pickets; not for them any illusions about what the state can and will do. They have seen the social activist machine at work and know it well. Lloyd James's time inside will be the hardest of them all. But only for a time.

'TIMES ARE CHANGING'
Race Today, November 1975

The issue of police brutality to and harassment of the black community is not new. The trial of the Cricklewood 12, the Stockwell 10, the Cliff McDaniel case, are examples of what we in the black community have been experiencing for some years.

When approached in detail, these trials indicate that where the battles are confined to the courts (in Northern Ireland they are not), police officers will explore every avenue, manipulate evidence, and verbal defendants in order to secure a conviction. This they cannot do on their own. They depend on magistrates who, almost by instinct, accept and rubber-stamp the evidence of the police.

With jurors, they appeal to the hide-bound prejudices of whites, whom they hope will accept any version of black activity. In this, the press are their loyal allies.

Of course, older blacks must be approached differently. Here, they sense that the first generation are finding it difficult to come to terms with how their children see the world and what they do or do not do as a consequence. Down to the last verbal – that is, what the defendant is supposed to have said in custody – an appeal is made to older blacks to stand aside from and cast adrift these younger blacks who 'let the side down'.

These are fundamental political questions which can only be approached in a political way. We say that this because Berris Edwards, Donald Richmond, Dennis Bovell and Cliff McDaniel sit in the dock, listening to police evidence against them that they know is not true. Whether or not a magistrate or a jury believes it depends on which force has the predominant moral influence in the society at large. Jurors, or magistrates, do not begin to think on the bench or the jurors' box. That process begins before and continues long after.

In this context, magistrates and juries must be separated. The former are conditioned by background and social influence – school, church and the like – to believe the police. The latter, although attempts have been made to condition them by loyalty to the nation, are less reliable. That is why the option of trial by jury is infinitely better than trial by magistrates. Ask Cliff McDaniel. Look at the overwhelmingly white juries who refused to convict the Cricklewood 12 or the Stockwell 10.

We should not jump to instant conclusions that whites have suddenly taken our side. Some history is in order. Many of us remember the times when whites would not hesitate in convicting blacks on any evidence whatever. The police could do no wrong. But their own experiences, together with the unending propaganda from the black community, have had an impact. After all, we have been here in Britain for 25 years. We have worked and lived alongside whites. That counts for something.

Older blacks too have been on juries and those who were formerly dismissed as 'Uncle Toms' have, even with their characteristic caution, come down on the side of West Indian youths.

So what is the opposition ranged against us?

The *South London Press*, read by thousands, gave pride of place to Commander Randall's mugging figures in Lewisham. You only have to read their report on the verdicts handed down in the Stockwell 10 trial to know that they have not and will not subject to microscopic treatment the evidence of police officers operating on the South London Underground. Even following the recent conference on Race and the Media, at which so many journalists gave pious pledges to report black issues, not one serious in-depth analysis of police evidence in the recent trials has appeared. Perhaps the editors believe that potential jurors are best left alone.

And then there is Robert Mark, Commissioner of Police – Mr Shrewd himself. His attack is two-pronged. First, jury trials should be done away with and second, he announces the recruiting of black police officers, to be his most immediate preoccupation. Verdicts, favourable to the police, will be so much easier to come by if West Indian youths are framed by black policemen. It is his way out of the crisis that faces policemen who are defeated by juries who won't buy what is sold to them by police officers from the witness box.

Times are changing and our political task is clear. There can be no deviation now from the path of constant exposure of police corruption and brutality.

'THE GUILTY VERDICTS ARE UNACCEPTABLE'
Ian Macdonald, November 1976

Six young black women from Harlesden were arrested and viciously beaten up on the night of 24 June 1976, following a battle between the police and black youth who were making their way home from the Burning Spear Club. The police instigated the confrontation when they attempted to force a 15-year-old youth into a police car.

Yet, in evidence to the court, the police denied the incident involving the 15-year-old youth. They claimed, instead, that they came into contact with the defendants when they saw the girls knocking on doors in the early hours of the morning.

The following day more than two hundred members of Harlesden's black community demonstrated against the brutality of the police and mounted a picket on Harlesden police station. They have also been packing out the public gallery of Willesden Magistrates' Court while the case has been fought out.

Below, we print extracts from the closing speech of Ian Macdonald, one of the defence barristers, together with the verdicts handed down by the magistrates.

Hyacinth	–	Using Threatening Behaviour	–	Guilty
		Wilfully Knocking on Doors	–	Dismissed
		Assault on a Police Officer	–	Guilty
Virginia	–	Using Threatening Behaviour	–	Dismissed
		Wilfully Knocking on Doors	–	Dismissed
Rosa	–	Assault on a Police Officer	–	Guilty
Monica	–	Assault on a Police Officer	–	Not Guilty
		Assault on a Police Officer	–	Guilty
Shirley	–	Obstructing a Police Officer	–	Guilty
Olive	–	Wilfully Knocking on Doors	–	Dismissed
		Assault on a Police Officer	–	Guilty

We were told by the prosecutor, in his opening speech, that we must all keep a low profile. Mr King-Lassman called for calm. He said that this was a storm in a teacup. I objected at the time. No prosecutor has a right to say that. It is not his function. It is not the function of the court to act as some kind of fire brigade on the racial situation in Brent because, let's make no mistake, that's what he is talking about. The function of the court is to see whether it can get at the truth. It has to look at the events as real live people describe them. One side says one thing happened, the other side says something else happened. Your function is to say whether the prosecution's version of what took place carries conviction or not.

As defence counsel, if I am told that events took place in a certain way, and it is obvious that what my clients say is in total contradiction to what the police are going to say, then I have to be prepared for a confrontation. The day that any defence advocate starts censoring the case of his clients for the kind of political interest that Mr King-Lassman is suggesting, then the candle of liberty begins to be snuffed out. I, for one, will have no part of that.

Police Officers Do Lie

I want to put to rest the suggestion made by the prosecutor in re-examination of a number of police officers, that no police constable would jeopardise his career and his pension by acting in this way or, by coming to court and telling a pack of lies. The truth is, that the normal thing when police get into court and give their evidence – especially in Magistrates' Courts – is that they are 98 per cent sure they will be believed. That is a statistical fact. A few years ago, during an anti-apartheid demonstration against a South African rugby tour, a young man was arrested and convicted of threatening behaviour and assault on a police officer. The evidence of the police officer was believed. It was only some years later, when that police officer found religion, that the truth came out.

You, as a Bench, probably get to know the many different police officers who come regularly to this court. Also, you have a lot in common because you are both concerned with law and order and the stamping out of crime. It's very difficult in that situation to be suddenly told that that person is a liar. I understand that. It's also a well-known fact in the legal profession that, if we confront police evidence as in this case, then we run very high risks. If we attack too hard, we're told that our client will get a bigger sentence. So, we soft-pedal. We advise our clients to plead guilty because they'll get a lighter sentence.

Given all the assumptions about the police, given the reality of legal representation, the police have enormous scope for abusing their power.

Police Assault Defendants

No one can persuade me that Rosa T. got her injuries colliding with PC Taylor. She might have caught her eye on one of his shiny buttons, but I've never heard of a swollen eye being caused by a button. And this leaves unexplained her swollen lips, and the bruising on her chest and back. What is beyond dispute are the doctor's findings. You have to ask, did she get these injuries because she collided with PC Taylor or, did she get them because she was kicked and punched? The injuries to Hyacinth M. are even more mysterious if you accept the evidence of PC Fraser. Her injuries are beyond dispute – tender right jaw, tender left cheekbone and bruising on lower abdomen and tender on her back. PC Fraser says he saw no injuries on her and is adamant that he did not touch or punch her. If you believe him, then how did Hyacinth M. get her injuries?

Figure 5.1   Outside Royal Courts of Justice, September 1977, following Darcus's successful appeal and release from prison: Selwyn Baptiste, Darcus Howe, Ian Macdonald, John La Rose and Barbara Beese.

'UP AGAINST THE LAWYERS'
Ian Macdonald, February 1977

In the October 1976 issue of Race Today, *the Black Parents' Movement rejected the practice which stems from the widely held belief that lawyers know best and that defendants are passive partners in the court scene. Gavin McKenzie and*

Ole Hansen, both solicitors, wrote to Race Today *expressing how appalled they were at the 'likely effects' of what the Black Parents' Movement advocate. In this article, Ian Macdonald, Barrister-at Law, argues the opposite.*

I must take issue with my friend, Gavin McKenzie and his colleague, Ole Hansen, over their criticism of the Black Parents' Movement.

They say that the object of fighting a criminal trial is to minimise the damage to the defendant, and then suggest that the way to do this is to find a 'good solicitor' and rely entirely on his or her expertise. These assertions are based on two assumptions: that the defendant is a victim, someone who is powerless and essentially passive, and that the professionals know best, or certainly, that they know better than the members of the Back Parents' Movement. My disagreement is total and fundamental.

First, the defendant as victim. In the black context this means you see the defendant as black Sambo but never as the rebel, Nat Turner. The self-activity of the defendant in the court proceedings is denied. However great the defendant's rebellion up to the time of arrest, it must stop at the door of the court. Courtrooms are places for professionals, and defendants must follow a certain code of behaviour and sit docile and passive in the dock. The 'good' lawyer then bargains with the court about their fate.

Unfortunately, this is probably a correct description of the normal lawyer-client relationship in criminal cases, except that a large number of lawyers are incompetent at carrying out even this relatively simple task. The traditional treatment of the defendant as passive victim has certain clearly defined consequences on how a case is prepared (which Gavin and Ole go into) and on the style of advocacy used in court (which they leave out).

So far as preparation is concerned, solicitors are in sole charge over the client. From the moment they are instructed they tell the client what to do, what to leave out of statement, often, what to put in, which witnesses to call, how to dress and how to behave in court. A 'good' solicitor is one who does these things with care and sympathy, who takes time, and trouble and who knows legal loopholes. And there are not too many of these around.

The solicitor's role is reinforced by the advocate. If you see your client as victim, then basically your role is to strike the best bargain you can for him or her with the magistrate or judge. Your style of advocacy will be deferential and accommodating. Your success depends on their goodwill and sense of fair play. So you will not press points that might offend. You will leave the substance of the case untouched, but will jump at any technicalities or nice legal points which offer a chance of escape for your client.

In short, this type of case preparation and advocacy accepts the myth of judicial impartiality, and never challenges the power of the court. And all the time it assumes that your client will be sitting there in the dock, dumb and passive, except for his or her brief and often painful sojourn to the witness stand and back.

I accept that there are certain cases where this kind of bargaining process may be the best option open. But in most cases it simply doesn't work. Clearly, something else needs to be done. Some other way has to be found.

Gavin and Ole recognise this. I have no doubts about their care and concern. But what do they propose? A defence committee. Fine. Very radical. But what kind of committee? Essentially, theirs is one which in no way trespasses on the lawyers' territory, leaving the tactics and conduct of the case in their 'expert' hands, and devotes itself to the good works of soothing the troubled victim's brow, finding witnesses and dealing with the press. And what is the result? The same kind of deferential bootlicking in court, only now you have a few pickets outside. This way you strike a radical pose and change nothing.

This brings me to their second assumption: that the professionals are the experts and know best.

The traditional methods of defending court cases do not generally work. There are exceptions. But they certainly do not work in the situation existing between the police and black youth with which we are dealing. Solicitors and barristers may be well-versed in the do's and don'ts of the traditional craft but they have no idea what to put in its place, and, by and large, they don't want to know, because they make a lot of easy money doing things in the traditional way. That is the extent of their expertise.

What Gavin and Ole ignore completely is that the people in the Black Parents' Movement have not just dropped out of the sky. They come into that organisation with a very particular history and experience of dealing with courts and police. In particular they have the Mangrove experience. I believe that the Mangrove trial was a watershed, not because I took part in it – I know a lot of things now that I didn't know then – but because we learned, through that experience, how to confront the power of the court and in the end to break it. That was because the defendants refused to play the role of victim and to rely on the so-called 'expertise' of the lawyers, and because they were so organised that they could carry their intentions through.

Once you recognise the defendant as a self-active and self-assertive human being in the court everything has to change – the power and role of lawyers, the style of advocacy, and the method of case preparation. The lawyer can no longer act as a buffer, mediating between the judge and his or her client. The power confrontation is sharp and direct and the myth of judicial impartiality fades away.

The main point of the criminal trial is not the lawyer sheltering his or her client from damage. The main question is how strong and powerful you are. That is purely an organisational question of which the Black Parents' Movement, I believe, are fully aware. If you are weak, you will be annihilated. If you are strong, then the court, like every other state institution, will seek to make some accommodation with you.

What Gavin and Ole and all the other radical lawyers have to decide is whether they want to retain their slice of the traditional lawyers' cake or to participate in a bold new experience.

'THE BRADFORD 12: REFLECTING ON THE TRIAL OF THE DECADE'
Race Today, August 1982

In the following three related articles, members of the Race Today *Collective describe and analyse the historical importance of the trial of twelve young Asians who were charged with conspiracy to make petrol bombs at a demonstration against the National Front in Bradford.*

The Mass Youth Movement and its Origins

First, who are these young men and what are the forces which shaped them and their actions? The twelve defendants are all young Asians, that is to say the offspring of immigrants who arrived in Britain from India and Pakistan. They are products of the British education system and are aged between 17 and 25 years. With the exception of Jayesh Amin, a university graduate, and Ishaq Kazi, a bank clerk, they were, at the time of their arrest, either unemployed or employed in working-class jobs in the city of Bradford.

Politically they were members of the United Black Youth League (UBYL), a small organisation which, at the time of their arrest, was three to four months old. Although by then no statement of policy and position had been drawn up, an interpretation of their activities in campaigns indicated a radical approach to two issues: racial attacks on the Asian community and deportations of Asian workers.

What is certain is that these young men did not fall from the sky, nor are they oddballs prone to irrational behaviour. They are products of an histor-

ical movement which first made itself felt at the heart of British society in
the summer of 1976.

Every new historical movement invariably emerges around a single issue
and has as its objective the transcending, perhaps the shattering, of the
old. In this case, the issue has been and continues to be the constant and
murderous stream of racial attacks against the Asian community. The 'old'
was and is represented by the moderate approach of the traditional Asian
organisations backed by the British state. The moment? The murder of
18-year-old Gurdip Singh Chaggar by a gang of racialists on the streets of
Southall on 4 June 1976.

From the late 1960s onwards, the Asian community throughout the
United Kingdom had been complaining about the racial attacks carried
out by right-wing fascist organisations or disaffected young whites. Their
complaint that the British police showed a marked reluctance in tracking
down and bringing their assailants to justice was right. The official position
was that the term 'racial attack' was a figment of the Asian imagination.

Another factor needs to be considered. During the late 1960s and
throughout the '70s, the Asian community had developed a remarkable
militancy on the shop floor. These militant activities won recognition which
in turn led to some being rewarded with jobs inside the trade union bureaucracy, others becoming local councillors. Add to this the vast race relations
bureaucracy and the Manpower Services Commission with its vast and
paralysing sources of state funding, and the corruption of the traditional
Asian organisations was complete by the time Gurdip Singh Chaggar lay
dying on the pavement of a Southall street. The effect of this corruption
was and continues to be the stifling of the traditions of militancy in the
Asian community.

By that time, however, a whole generation of Asian youth had grown
up in Britain. They rose en masse to challenge the old ways and methods
of dealing with racist attacks and to break through the solid wall of Asian
organisations which maintained the status quo.

The first major expression of this new force came in the aftermath of
Chaggar's murder. The terrain was Southall, a West London suburb in
which some 30,000 Asians, mainly from the Punjab, reside. They work in
local factories and at Heathrow Airport and, as in every Asian community
in Britain, the Indian Workers' Association, the Sikh Temple and the local
race relations industry dominate.

In the days following Chaggar's murder, the youth took to the streets.
They organised patrols, attacked white motorists and opposed the police.
When two of their number were arrested, they surrounded the local police

station and secured the release of their comrades. Very soon, young Asians in other parts of Britain stirred similarly in response.

This was a massive social upheaval involving thousands of young Asians throughout Britain who were prepared to throw the caution of their parents to the wind and employ militant and violent methods to defend themselves against racist attacks. The rest of British society had to take notice. No longer could the issue be clouded by the smokescreen of official jargon and police semantics. Thousands of whites, mainly political radicals and well-meaning liberals, responded in support. And the first-generation Asians, who had got nowhere with their moderate approach, were willing to go along with the youth.

It was in this mass movement which the Bradford 12 had cut their teeth.

The British state was cautious at first, leaving matters to the entrenched Asian organisations. But they did not manage well, barely containing a mass revolt against the demonstration which followed Chaggar's murder. As one young protester put it: 'These people [the elders] have done nothing. Some of them have got rich. The party wallahs are asking us to join them when what they need do is join us, otherwise they are finished.'

Posit these comments against those expressed by traditional moderates: 'These people [the youth] are not political, they have no politics. It is we who have the political experience.'

Those were the political lines to emerge in the cut and thrust of events surrounding the Southall murder, but they replicated themselves among the Asian community throughout the country. Young Asians set up youth organisations which challenged the old organisations; the old struck back. Very often, the youth leadership was courted with persuasive offers to sink differences and join up with the old, or encouraged into state-funded projects.

These manoeuvrings penetrated large sections of the organised youth leadership, but the mass movement remained largely unaffected. When the front line fails, it is the turn of the rear guard to prevail. In this case, the rear guard was the coercive forces of the British state.

During the General Election of 1979, the fascist and racist National Front put up candidates in constituencies where there were large black communities. They had no change of winning but it gave them the right to hold public meetings in black areas, as in Southall. Young Asians gathered in their thousands to prevent the meetings taking place. The police mobilized in enormous numbers. They proceeded to attack the protesters with a savagery which no section of society, except the Irish in Northern Ireland, had experienced in years. One person, an anti-racist schoolteacher,

Blair Peach, was bludgeoned to death by police batons. Over three hundred people were arrested and the cases were heard by carefully selected magistrates who returned a disproportionate number of guilty verdicts. Only by such vulgar, empirical violence could the British state hope to contain the Asian mass movement and its white support.

There is the time-honoured conclusion, born out of centuries of social and political experience, that repression of this order only serves to strengthen the resolve of the mass movement. In a period of five years, thousands of young Asians had transformed the balance of power in this crucial struggle. One moment of violent excesses on the part of the police would not crush it.

All twelve defendants had at one time or another been activists in that general movement. Their membership in the UBYL, however, placed them in a special category because this openly repudiated the traditional Asian formations which dominated the Bradford community. They were, therefore, consciously laying down the challenge to the state and its Asian phalanx for the hearts and minds of the Asian community.

In the cut and thrust of attempting to transcend the old, a faction within the Bradford AYM succumbed to the carrot of state funding and welfare activities. Gata Aura and Tariq Ali walked out and set up the United Black Youth League through which they aimed to draw membership from the West Indian community and to travel along a radical and revolutionary path, for example, manufacturing petrol bombs for use in the event of a racial attack. They also organised campaigns, for example, for Anwar Ditta, an Asian women prevented by the immigration laws from having her children join her. This campaign was national in scope and made Gata Aura in particular a national political figure.

The Campaign to Free the Twelve

As in Southall in the General Election of 1979, the British state drew the line, in this case the Director of Public Prosecutions being the cutting edge. Instead of charging the defendants with manufacturing petrol bombs, as many more had been during that summer of riots, he chose the highly political course of charging them with conspiracy.

By opting for this, the DPP laid down a major challenge to the youth movement and its organisational activists; here was a political opportunity, par excellence, to galvanise the thousands of young Asians into motion. They had shown their mettle over five dramatic years and all the evidence indicated they were on the move. Only weeks previously, when skinhead fascists had been bused into Southall for a pop concert at a local pub and Asian shops had been attacked, the young Asians of Southall had organised themselves, marched on the pub and, despite police protection, burnt the building down.

A group of activists from the Bradford AYM, in alliance with other forces in the community, formed the July 11th Committee to free the 12. The issue which at once preoccupied the committee was the political line they would adopt as regards the defence of those arrested. Courtenay Hay, a former member of the defunct Bradford Black Collective and now chairman of the Committee, visited Gata Aura in prison. Gata Aura tells us that he informed Hay that the line was self-defence. Hay moves in mysterious ways his wonders to perform. He returned to the Committee with the line that the defendants were framed. His campaign message was: 'The UBYL, because of its political activities of fighting racism, its resistance to fascism and carrying forward the anti imperialist struggle, has been made a victim of political persecution by the state police.'

It was obvious that he had elevated the UBYL to a position which did not accord with reality. The organisation was all but four months old, just about cutting its teeth, and had made to date little impact locally or nationally. Had political activists been operating in a situation in which the British state would deliberately frame an entire organisation on conspiracy to make petrol bombs, then we were living in dire straits indeed. There was ample evidence in the trial that Special Branch trailed the UBYL, waiting to pounce once a mistake was made, but the frame-up line was indigestible to all but the most gullible.

The July 11th Committee went to the public for the first time on 12 August 1981 at the Arcadian Cinema in Bradford. The leaflet inviting the public to the meeting screamed 'Framed by the police'. Some nine hundred Asian youth attended that meeting but the explanation for the arrests was difficult, almost impossible to swallow. The twelve defendants were their peers whom they know politically and socially and they knew that they were quite capable of making petrol bombs. The frame-up line fell on deaf ears.

In addition, the platform boasted Councillor Ajeeb, Councillor Hameed and J.S. Sahota of the IWA, all of whose political practice had been in mortal opposition to the mass radical and revolutionary movement of Asian youth. From that meeting onwards, the mass of Asian youth voted with their feet. They went away and stayed away.

Meanwhile the Yorkshire police had been visiting the elders of the Asian community, warning them away from supporting the 12 who, they said, were terrorists. The elders bought this and spewed it out to their followers.

The Committee persisted with the frame-up line and it became clear that the campaign was in the grip of the Asian middle classes (predominantly students), together with every left tendency and radical outfit. Significantly, in November, a campaign meeting in London was not held in the traditional strongholds of Asian youth revolt, but at the London School of Economics. Whatever else the campaign would do, it certainly could not take the mass movement one step further.

The only line which would have generated support in the Asian community was the self-defence line, but though this was debated week after week in the Committee, it was defeated, overruled by the solicitors. The solicitors? Yes. The legal team advised that it would be the correct course to keep the defence secret and surprise the prosecution with the self-defence argument. They carried the day, though we defy a single lawyer to explain what the prosecution could have done to strengthen their case if the self-defence issue was made public. Nothing at all.

A word about lawyers in general. They, most of them, have the tendency to dominate the client. Their word is law. It needs a powerful, political campaign and equally strong defendants to hold the fort. Otherwise, lawyers do as they please, requiring of campaigns mere orchestration and stage decoration.

In time, the campaign switched its line to the obscure and liberal position that conspiracy charges were legally oppressive. Listen to this: 'Conspiracy charges relate more to defendants' political views and activity than to anything else. They have been used before as a political weapon by the British state to repress opposition.' Though this may have been true, it was not an argument which would mobilise a single Asian youth, who would have responded to the line which said, 'Yes, we made the bombs. We made them in defence of the Asian community. Self-defence is No Offence.' They would have flocked to that position from every Asian community in this country.

Ironically, the campaign eventually did adopt the self-defence position, but only after the trial was halfway through.

However, all was not negative. The 12 entered Leeds Crown Court with much behind them. The mass movement's actions over a period of five months ensured that no jury in this nation could be unaware of the general issue of racial attacks and the defence secured a major weapon when a Home Office study revealed the existence of 2,581 instances of racial attacks in two months. William Whitelaw, Home Secretary, was forced to change the official position, admitting: 'The study has shown quite clearly that the anxieties expressed about racial attacks was justified.' This was the context within which a team of radical lawyers, blooded in and shaped by the black revolt in Britain, would take the fight to the judicial authorities.

There was, however, one major hurdle to overcome. Tarlochan Gata Aura, on arrest, made two statements to the police. They had offered the inducement that he would be granted bail if he came clean and had prompted him with the information that his fingerprints were found on one of the bottles. In his statement, he mentioned Ishaq Kazi, Praveen Patel, Jayesh Amin, Bahram Noor Khan, Sabir Hussain, Tariq Ali and Vasant Patel as part of the general organisation. He admitted to making the bombs for use 'in case the National Front were there causing trouble'. Following Gata Aura's admission, all the other defendants crumbled and made varying admissions. Without these statements, the prosecution would have had no case.

Gata Aura's admission created a great deal of acrimony among the defendants. The rank-and-file membership expressed a serious hostility to the leadership trio of Aura, Amin and Ali. The three, they claimed, got them into the mess and created extra difficulties by being the first to sign statements of admission. Although this attitude is understandable, and could point to a serious question of leadership, it is also understandable that a youth of 25 years, as Gata Aura was, working in such a new organisation, in virtual isolation, would crumble. As he said, he thought 'it was the end of the world'; he had little experience of police stations and he could see no other way out.

The Trial at Leeds Crown Court, 26 April 1982

The first major issue at the trial turned on jury selection. Defence counsel challenged the fact that none of the jurors were from the Asian community in Bradford, and only two prospective jurors were Asian. Old legal statutes were invoked, complex arguments were offered, specialist and technical jargon was employed. Eventually, Judge Beaumont, by an administrative sleight of hand, met the defence halfway, having expressed his sympathy with the view that there should be some black representation on the jury. Eventually of the twelve jurors sworn in, seven were white and five were black.

Paul Kennedy opened for the prosecution. Not a man of great sparkle, wit and incisive intellect, he referred the court to events of 11 July 1981 when, he recalled, 'There was considerable disturbance in Bradford City Centre in which windows were broken, property was damaged and the crowd behaved in a menacing way and had to be dispersed.' Tariq Ali, he offered, was identified by police officers as moving between groups of

Asians. Tarlochan Gata Aura, he added, was organising members of the UBYL to attend a meeting in which 'Tarlochan made it clear that trouble was expected that evening and that petrol bombs should be made.'

And here was the major point of contention. He claimed: 'There was no threat from skinheads and the National Front ... they [the bombs] were to be used against the police .... against large shops where they would have a larger effect ... they were to be used in a riot.'Then he outlined the specific allegations against the 12:

Tarlochan Gata Aura: Co-leader of the United Black Youth League (UBYL). Organised the meeting and the manufacture of petrol bombs. Obtained the petrol, stuffed the bottles with wicks. Wiped the bottles clean of fingerprints. Went to the town centre to participate in a 'riot' and was arrested and charged with threatening behaviour.

Tariq Ali: Co-leader of the UBYL. Took decision with Tarlochan Gata Aura to make petrol bombs on 11 July. Went to town centre to agitate and incite a riot in which petrol bombs would be used. Arrested for disturbing the peace.

Jayesh Amin: Leading member of the UBYL. 'Reluctantly' allowed his home to be used for the manufacture of petrol devices.

Giovanni Singh: Bought rubber tubing for syphoning petrol. Arrested in town centre for intervening in Ali's arrest.

Parveen Patel: Present at UBYL meeting. Obtained milk bottles, filled with petrol siphoned from car.

Ishaq Mohammed Kazi: Present at meeting. Allowed his car to be used to obtain necessary materials.

Bahram Noor Khan: Present at meeting. Obtained petrol. Kept watch while others made devices.

Masood Malik: Present at meeting. Obtained materials for petrol bombs. Kept watch while others made devices.

Vasant Patel: Present at meeting. Obtained milk bottles and material for wicks.

Saeed Hussain: Present at meeting.

Sabir Hussain: Present at meeting. Arrested in town centre intervening in Ali's arrest.

Ahmed Mansoor: Present at meeting. Obtained bottles, kept watch, wiped bottles clean to remove fingerprints.

The basis of all this information lay in the statements of admission signed by all defendants.

There then followed some 37 officers, most of whom testified to the fact that they accurately recorded, in the language and wording of the defendants, hundreds of questions and answers. The defence counsel aimed to show that sizeable areas of the police documentation were fabricated and that they intimidated, harassed and used violence against the defendants to sign the admissions.

The major issue turned upon the use for which the bombs were manufactured. The police claimed that some defendants admitted that they were to be used against police and property. The defence denied this allegation and claimed that those words were fabricated by the police.

The high point of the fabrication issue was reached in Helena Kennedy's cross-examination of Officer Maloney. He claimed that he questioned Sabir Hussain extensively (196 questions and answers) without taking any notes; he had later recorded them verbatim.

'Did you do that from memory?' teased Ms Kennedy.

'Yes, I did', replied Maloney triumphantly.

'What was the first question I asked you today?' demanded Kennedy, a sharp edge to her Scottish brogue.

'I can't remember', surrendered Maloney.

And then there was the crafty 'hatchet job' on Detective Inspector Sidebottom, executed by Paddy O'Connor, counsel for Masood Malik. Paddy enquired of Sidebottom whether 'Further to my previous statement I would like to clarify the points which I did not mention before' were really the words of 'an 18-year-old Yorkshire lad'?'Yes', replied Sidebottom.

O'Connor then read from Sidebottom's own statement: 'Further to my previous statement I would like to clarify the point I did not mention before.' Out came O'Connor's sledgehammer: 'Did the 18-year-old lad draft your second statement for you?' Sidebottom was demolished.

Highlights those were, but there were many similar moments in the rigorous cross-examinations by defence counsel.

The other key issue pressed by the defence was whether racial attacks were prevalent in Bradford. Officer after officer described Bradford as a haven of multi-racial peace, not budging even in the face of clear evidence to the contrary. They made themselves sound and look ridiculous.

At the end of the prosecution's case, after defence submissions, Sabir Hussain and Saeed Hussain had count 1 dropped and Jayesh Amin was set free, there being no prima facie case against him.

It was now the turn of the defence. Mansfield opened for Tarlochan Gara Aura who then went into the witness stand.

His soft features belied a formidable political experience. Tarlochan had just turned 25. He was blooded in the anti-fascist, anti-racist movement of Asian youth and had sought relentlessly for some organisational and ideological clarity through which to advance the Asian struggle. He had been part of a black caucus within the Trotskyist International Socialists, leaving it when 'Black and White Unite and Fight' was all the leadership could muster. He had then been part of 'Samaj inna Babylon', a combination of Asian and West Indian activists who produced a newspaper, then the Indian Progressive Youth Movement in Bradford, then to the Bradford AYM, the Black Socialist Alliance and finally the UBYL.

Tarlochan gave his evidence quietly and moderately, if somewhat nervously. His delivery under examination in chief and cross-examination could be described as *'suaviter in modo, fortiter in re'* – moderate in manner, strong in content.

Yes, he had made the bombs; yes he had organised others to manufacture them. He would take full responsibility. He had pursued the course because he was told that the fascists were coming to attack and a wall of flame would deter them. No, he was not a man of violence. He had not left the Bradford AYM because he wished to pursue violent methods. He left because the organisation had degenerated into living off state funding. Coolly and calmly, he informed the court of the different campaigns in which he had been involved. At the end of his three-day ordeal, he impressed the jury and the public as a young man of moderation and sensitivity, searching for ways and means of alleviating the Asian condition. It was a splendid performance and the high point of the trial.

Evidence was called to show that the Asian community throughout Britain had been living under a reign of racist terror, and that on 11 July 1981, the whole community was under virtual siege once news of an impending racist onslaught spread like wildfire. Evidence was also put forward, and not questioned by the prosecution, that a Chief Inspector was actually informed of the impending attack and the police did nothing to protect the community.

Then came the dramatic moment. Not a single defendant, apart from Tarlochan, would go into the witness box. They would make statements from the dock on which they could not be cross-examined. This included Tariq Ali, a formidable political activist. It was a curious decision. Thousands throughout Britain would have been moved by their responses to the prosecutor's questions.

The lawyers advised on this course because they speculated that the defendants were too naive to withstand lengthy and hostile cross-examination. We beg to differ. Five years of mass revolt do not docile Asians make. All of these young men had experience in organising demonstrations, campaigns and other militant activities. They had lived through the jungle of the school playground, the cut and thrust of working-class life, three to four months in prison and the rigorous discipline of the bail conditions for close to a year. The mass of Asian youth would have warmed to the spirited defence which they surely could have mounted.

In the summing-up, the five black and seven white jurors were asked by the defence to scale two formidable hurdles.

First, they were asked to say that the manufacture of petrol bombs was a legal act required to meet the threat that racialists posed against the Asian community. And, further, that the petrol bombs were necessary because the police failed to protect Asians from racial attacks.

Second, they were required to accept that the 'best police force in the world' contained men and women who would fabricate evidence against defendants.

The jurors deliberated for a day-and-a-half before returning verdicts of not guilty. They accepted the defence's version of events, and defied the propositions placed before them by the police.

In this, the mass movement of recent years was expressing itself.

'THE MOSS SIDE POLICE FORCE: A LAW UNTO ITSELF'
Race Today, May 1985

Police officers in Manchester, the Moss Side police in particular, are back on the agenda of black political struggle. Only this time the barbarism for which they are known, and about which countless allegations have been made, has reached unparalleled depths. Jackie Berkeley, a 20-year-old West Indian woman, accused two policemen and two policewomen from the Moss Side police station of organising and participating in the sexual rape of her body. After investigation, she was arraigned by the Director of Public Prosecutions on charges of wasting police time, obstruction and assault on police officers.

She defended the case at the local Magistrates' Court, was found guilty and given several suspended sentences.

As we write, Jackie lies in a hospital bed in Manchester after she attempted to take her own life.

Jackie's allegations, and the support for the police extended by the Director of Public Prosecutions and local magistrate, are part of a consistent pattern to emerge in Manchester over the last decade.

We need only to look at a few cases over the past three years to prove this.

In 1982, coshes, chains and clubs, weapons more appropriate to thuggery and sadism, were found in the lockers of police officers at the Moss Side police station. When asked to explain officers said that these were seized from football hooligans and were stored in lockers for convenience or were in use as paperweights. To date, all the officers involved continue to work in the Manchester police force.

The second incident concerns a black youth worker who witnessed a fracas involving police and youths in Moss Side in 1983. He went over to assist in calming the situation and there witnessed police attempting to slam a car door shut on a prisoner's head. The youth worker, Harley Hanley, protested. As a consequence, Hanley was so badly beaten that doctors fought to save his eye. He was charged with obstruction and assault against police officers, and, like Jackie Berkeley, he was found guilty by the local magistrate. He persisted and won his case on appeal. Such was the uproar that the Director of Public Prosecutions brought a charge of assault with intent to commit grievous bodily harm against PC Marshall of the Moss Side police station. When that charge was defended at the Crown Court, the only witness called by the prosecution was Hanley himself, in spite of the availability of witnesses who would corroborate his story. Marshall walked from court a free man, confirmed in the fact that he had the support of the DPP.

And it does not end there. The prisoner on whose behalf Hanley had protested, a Mr Sam White, found himself under arrest a few months later, again at Moss Side police station. In defending charges of assault and obstruction, he told a jury that he was handcuffed at the station and badly beaten. The jurors believed him and set him free. He is now in the process of instituting civil proceedings against the officers involved.

These incidents constitute a mere handful of what has been alleged against the Manchester police. Elected representatives on the Manchester Police Authority sought to rein in and keep on a short leash the Chief Constable of Manchester, James Anderton, and his police officers. The issues were fought out in public and in the course of this struggle, Anderton uttered the now famous statement: 'It is the duty of the state to protect the police.' It becomes clearer by the day that the British state is extending this protection through magistrates, judges, the Director of Public Prosecutions, the Executive and Parliament.

Ranged against this formidable array of power are the black and white working-class communities of Manchester with the residents of Moss Side in the vanguard.

All exploded in the insurrection of 1981 and the fiercest battles, between black and white youths on the one hand and the police on the other, were fought in Moss Side. We need only to extract from the Hytner Enquiry which followed the Moss Side disturbance for proof:

> at about 10.20 p.m. a responsible and in our view reliable mature black citizen was in Moss Lane East, and observed a large number of black youths whom he recognised as having come from a club a mile away. At the same time a horde of white youths came up the road from the direction of Moss Side Police Station ...

The youths attacked the station with such ferocity that police officers abandoned ship. Revolts of this kind always contain within them violence of equal intensity to that experienced by those who are revolting – in this case, the intolerable violence that had been heaped upon generations of Irish and black immigrants by officers who manned that station.

The rape of Jackie Berkeley is a continuation of that experience and the campaign to free her and to bring the rapists to justice is a continuation of those traditions of revolt.

We welcome support from the hundreds of women who are taking the fight to the authorities on the issue of rape, but the Jackie Berkeley campaign, if it must remain faithful to history, needs to incorporate in its thrust the Harley Hanleys and the Sam Whites on the one hand, and the bold and uncompromising actions of those who stormed the Moss Side police station on the other. The struggle against the Moss Side police did not begin when those women who campaign on the issue of rape discovered it. All must meet at the confluence of history.

'THE TRIALS OF JACKIE BERKELEY'
Gus John, May 1985

An historic 14-day trial came to an end at Manchester Magistrates' Court on Thursday, 14 March 1985. Jackie Berkeley was answering charges of breach of the peace, criminal damage to a police van, obstruction and assault on three police officers, and wasting police time by making a false complaint of rape.

She was found guilty of all charges except criminal damage to a police van and given suspended prison sentences of varying lengths.

Before the case came to court, however, it was apparent that even though Jackie was the accused, the central issue of the trial would be her allegation that she had been raped by police officers whilst in custody at Moss Side police station.

Gus John describes the events leading up to her conviction and examines the issues raised by the affair.

Jackie was a mere 20-year-old, five feet three inches in height and weighed about nine stone. On 19 April 1984, she was walking down the street with two young women friends when another group of women, who had a score to settle with Jackie's friends, started to attack them. Jackie intervened to stop them fighting. Police officers arrived on the scene and indiscriminately grabbed those nearest to them. Jackie protested that the police were arresting the wrong people but was ignored. She was lifted off her feet by four police officers, and thrown into a police van.

Jackie was taken to Moss Side police station where, on arrival, she alleges she was put alone in a single cell, stripped, racially abused and raped by two policemen whilst two policewomen held her down. Jackie further alleges that she came round in a corridor where she was further abused and assaulted.

She was detained in custody until she appeared in court on Saturday, 21 April, charged with assaulting police and criminal damage – i.e., tearing police clothing. She was granted unconditional bail, which means in effect that she could have been released any time between her arrest on the Thursday night and her appearance in court the following Saturday; the delay meant that any evidence of her rape would be absent.

Three days after her release, she complained to a youth worker that she had been beaten up and raped while detained in Moss Side police station. The following day, an official complaint was made on her behalf by her solicitor. The police launched an investigation led by Chief Superintendent Glover, Chief Inspector Birkenshaw and Detective Sergeant Christine Knott.

The Police Offensive Begins

From the outset, the police went on the offensive, casting doubts on Jackie's allegation and projecting her in the eyes of the public as a malicious and wicked woman who had made an unthinkable allegation against policemen and women whose honour and word were beyond doubt.

Jackie was subjected to a series of identity parades lasting six hours and involving hundreds of police officers in one afternoon. She was able to identify three of those who she claimed had been active in the rape – two policewomen, Dyson and Askew, and Police Constable Reubens. The fourth accused, PC Fellowes, who had been in plainclothes on the evening in question, was identified by a description of his clothing. All had been at Moss Side police station that night. The investigation was forced to continue, but none of the officers were suspended, pending the result of the investigation.

The police interviewed Jackie repeatedly; endless statements were taken from her. The four police suspects, on the other hand, were allowed to make self-recorded statements, in December 1984, two months after Jackie had been charged with making a false complaint and wasting police time.

Jackie and her family had to face the fact that what should have been a rape trial, with Jackie as accuser, became, at the instigation of the police and the DPP's office, a Magistrates' Court trial with her as defendant. She was given charges for which she could not elect to be tried by jury and the police case was further strengthened by prejudicial media reporting.

Jackie and her family went on the offensive and with friends and supporters, organised a defence committee. The Committee publicised the case and the manner in which the police, court and media were hell bent on crushing Jackie. Ian Macdonald, steeled in black and working-class court struggles was appointed barrister. When the trial started, on 25 February, people queued to get into the public gallery and a large picket was held outside the court.

The Prosecution's Cover-up

During the trial, all four police officers contradicted fundamentally their own self-recorded statements and those of their colleagues. They chose instead to weave a tissue of lies in the witness stand, as the defence unmasked their squalid cover-up. For example, PC Fellowes, in his evidence in chief, gave a graphic description of how he went into the cell corridor to tick off Policewoman Askew for wrongly assigning a job to him. In the corridor, he came upon PW Dyson, PW Donald and PW Askew in some difficulty with one of the two women prisoners. Fellowes described how he 'stopped that woman running forward' and how Jackie Berkeley started swinging at PW Askew and screaming and shouting 'fat cow, lesbian ... fucking and blinding'.

Fellowes said he detailed two other policewomen to go from the charge office to assist the others in sorting out the matter. Later on, he left the office because as far as he could remember, he had split his trousers, but he couldn't be sure whether they were split or not. In any case, on entering the cell corridor again he saw PW Dyson with 'the whole front of her shirt ripped open, and she was trying to cover herself with her hands.' So he removed his jacket and gave it to her to cover herself. However, when it came to the policewomen to give their evidence none of them remembered seeing Fellowes, except for the one time that he performed the gallant act of giving Dyson his jacket.

Since this experience at Moss Side police station, Jackie, previously an extroverted, happy young woman, had become a depressive, refusing to communicate with anyone. She took the witness stand looking worn, her face empty of any expression and manifesting all the signs of someone feeling that what was going on around them was unreal. Ian Macdonald led her evidence in chief. The street incident she dealt with easily, but as he took her through what occurred in the police station she became more and more distant, hardly audible and switched off from the court entirely.

The magistrate expressed stony-faced indignation by commanding her to speak up and observed: 'I'm quite sure you speak much more loudly than that at home.'

The emotion in the courtroom was such that most of the public gallery were in tears, and Jackie's barrister had to steel himself and try and get her through her evidence as succinctly as possible. The magistrate's remark therefore was like salt on an open wound. The magistrate, in order to facilitate a 'fair trial', ordered that a public address system be installed inside the court; that she be given doctor's attention and psychiatric reports be provided. All to no avail. Her barrister was only able to get 'yes' or 'no' answers from Jackie; the prosecutor got even less. The prosecution case relied upon a police cover-up and the discrediting and destruction of Jackie.

The Case for the Defence

The defence case brought forward expert, circumstantial and forensic evidence. Those involved in the fight testified that Jackie had acted as a peacemaker. The girl who started the fight told the court that she had asked the police why they were not arresting her since she had started the fight but was simply ignored. Defence forensic evidence showed that the condition of Jackie's knickers was consistent with them having been removed with force.

Psychologists, rape counsellors and academics testified on the high incidence of rape and the effect it has on its victims; in particular that those who have been raped find it difficult to reveal their ordeal to anyone, particularly those nearest and dearest to them. The time span varied from days to years, or in some cases never. The fact that Jackie had told a youth worker five days after her rape was consistent with their findings. That she was unable to relate the experience to the court, was withdrawn and depressed, was also a common symptom.

By the time it came to the summing-up speeches, there was still no agreement on a single detail that led up to Jackie's detention and subsequent rape. Ian Macdonald was faced with the hurdle of penetrating the world of Stipendiary Magistrate Glynmoor Jones. He had to convince him that Jackie Berkeley was telling the truth and make him accept that British policemen and women could act in the way she had described.

Macdonald addressed the bench for three hours. Dealing with the evidence of the police witnesses, he demonstrated how totally unreliable it was. He singled out for detailed consideration the evidence of Reubens, Fellowes, Dyson, Askew, Eccles and Donald. He dwelt at length on the fact that Jackie had no motive for falsely accusing the police of rape and had been warned repeatedly about the consequences.

Much of his speech was devoted to how society deals with rape and the social, political, racial, emotional and physical reactions to rape, particularly of a black woman. He dealt with the attitudes of the policemen and women to Jackie and the other black women prisoners and further that Moss Side police station was an outpost of barbarity. Macdonald's speech, like the trial itself, confronted the political, social and racial attitudes that dominate Britain.

The Verdict

Glynmoor Jones' verdict was not based on what he had heard in court for the 14 days of the trial. He refused to acknowledge even the slightest possibility that Jackie Berkeley had been raped. His major plank, like that of the prosecution, was that Jackie did not complain about her rape until five days later. He used the fact that Jackie's mother had visited her in the central detention centre the day after her arrest to support the case against her, saying: if indeed she had been raped, 'one would have expected her to have blurted it out to her mother.'

He found her guilty of all charges except criminal damage to the police van.

Ian Macdonald told him that he wished to make it clear that the verdict was unacceptable. The courtroom erupted to deafening applause and shouts of protest. The courtroom of the Stipendiary Magistrate had rubber-stamped the prosecution case; the people's court had found her innocent.

The *Manchester Evening News*, reporting on the trial every day, lent their weight to the prosecution's case. It gave space and headlines to their presentation and curtailed or omitted the defence's case. To give but one example: '... the strip search that did not happen', as evidenced by one police officer, was highlighted in the press but the testimony of a police-woman given the following day who herself 'strip searched Jackie Berkeley' was ignored. Moreover, the very serious issues raised by Ian Macdonald's closing address, were never aired in the press.

In sentencing her, Glynmoor Jones chose to ignore the social enquiry report he had ordered, which recommended that Jackie was a woman at the end of her tether, required care and assistance, and should not be given a custodial sentence.

Instead, he proceeded to sentence her to 14 days' imprisonment on the charge of breach of the peace; one month's imprisonment on each of three counts of assaulting a police officer; one day's imprisonment for criminal damage to police uniforms, and three months' imprisonment for wasting police time. All six sentences were suspended for twelve months.

The verdict and sentence demonstrate two things. The magistrate had fulfilled his obligations to Moss Side police, the DPP and the Police Federation. At the same time, the power of the campaign ensured that he found it impossible to send Jackie Berkeley to prison.

6

'Creation for Liberation':
Race Today and Culture

INTRODUCTION
Farrukh Dhondy

In my childhood I was taught that a noun was 'the name of a person, place, or thing'. That seemed to cover almost anything I could think of as I was told even abstractions such as anger or love were nouns.

So also 'Culture' being all-encompassing, is difficult to pin down. Without the help of a dictionary or the Internet I would say it's the sum of how we, as a nation, society, class, group, race, tribe, or religion, do what we do. The culture of all societies evolves. We don't wear the same clothes, indulge the same entertainments, adhere to the same morals as the generations of our tribes and nations that went before. The culture of religious ritual, supposedly dictated by supra-human necessities, is slower to change and when it does, orthodoxy struggles to pull it back.

In a time of international movement, of settlement in new lands, of immigration in the twentieth and twenty-first centuries, there arises the necessity to define the culture of the groups of people who move. Immigrants from one culture to another carry with them the cultural habits and memories of the places they left behind. Material necessity and social pressure in and from the places to which they come compel them to acquire new ways and norms and modify the ones they inherited. The Pilgrim Fathers, battling against the landscapes and sometimes the natives of the New World didn't remain English or Scottish for long. They evolved a distinct American culture with its own version of English and later an American literature. The racial mix of European immigrants with the slaves they brought from Africa gave birth to what can be described as America's own classical music: Jazz.

The essays in the selection below trace, embody, review and tell the story of the evolution of Black and Asian British culture in the historically short period from the beginning of immigration in the decades after the Second

World War to the last decades of the twentieth century when *Race Today* stopped publishing.

In a sense, this very demise was a symptom of the initiation, growth and success of spaces and forums, in theatre, in visual arts and principally in the broadcast media, which gave platforms to these 'cultures' to be featured and celebrated.

Through the period of writing of these articles, which deal principally with the gestation and emergence of the artistic voices and careers of actors, writers, visual artists, and the dynamic musical forms from ska to reggae to dub poetry, Britain acquired the concept of 'multiculturalism'.

Race Today, not being in any sense a religious, psychological, or sociological platform, restricted itself as is evident from the selection, to the arts and to the political thrust and conscious or subconscious drives and determinations that infused them.

C.L.R. James, in very many ways an ideological guide to the *Race Today* Collective and its writers, insisted that after centuries of the brutal erosion of slavery, the culture of West Indians and African Americans was part of the 'Western Intellectual Tradition'. Of course he acknowledged the influence of African memory on jazz, calypso, reggae and choreography, but saw these as art forms influenced by Africa but nurtured as presences in the West.

Several of the essays, one by Roy Caboo on his evolution as a painter, and one in which Gerry Adams charts the growth of his political consciousness, for instance, are unique insights into the circumstances of life in a minority community which give rise to artistic, literary, or political determinations.

Some of the essays are catalogues of the artistic products of those years and even assessments of the rapidity, from a negligible and neglected presence, through which the new communities of Britain emerged from the shadows or wings, onto the page, the stage, the canvas and screen.

Race Today was never a publication with an aesthetic focus. The cultural articles represented here demonstrate the conscious interplay of political and material reality with the act of creation and the lives of the creators. Two of the contributions tell of the tragic stoning to death – Yes! Stoning to death – of the Jamaican poet Michael Smith on the streets of St. Andrews, Jamaica.

The editorial by Darcus Howe in a round-up of the flowering of the particular (rather than the 'multi') culture whose growth is traced in these essays, points to the institutions, such as the Black Book Fair and the Keskidee Centre for Black arts which activist insistence and struggle created as platforms for the propagation of various traditional and innovative forms.

Compiling this selection decades after *Race Today* ceased publication, one can look around in qualified amazement at the progress that has been made. One goes to the National Theatre and sees a Black actor playing Cleopatra, as Shakespeare should have imagined her; but you also see a Black actor playing Julius Caesar as he certainly didn't. There are theatres almost entirely given over to the work of ethnic minority playwrights, and directors and galleries which display the work of Black artists.

Television contents itself with the inclusion of Black faces on screen in 'positive' roles and with hiring Black talent off screen. Its commissioners seem impelled to contribute in this welcome way to social equality and anti-racism. What the positive policy of 'diversity', as it has been called since the era of the writings here, is not mindful of is that the impulse of the early arts and even the first years of a television channel such as Channel 4 were given to a no-holds-barred exploration of the lives of the new communities.

Arts for equality is good. Arts for the merciless exploration of truth is necessary.

'CABOO: THE MAKING OF A CARIBBEAN ARTIST'
Race Today, February 1975

The permanent army of unemployed located in every urban area in the Caribbean has been and still is the focal point of Caribbean artistic expression. Reggae, calypso and steelband are their creations and they have imprinted this on Caribbean social life. Their counterparts who inhabit the urban centres of Britain are no less talented, but it is only after 25 years of existence in Britain as a distinct social grouping that the black unemployed have thrown up their first major artist. Roy Caboo is an artist who has chosen the medium of painting, in which there is no Caribbean tradition to speak about. Below he talks to Race Today *about his work and the forces that have shaped his life.*

I left Trinidad at the age of 15. I was brought up in the Shango cult – a form of worship that survived slavery and persists right up to today. Shango is the god of lightning and it is Yoruba in tradition. It is a way of life really and an overwhelming influence on what I think and do. I lived with my parents in the small market town of San Juan, five miles outside Port-of-Spain. I left school when I was 13 and I worked as an office boy at a wage of 6.50

(£1.25) per week. By then, all over urban Trinidad, youth gangs were in existence and I was part of that cult. So Shango, the urban gang life and this job were the major influences that shaped me then. There was no tradition of painting in Trinidad that I knew of. Nothing that I could learn from, accept, or reject. If you had a leaning to painting, you became a sign painter or a commercial artist.

On arrival in Britain, I went to grammar school in Surrey for about nine months and got my sole qualifications – three O-level passes. Then I came down to London and my uncle found me a job as apprentice to a chandelier maker. I stuck that out for a year, but I knew that at that time, spars of mine were earning a lot more bread than me. I was getting £7 per week and they were coming home with £30–33. And also, when you are making chandeliers worth thousands of pounds and getting £6 and £7 a week, you know you're being exploited. So I decided to go and make some money – buy some clothes, the whole trip. I went to work in the meat cold-storage department of Lyons, handling cold dead meat for about eight or twelve hours every day. Well, that was jumping from the frying pan into the fire. After eleven months, I started freezing up. It was like winter inside and outside. So I decided, I can't make it. I can't get up at 8 o'clock in the mornings in winter and go to Lyons in the cold. So I left. After that, I stopped working altogether, in rebellion against the whole kind of enslavement of jobs. It didn't make much sense to me and a lot of guys were saying the same. In the communities of Ladbroke Grove and Brixton and Shepherd's Bush and all them places brothers and sisters were getting into that way of life – having nothing to do 24 hours a day except survive. Some of them wanted work and couldn't get it and some could get work but wouldn't for that money because they figured they deserved more than that, or they just didn't want to be a tea boy or sweep the floor. So most of them preferred to be 'nothing' rather than to be what 'The Man' want them to be.

I was always able to maintain myself outside of the factory. I realised that this was different from most of the brothers and sisters around me. I had chosen to refuse to work and I understood the consequences. I had the choice because I was an artist. Whatever happened I had that. In Ladbroke Grove, I could always do a painting and sell it for £2 and go down the Mangrove and hold a plate of food. Even though I knew it might be worth £50 or £30, that wasn't important then.

That experience of survival destroyed some of us completely. But with others it doubled our power – the power of intelligence, the power of reasoning – whatever qualities we had to start off with. Some found the best thing for them was to separate themselves from it as far away as possible, going completely into themselves, not talking to anybody. The police situation has a lot to do with it, the police being the guard dog to the whole set-up. The minute you're a wanderer, you are in a jungle. You then realise you have to survive, so you join some tribe, some clan, some gang, some form of protection, some centre, some organisation. That is why Black Power rung the bell to all them youths who were vibrating with this particular kind of consciousness. And the idea of violence as a solution seemed a possible way out. Total rebellion was my motto, giving me energy and inspiration all the time.

These experiences have a great deal to do with where I have arrived in my work. The whole political trip was the walking-stick I had propping me all the time. Every time I put myself in a group situation I start recording the thing, so it's a channel for my ideas. This is how a painting like *Man Versus Man* came into being, where you see a man with a sword digging out his brother's eye. Because I stand up round the gambling table and see it or stand up in a blues dance and see it. I stand up in the street and see two brothers stabbing each other. I see the sisters taking the brothers to the police and the police digging out the brother's eye.

For the period of seven years, it was a problem finding materials and living at the same time so I spent about six or seven years just doing quick, quick paintings just to be painting but the last nine months, coming to work here at Keskidee has given me the opportunity to hold a studio, hold some material and start working seriously. So what you see at the recent exhibition is the beginning of my painting career as such.

The exhibition took place at the Keskidee Centre, which is the black community centre in North London. A lot of young people attended. I paint with them specifically in mind and I am concerned when a little guy goes and looks at a painting and he don't quite understand because he is not taught that at school. But I have found that even though he does not understand the meaning, he knows it relates to him; he can feel it or parts of it and maybe he would learn something. One of the main things that I try to do is to inspire people who feel that they can't do this and they can't do that, which lots of the younger brothers and sisters out there feel. That is why at times I will paint something that will seem totally ridiculous in terms of traditional art – the way I put my colours together or the structure or whatever. But I would do it like that deliberately, to give him a different concept of art so that he could say, 'Well, I've being doing that for a long time and I have been thinking that I can't do nothing.' He is usually afraid to show his sketches to people because it is not up to the standards they teach you in school; you carry it to the teacher and he tells you that it's nonsense. But now he sees somebody doing it for real. Even though he doesn't understand exactly what you are saying, he understands the attack upon the traditional structures. He feels rather than sees what it is saying, and then he goes back home and starts relating his own feeling into his work. But once that seed is in him – that seed to get up and do something – art or something quite different – it's a trigger to do something constructive and that would be bettering himself and the people around him. This is what is very important to me. I want to translate my work into postcards and calendars and so on, so that it can go further into the kind of people I am working for, into the communities, villages or whatever.

It is for me, or any artist who wants to open the eyes of people and expose the truth, to find the time to observe. And he has got to have the time to sit and analyse. That is why he is not in the factory. Take *Man Versus Man*. Most people wouldn't buy that picture because it hits them hard and they say they couldn't live with it because the violence in it is so startling. Two guys holding a sword digging out another guy's eyes. When you paint something like this, people say, 'Well, he is full of hatred', and they can't see that you are putting down what you see, what you see going on around you. You are being very unemotional about it, but that is the reality. That is the modern world as it is. Raw. Man at the moment is in the process of massacring thousands of people. The hate and the lust and the greed and the scorn and everything else, all that nastiness constitutes the world today. 'I have more power than you and I will drop a whole lot of bombs on Vietnam', and as far as he is concerned he has sufficient reason to do that, never mind all the children, all the people who are destroyed. So man is in this tangle of aggression and then on top of that he turns to nature itself and rapes it. Man is dropping these heavy iron drills into the earth because he wants oil. He wants everything from the earth; he wants food and then more food; he wants water; the earth gives him water in abundance but he wants more; everything earth or life gives he wants more. If he could charge for the sunshine he would charge for it; if he could charge for fresh air he would charge for it; if he could charge for light he would charge for it. So in *Man Versus Man* all I did was put that situation in front of us, so that we could see that we are just digging out each other's eyes. I don't care how disturbing it is because to me it is the truth and if young blacks see the truth they might say, 'Shit I ain't getting involved in that, I am going to find something else, at least to try and keep me out of that.' Even if I say that to half a dozen of them I have done something. That is *Man Versus Man*. I don't make a distinction between white man, black man, different types of man. All that is part of the excuses, you are white, I am black, he is Chinese, he is Russian, he is Cuban, he is this, he is that, he is a shithouse, he is a thief; everybody just digs up all these labels and all they have to do is stick it upon you and shoot you – and then justify it. I wouldn't like to believe that black people are totally brainwashed by the white man, because that would mean that this white man can brainwash a whole nation of black people but hasn't been successful in brainwashing his own. So I'm saying that this guy hasn't got the power that we have given him. By giving him this power, we are blinding ourselves to the fact that we are intelligent beings and nothing is impossible. You have to be able to criticise yourself, see your weaknesses, see your advantages and learn to take full advantage of them. We have to grow, whether we use art or music or writing or rapping with brothers and sisters to develop ideas.

To go back to the pictures. *Towards Enlightenment* is a purely spiritual picture which reflects the level that I have reached at this moment in terms of my own spiritual development. Now I don't have to try to work out ideas. I just go into meditation and ideas come. What I needed was the ability to put ideas on to canvas which isn't as easy as copying something. I never paint or draw models. For me it takes away the seed of creative power, that element of creative force which comes only out of yourself. So I have very little respect for nude drawings. You draw them and people say fantastic, all the colours are brilliant. But to me, it ain't saying nothing at all; to me, the artist is trying to bring his picture to a state of reality when the reality already exists. If you really want to see art in its true form, then you just strip a chick naked, lay her down on the bed and you are cool. You look at her for as long as you want to look at the painting. But when you go into yourself and really see this woman, see her nature, see how that personality develops in your mind, and you observe her behaviour, her attitude to people and to things and to life, then you are painting the personality of the woman, the woman herself, not this piece of flesh that pretends to represent the woman. The splendour of the work is not simply in how well the form is painted; it rests on capturing the complete meaning.

I try to approach my work with the same discipline as a factory worker with the boss over you watching. I can't stop doing that picture until it is right – there is no halfway. When I've done a piece of work, it is as if I have never seen it before. This is when I really start looking at the work objectively. I have a picture that I personally like a lot called *First Creation* which is an extension of *Mothers of the Amazon*. Charcoal-black women, most of them pregnant, are sitting or standing in this yard where they are going through the ritual and I like that because it takes me far back into time. It must have been a heavy period to be living in and it gives me a lot of confidence that we have lived through that history, even slavery, and reached where we are today. The beauty radiates from these big shapeless black women because it's the beauty of naturalness. So I like that picture because of the history, as well as the message.

'BOB MARLEY AND THE REGGAE INTERNATIONAL'
Linton Kwesi Johnson, June 1977

It is now four years since Bob Marley – the only reggae artist with superstar status – entered the stage of international popular music along with the Wailers. *Catch a Fire*, the album with which they made their historic entry, with its far-reaching innovations at the levels of production, marketing and, most important of all, in the music itself, heralded nothing less than a revolution in Jamaican music. It is not at all surprising, therefore, that for the average non-West Indian listener, the word 'reggae' is synonymous with Bob Marley and the Wailers. With their obvious talent, ability, intelligence and natural creativity, the group has managed to create a sound that transcends the local, national limitation of popular Jamaican music, taking it into the mainstream of the popular music of Europe and North America. Given the particularity of reggae and its rootedness in Jamaican history, society and culture, this is a remarkable achievement.

Such a giant step has not been taken without concessions and compromises, contradictions and ambiguities but these do not detract from the importance of the enormous success of Bob Marley and the Wailers in breaking down the rock barrier and penetrating the international rock music market. This success has in fact generated a whole new style of reggae music which *Race Today* has dubbed 'international reggae'.

The recent European tour of the group which culminated at the Rainbow Theatre on Saturday, 4 June, where thousands of enthralled fans, black and white alike, were taken once again through the 'Trenchtown experience', and their new album, *Exodus*, shows quite powerfully that Bob Marley and the Wailers are still the leading exponents of international reggae. Marley himself has become the *ambassador of reggae*, a role which he has played with confidence and competence and, as his biography and career show clearly, a role for which he was well rehearsed. He has been exposed to and influenced by the diverse musical forms indigenous to his native Jamaica as well as other forms of internationally popular music, in particular black American (rhythm and blues, soul and funk). Moreover, his travels through Europe and the US have brought him into further contact with the metropolitan sounds of modern popular music culture.

Since the revolution of *Catch a Fire*, the next five successive albums, including *Exodus*, have been successful steps in consolidating the revolution. The music on *Exodus* is characteristic Wailers' music. It is a taut, terse sound wherein Jamaican roots are creatively combined with elements from the metropolitan sounds of Europe and North America. With the exception of the title track which is a fusion of rockers' beat and funky rhythms, there are no new innovations in the music but, as is the case with *Equal Rights*, another international reggae album by ex-Wailer, Peter Tosh, there are new combinations of old ones. And, as was the case with *Rastaman Vibrations*, Marley's last album, there is a strengthening, a solidification and accentuation of the input of Jamaican roots in the rhythm section, the nucleus of the music. Aston Barrett's bass is as bouncy as ever and a little more jazzy and accentuated. Carlton Barrett has developed and updated his highly individual style of drumming, incorporating elements from the military style into his rockers' repertoire. Tyrone Downie has, since joining the group, added gyrating, crooning, sweetening, soaring touches to the music. The new sensational lead guitarist, Julian Marvin, adds a new toughness to the hard-rock element as the song 'The Heathen' exemplifies. The use of brass which was first used on *Natty Dread*, the rock critics' favourite Wailers' album, is here continued on three songs. The backing vocals of the I-Threes, who have never been real substitutes for Peter Tosh and Bunny Wailer, are here effectively used. On the whole, the new combinations of beat, rhythm and melody on *Exodus* achieve a comfortable balance between roots, rock, soul and funk.

Thematically, *Exodus* was born out of the drama which preceded Bob Marley's 'Smile Jamaica' concert in support of Michael Manley's PNP during the last Jamaican general election. 'Smile Jamaica', Marley's current hit single at the time, was a call for national unity, imploring the gun-shocked Jamaican populace, referred to in the song as 'soulful people', to 'smile' as they are in Jamaica, a 'soulful town' with people having fun. This was, ironically, during the period of heavy manners in spite of which an assassination attempt, which he narrowly escaped, was made on Marley's life. Hence the first song, 'Natural Mystic', on the first side of the album. Marley here interprets his violent experience in terms of some preordained, natural mystical order of events. As a professed Rastafarian, he no doubt sees the 'miracle' of his escape from the jaws of death as the work of a divine mystical force. Furthermore, there was a quotation on the sleeve of the last album to Joseph, whom the 'archers have sorely grieved ... and shot at him and hated him'. Marley is Joseph, according to Twelve Tribe principles, and this, presumably, is prophecy.

There were a lot of conflicting rumours as to who was responsible for the assassination attempt and the reasons behind it. One rumour was that it was the work of the JLP opposition party, fearing the impact of the 'Smile Jamaica' concert on the outcome of the election. Another was that it was the work of the PNP trying to win support and sympathy by discrediting the opposition. A third was that it was linked to Marley's alleged involvement in the ganja trade. These were three of many rumours and hence the songs 'So Much Things to Say', 'Guiltiness' and 'The Heathen'. The first of these songs, 'So Much Things to Say', is a verbal castigation of those rumour-mongers who wrongly implicate him. Here he declares that Rasta does not come to fight flesh and blood, 'but spiritual wickedness in high and low places'. 'Guiltiness' is a similar reprimand of those responsible for the assassination attempt and Marley cries woe to them. 'The Heathen', with its awesome beat, soaring rock guitar, stabbing piano rhythms, and its prophetic and defiant stance, is as much an expression of retributive justice as it is an expression of sheer jubilation at his escape. Here Marley is Shadrack, Mescheck and Abednigo who were cast into the fiery furnace but did not get burnt. He is the unscathed Daniel who was 'cast into the lion's den'; he is the person who 'fights and runs away', living to 'fight another day'. Having drawn comparisons between his own fate and that of Marcus Garvey and Jesus Christ in 'So Much Things to Say', in the song 'Exodus' he describes himself as 'another brother Moses from across the sea'. So that it becomes apparent that whilst Exodus may be 'the movement of Jah people', it is more specifically the movement of Marley, the rasta rebel and fallen fighter who lives to fight another day.

The song 'Smile Jamaica', as I pointed out in a *Melody Maker* article of 5 February, contradicted the previous anti-establishment stance of songs like 'Small Axe', 'Them Belly Full', 'Revolution', 'Burning and Lootin' and many others, including 'Exodus'. For if Jamaica is such a 'soulful town' with such 'soulful people' having fun, why the 'Exodus'? It would seem that if Marley's perception of Jamaica as 'Babylon' had been blurred in 'Smile Jamaica', then the assassination attempt has shocked him back to his previous perception. 'Smile Jamaica' was clearly propagandist; now Marley is 'leaving Babylon' for his father's land.

The songs on Side Two of the album are somewhat different from the private/public themes which dominate Side One. Here the emphasis is more on the entertainment aspect of the music. 'Jamming', like 'Lively Up Yourself', 'Roots Rock Reggae', etc. is an open invitation to participate in the music of Bob Marley and the Wailers who are a 'living sacrifice' and who are 'jamming right straight from the yard'. It is a jazzy sing-along song with a hint of ragtime. This is followed by two very different love songs – 'Waiting in Vain' and 'Turn Your Lights Down Low'. The former is an invigorating rockers' hopper with a jazzy, bouncy bass line, a gyrating organ grind that pumps the rhythm along, and some very pretty guitar picking. The latter, 'Turn Your Lights Down Low', is pure soul; a ballad in the same vein as 'Johnny Was', though a different theme. 'Three Little Birds', with its rhythm-and-blues and ska resonances, is a song of reassurance. The message here is not to worry, 'cause everything is gonna be alright'. The bass line here echoes strongly the Skatalites' 'Beardman Ska' and, like 'Waiting in Vain', has a dated sound that is nonetheless refreshing to the ear. The final song on the album, 'One Love', is an updated version of an old Wailing Wailers' song from the ska era of the '60s which, as the title suggests, is a lyrical expression of the Rastafarian dictum calling for unity, love and oneness amongst the oppressed black Jamaicans. The new version is a little slower in tempo and less vibrant, thought equally entertaining.

Since his entry on the international stage, Bob Marley has made six highly individual albums whilst maintaining a certain degree of continuity in his art. Together with the Wailers, he has had a great impact and has also made an invaluable contribution to popular music, internationally and to the reggae international. What direction his music will take in the future remains to be seen. One thing is certain: that *Exodus* is a fine album, though not a great one. People all over the world are 'jamming' to the music of Bob Marley and the Wailers and, like them, we too 'hope the jamming last'.

'THE BLACK WRITER IN BRITAIN'
Farrukh Dhondy, May 1979

When I began to read English, I read what generations of British school-teachers, booksellers and makers of opinion had established as good reading for colonials. I read Enid Blyton and then Kipling and all the comics, mostly American, that I could lay my hands on.

When I was six, I lived in Madras and remember the bookshop called 'Higginbotham's'. It was the first place I knew that smelt of books, the first place to cast the enchantment of print and covers and browsing on me. Every time we were taken there, my sister and I pestered our parents to buy us a copy of *Classics Illustrated*, the classics in comic form. The adults probably thought that if we were going to read comics anyway, it might as well be the classics; they didn't approve of Gabby Hayes, Hopalong Cassidy,

Roy Rogers and Lash Larue with his black cocked hat, sadistic whip and gangster lips.

At that age, I couldn't read the comics but I culled the story from the pictures and by asking my sister. I knew the stories of *Wuthering Heights*, *Lorna Doone*, *Ivanhoe* and the rest before I was eleven, without ever knowing who wrote them, why or when. (As a schoolteacher in Britain, I've often looked for these comics for use as a teaching aid, but haven't found them.)

When we could, my sister and I read the American funnies. I couldn't stand or understand the English comics; they seemed to be full of healthy heroes and moral endings. Even British adventure books written for boys didn't get me where it counted. I remember winning a book called *Biggles Hits the Trail* for being good at maths or something. I liked the book because it had a certificate in the front, but of the story I could make neither head nor tail. I was puzzled by the plot and the way the characters talked was more bizarre to me than the dialogue of Mickey and Minnie Mouse.

Kipling enchanted me in my later adolescence because he wrote about India. One of the most powerful appeals of literature is that it makes you aware of what you already know. Recognition is all. That was the appeal of *Kim*, even though I lived a thousand or more miles from the North West Frontier or from the bazaars of Lucknow. It was the appeal of *A Passage to India*, even though Aziz and Godbole had passed away with my great-grandfather's generation. It was *The Plain Tales from the Hills* and *Passage* itself which first suggested to me that stories were most powerful and engaging when they tackled the insoluble encounter between races and classes, between white and brown, between rulers who weren't rulers in the end and ruled who weren't ruled.

That was the mood in which I discovered the writing of Lawrence Durrell and his purple encounters with Arabs and the Mediterraneans with whom I instantly identified. I read *The Alexandria Quartet* on the tram to college in Bombay. I got so involved with it that I missed my lectures for a few weeks, reading and re-reading the sacred texts from one tram terminus to the other, with a two-way ticket tucked between the pages of the dictionary on my lap. It made me want to write. Made me feel that if only I could learn all those hard words and look up a few more, I would be ideally placed to supply the waiting world with the next encounter between Englishness and an exotic setting, my own, which Mr Durrell could know nothing of. I even found myself hoping that Lawrence Durrell had found fame and fortune enough to prevent him from leaving Alexandria and buying a ticket to India, writing about it and so stealing my destiny. I knew it was a fanciful destiny, but I seriously thought of getting down to work. My only problem was that I didn't know any Englishmen.

By the time I ran away from engineering college, a year later, my taste in reading had changed and with it my impression of what writing was about. I realised that Durrell was a passion of the immature, and irrelevant to the people I met every day. Now I had started reading writers who seemed to force the reader to do most of the work: Albert Camus in translation, the poems of Yevtushenko, the muddle of Kafka. This seemed much easier than writing like Durrell; all the writer had to do was get hold of a pen and some paper and suffer. The pen and paper were there, and the bewildering millions of Bombay reminded one constantly that not passing exams and not getting a job would plunge one into an abyss in which suffering was inevitable.

It was impressed on me that the firmest step away from the abyss was a 'foreign qualification'. A certificate from a university abroad was a life-insurance policy second only to family money and for me the choice was easy: literature, or some books, I should say, made me choose Cambridge. The hard work was the question-spotting on the Physics paper which would get me the scholarship to go there.

It was at university in Britain, in the mid-1960s, that I discovered that there were theories about how we read books, orthodoxies which, at that time, stated that all writing, whatever its purpose, was innately political. You could win applause by saying 'all literature is class literature' and win all manner of abuse by professing to like a book because its story was unusual or that Shakespeare's understanding was valuable in itself. When this line of thinking progressed even further, it reached the idea that doing was good and writing was second-hand. It wasn't a climate that encouraged anyone to write.

I won't trace here the process by which I found myself, after two universities, in London and in the Black Panther Movement. I'd already been a member of the Indian Workers' Association in Leicester which, at the time was a demonstrative movement. It didn't envisage having writers or any form of cultural platform built out of the lives of Asians here. It didn't envisage even the sort of writing that makes James Baldwin and Richard Wright essential influences on black America. It certainly didn't encourage the emergence of voices like Le Roi Jones, Eldridge Cleaver, or George Jackson, though even in Asian organisations, as distinct from West Indian ones, the message of those writers had a vogue.

It was in the Black Panther Movement, in London, where writing again emerged as an idea to me. There were several young West Indians in the movement who wanted to write, and some actually did. Most of them kept it secret, however, because the leadership had never seen the political movement as the establishment of blacks culturally and politically in Britain. Although part of an important political explosion in Britain it had not clarified what its service to the masses ought to be, though occasionally it growled that writing could be a part of it. The poems and short stories, therefore, which were being written, were talked about sotto voce or kept in the drawer at home.

The Movement, therefore, didn't encourage me to write, though I did some of it on the sly, writing articles for Indian newspapers. In the ranks of the leadership, the intellectuals, with degrees and so on, were suspect. And rightly so, because the late 1960s and early '70s were producing, in Britain, a class of intellectuals who used their certificates to hustle jobs and positions in the Community Relations industry and in the echelons of the controlling institutions which channelled the energies of the black population. We were throwing up a bureaucratic middle class, and writing and its purpose came under careful surveillance.

Partly because of the attitude it took to black creativity, the Black Power era was a short episode in the history of blacks in this country. A community does not live by rhetoric alone. Because of this, some writers broke with the Movement, some later writing about black suffering or black nostalgia and one or two, such as Gus John, producing sociological works with vigour and guts. And there emerged at least one West Indian poet and one political writer who went on to make their mark and exercise to full measure talents which the early Black Power Movement suppressed.

The political writer was Darcus Howe, who had now seized the editorship of the *Race Today* magazine. He invited me to write about blacks and schools in the second issue he edited. I wrote that piece, and, for a couple of years after that, continued to contribute to the journal which was knitting itself into a collective. The journal addressed itself to the blacks in this country and to readers who would support independent thought and action. It sought to make its writers into activist journalists. Out of the journal came the organisation called the *Race Today* Collective, which said, to me at least: 'Write what you must, we'll judge you, assess you, but we won't stop you.' The organisation pushed me to write, forced me to find out and write about people and areas I wouldn't have discovered of my own sweet will. The magazine sent me, for instance, to the East End of London as a political activist. We were working around the housing question and it was there, in Spitalfields, that I met, for the first time, the Bangladeshi community.

What I haven't said yet is that at this time, I was teaching in London secondary schools. Teaching English taught me what 'English' children (black and white) read and avoid reading, which I'd never thought about. Teaching soon taught me why they couldn't and don't, because as an Asian 'supply teacher' in a South London comprehensive, I was lumbered with the classes that had displayed a heroic reluctance in the field.

In the stock cupboard, to which I was led after three days of hell with a stick of chalk and dwindling ingenuity, the projected reading of the future generations came into focus on the spines of paperbacks. I spent an hour in the arsenal that first time. There they all were, waiting for me to lob them into 3.10 or 2.8 (which is what the classes were called). I would devastate the unruly with *To Kill a Mockingbird*. I would toss Wilfred Owen in their entrenchments of indiscipline like a grenade. Then reality caught up. I thought of Delroy and David and literacy and leafed through the books to see how hard the language was. The shelves were weighed down with stuff. There was Gorky and his wretched, blessed childhood. There was 'The Loneliness of the Long Distant Runner'; there were texts with extracts from *Cider with Rosie*, James Thurber's fables, poems by Charles Causley, a balanced diet of irreverence for class values and a reverence for 'human' ones.

I learnt a lot about writing by teaching it. Criticism is good for writers and instant criticism may not be the best but it is very instructive, and I've tried to remember that when reading my own stories to pupils. I also learnt a lot about the use of literature in schools. There are, for instance, teachers who will champion Sillitoe and expect pupils to write essays on why Smith in 'The Loneliness of the Long Distance Runner' doesn't give a bugger about the race, exhort them to care about why he doesn't care. The irreverence of modern literature gets reduced by the schoolroom to a play thing. No! To a work thing.

It was while I was teaching in South London that Martin Pick, editor at McMillan Publishing, sought me out, having read my stories in the Black Panther publication, *Freedom News*, to ask if he could publish them, because there was very little being written about multicultural Britain. I said I would write new ones and from this came *East End at Your Feet*, which is not about Bangladeshis in Spitalfields, or about Punjabis in Leicester, or Parsees in Poona, but about my perceptions of what makes up 'Asianness' and what makes young ones different from old ones.

East End at Your Feet was widely read in classrooms, introduced by English teachers who wanted material which was relevant to their inner-city students, black, white and Asian. Once, when I had been invited into a school to talk to fourth-year students about the stories, and my novel, *Siege of Babylon*, I asked them, when I'd finished my talk, why they were interested. They said they were following an alternative syllabus to the normal CSE, and these were among those they had to read. They had been set exam questions on the books. I asked the teacher to show them to me. They were good questions, but I swear I'd have ended up with a Grade 2 if I'd tried to answer them in one and three-quarter hours.

I say they were good questions because they were about culture and the clash of cultures. If you're a black writer in Britain and write about what you know, it is inevitable that culture and its clash are your material. And if you're a black writer writing stories for young people, you can't escape being seen by teachers and examination syllabuses as someone who will explain blacks to whites. Isn't that the essence of multiculturalism?

There is a partial escape from such a fate, and that is to acquire an audience independent of the good intentions of multi-ethnicity. The poet I spoke of earlier has not gained his reputation through being recognised as a man who has the power of dispelling prejudice by selling sweetness or increasing familiarity. Linton Kwesi Johnson is a reggae poet, a political poet who has made his way in the world in which reggae matters and

Figure 6.1   Claudius Hillman, Michael Cadette, Stafford Howe, Darcus Howe and Leila Hassan at Radical, Black & Third World Books, Islington Town Hall, 1982.

poetry is not in a book. He has a primarily black audience. That's not to say that his work and records and published lyrics won't enter the classroom. They certainly entered mine. Already, I see his influence in the work of pupils who write poems. But his work can't be used to put across the idea that harmony is the theme and object of writing about and by blacks. The message and method of his poems are antithetical to such an idea. I wish the same for my work, my writing, because as a teacher I know that good lessons have their purpose, but writing, good or bad, should have its own.

"I'M A POET" C.L.R. JAMES DISCUSSES NTOZAKE SHANGE'
Lecture at the Riverside Theatre, Hammersmith
C.L.R. James, January 1982

First of all, a necessary word about myself. Some people think that they have read my books and they know something about me: they don't know the most important thing. In 1936–37, I was writing a book, *The Black Jacobins* and the first sentence of that book is 'Christopher Columbus landed first in the New World at the island of San Salvador, and after praising God enquired urgently for gold.' That's what I wrote in 1937, and that is what I still believe in 1981. I haven't changed. What I have done is to develop and move intricately into the general idea that is expressed there.

At the present time, I believe the society in which we live is destined to developments of the most drastic kind. I am not going to try to make any propaganda here, but I will tell you that I believe that we are moving towards two different types of society. One of them is what is taking place in Poland. The world is moving to becoming a society in which the majority of people will form solidarity parties, or if we are not doing that, we are going on the other hand, to regimes that are described by Solzhenitsyn in his book, *The Gulag Archipelago*.

I have suggested telling you about these books because these three black women, in the United States, are doing as much as anybody else, in the way of literature and general propaganda, towards advancing the world forward; in bringing to bear, as an actuality, many of the things that we are talking about. That is quite an achievement.

For hundreds of years, black women in America have scrubbed, have washed, have run errands, have done all the dirty work in that society. During the last ten years, they have been brought from the backyard, the dirty old kitchens, the broken-down houses, and placed in the very forefront of America literature. It is a tremendous move. And it is very hard for these writers to make their way, because what they are saying is dealing with realities in a way most of the socialists and communist propagandists, today, are not doing.

These are tremendous things to say, and I can only say them because I am going to prove them to you. I am going to give you the opportunity to prove them. I thought I would let you have that introduction, so you will understand, from some of the things that I say, that I'm not being extreme, that I really believe that we have, here, some of the most important pieces of writing that are taking place in the world today, about the world which is to come, and which contain the most drastic attacks upon present day society.

I am going to take two books tonight. I am going to take, first, the book called *Nappy Edges*, by Ntozake Shange. She is not an African woman; she is an American woman. She comes from the American middle class, is in contact with many intellectuals, blacks and whites, went to a good college and then started to write. And she is writing chiefly poetry. There is only one thing that I have to say in advance about *Nappy Edges*. Shange uses words which are not used by polite people in polite conversation. When she uses that word, I shall say 'they made love to each other.' It is a four-letter word. You will know it, but I am not going to be one to introduce it to the platform while hiding behind Ntozake Shange.

Now, Ntozake Shange is a poet and she states it:

People keep tellin me to put my feet on the ground
I get mad and scream/there is no ground
Only shit pieces from dogs horses and men who don't live
Anywhere/they tell me think straight and make myself
Something/I shout and sigh/I am a poet/I write poems/
I make words/cartwheels and somersault down pages
Outta my mouth come visions distilled like a bootleg
Whiskey/I am like a radio but I am a channel of my own
I keep saying I do this/& people keep askin what am I
Gonna do/
What in the hell is going on?
... people keep tellin me there are hard times/what are
you gonna be
doing ten years from /what in the hell do you/I
am gonna be writing poems/I will have poems/inchin
up the
walls of the lincoln tunnel/I am gonna feed my

children poems on
rye bread with horseradish/I am gonna send my
mailman off
with a poem for his wagon/give my doctor a poem
for his heart/
I am a poet/I am not a part-time poet/I am not
an amateur
poet/ ...

Now, that is her case for being a poet. Today, people don't write that way. That is the way Keats, Shelley, Browning and such people wrote about their own day, with the feeling that what they did mattered. Shelley had a fine phrase, 'poets are the unacknowledged legislators of the world', and Shange belies that about poetry. She isn't writing poetry as a literary avocation. She is writing poetry about her own world, about the United States today, and she takes part in the world around her. Try to get this:

Every 3 minutes a woman is beaten
Every five minutes a
Woman is raped/every ten minutes
A lill girl is molested
Yet I rode the subway today
I sat next to an old man who
May have beaten his old wife
3 minutes ago or 3 days/30 years ago
he might have sodomized his
daughter but I sat there
cuz the young men on the train
might beat some young woman
later in the day or tomorrow
I might not shut my door fast
Enuf/push hard enuf
Every 3 minutes it happens
Some woman's innocence
Rushes to her cheeks/pour from her mouth
Like the betsy wetsy dolls have been torn
Apart/their mouths
Mensis red and spit//every
Three minutes a shoulder
Is jammed through plaster & the oven door/

Chairs push thru the rib case/hot water or
Boiling sperm decorate her body
I rode the subway today
& bought a paper from a
man who might
have held his old lady onto
a hot pressing iron/I don't know
maybe he catches lill girls in the
part and tips open their behinds
with steel rods/I cdnt decide
what he might have done I only
know every 3 minutes
every 5 minutes every 10 minutes/so
I bought the paper
Looking for the announcement
There has to be an announcement
Of the women's bodies found
Yesterday/the missing little girl
I sat in a restaurant with my
Paper looking for the announcement
A young man served me coffee
I wondered did he pour the boiling
Coffee/on the woman cus she waz stupid/
Did he put the infant girl/in
The coffee pot/with the boiling coffee/cus she cried
Too much
What exactly did he do with hot coffee
I looked for the announcement
The discovery/of the dismembered
Woman's body/the victims have not all been
Identified/today there are
Naked & dead/refuse to
Testify/one girl out of 10's not
Coherent/I took the coffee
& spit it up/I found an
announcement/not the woman's
bloated body in the river//floating
not the child bleeding in the
59th street corridor/not the baby
broken on the floor/

'there is some concern
that alleged battered women
might start to murder their
husbands and lovers with no
immediate cause'
I spit up I vomit I am screaming
We all have immediate cause
Every 3 minutes
Every 5 minutes
Every 10 minutes
Every day
Women's bodies are found
In alleys and bedrooms/at the top of the stairs
Before I ride the subway/buy a paper/drink
Coffee/I must know/
Have you hurt a woman today
Did you beat a woman today
Throw a child cross a room
Are the lill girls' panties
In yr pocket
Did you hurt a woman today
I have to ask these obscene questions
The authorities require me to
Establish
Immediate cause
Every three minutes
Every five minutes
Every day

She says that is happening every five minutes, every ten minutes, every day,
and she is asked for immediate cause. You see, that is what is going on, that
is immediate cause. She is passionately angry about what is going on, and
she interferes in her own say. Then sometimes, she entangles herself with
modern political life:

Today the cosmos satellite fell down over uranium city
British Columbia, Canada, with 100 pounds of uranium
235 on board, there were international secret meetings
for months, no one told me.
Today it all cda been over.

I wdn't have had to listen to governor turner refuse to
Pardon the Wilmington 10 cuz he didn't believe the lies
The liars recanted/I wdnt have to know that 4 or 3
Million American women who take the pill & smoke are
10 times more likely to have heart attacks than women
who don't take the pill or don't smoke?
What in the hell am I sposed to di?
.... baron empain waz kidnapped in paris today/by god
only knows who, for 20 million francs, surely 20 million
francs cd fix the pill, the wilmington 10 defense
committee cd use 20 million francs/20 million francs
wd assuage my troubles with rapid transit. I need a
cigarette cuz this is just too much for me. Plus there
are women who actually find sex boring/me/I'm gonna
have a heart attack.

Sometimes she writes poetry in the old Tennysonian style, but using
modern language and modern things:

You fill me up so much
When you touch me
I cant stay here
I haveta go to my space
People talk to me
Try to sell me cocaine
Play me a tune
Somebody wanted to give me a message
But I wuz thinking abt you
So I waz in my space
I'm so into it
I cant even take you
Tho I ran there with you
Tho you appear to me by the riverbed
I can't take you
Its my space
A land lovin you gives me
Shall I tell you how my country looks
My soil 7 rains
There's a point where the amazon meets the mississippi
A bodega squats on the Eiffel tower

Toward mont saint Michel
I'm so into it
I cant even take you
It's my space
A land lovin you gives me

Now, those of you, who are aware of literature, know that Ben Jonson wrote about Shakespeare, and how they used to meet Elizabethan poets at the Mermaid Tavern, and drink and eat and make jokes with them. William Hazlitt writes about himself, Samuel Coleridge, Wordsworth and others. Dostoevsky, Tolstoy and Gorki, they write about themselves. Here is Ms Shange writing about poets:

We usedta call ourselves the COSMIC-DU-WOP
COMMUNE, poets mostly and some musicians, thulani,
Jessica hagedorn, mashirantosha & pepe priester, pedro
Pietri, papoleto Melendez, etnaira rivera, gyan kai & caole le sanchez
& paul vane, Roberto vargas, alejandro
murgula, victor hernandez=cruz & tom cusan.

Do you realise that she is referring to an international body of people; that she is strongly associated with Latin American people, and that there are an African or two, an East Indian there, a white American. And she writes those names so you should understand. She says:

We are
All so transient, nothing changes too much for any of
Us, we write poems, we read the poems, we find out who
Pays money to read the poems, we go there, we read to
Each other, drink wine walk the streets with each other
Making poems, we like to fall in love & be poets. I'm not
Sure anybody enjoys our stuff as much as we do, or even
If people realize how essential poems are to our
Existence.

She is one of them. When you are familiar with the literature that these great writers write about themselves, and the life that they lived, you realise that she is a poet writing about the present generation of poets who have an attitude to poetry. That's a genuine poem about the poetic life and the poetic temperament. I don't know anyone better.

And here is one of the most beautiful of her poems, about a girl she knows. And this girl is her friend, Jessica Hagedorn:

Sometimes you remind me of lady day

Do you know whom she means by Lady Day? Does anybody know? That's Billy Holliday. That's one of the most marvellous women America has ever had. She is a great singer and she went to jail for drugs. Billy Holliday used to perform in New York. I have seen many great performers, but I have never seen a woman who walked onto the stage, commanded it by her performance and walked off – the dignity, the grace, the conscious power and style; unbelievable. And Shange is looking at this friend of hers and says:

Sometimes you remind me of lady day
& I tell you sadness
the weariness in yr eyes/the walk you have
kinda brave when you swing yr hips
sometimes serenity in yr eyes
& the love always.

Her range is very wide.

I will read one last poem. You know the story of Patricia Hearst? The millionaire girl who was fighting with blacks. She went to jail and they let her out shortly after. Have you read Richard Wright's novel, *Native Son*? Where a young black boy gets mixed up with some white people who take an interest in communists? He gets into trouble with her accidentally; he then burns her in a furnace and runs away. His girlfriend may know what he has been doing so he kills her. His name is Bigger. In this poem, Ntozake Shange is writing about Patricia Hearst:

(in the bay area in the spring of 1974
the black community waz besieged by the
hysteria created by the coincidental
S.L.A. patrician hearst kidnapping & bank
Robbery & the alleged 'Zebra' killings.
Everyday for three months the media
Announced 'the suspect is black & in his
Early twenties.' Every day every one of us
(women included) under 6ft, brown black beige,
waz subject to suspicion on wanton murder.

Wanton oppression the likes of which
Suggest the grips to tule lake, pinochet's
Stadium, the days of blood in buenos aires.)
I always hated bigger
thomas he treated bessie
sooooo bad a brown girl
trying to sing thru bitter winter young
& accustomed to brutes Bessie
waz a secondary murder an effect
dying with her in the vacant bldg.
bigger Thomas was no longer a man to me
bigger Thomas a a thus with no love
til I remember who
mary dalton waz
a hingty smark alect rich white girl
troubled bout the colored problems and the jews
concerned bout bringin some excitement to her
life/mary dalton cost bessie a possible lover
a gig in a a segregated tavern maybe
a new dress her grandchildren
it waz mary dalton her drunken ashes
her wanton charrd ones sent thousands of
bullets looking for a blk boy
any one nigger wd do the suspect is black
& in his early 20s
the suspect is our sons
again prey to whims and caprices of
grande dame white ladies
with tears and curses for their fathers
white ladies whose conscience drive them to
come to us drive them to join us
patrician hearst alias mary Dalton
has joined us
has paraded her debutante
bred body in fronta the 7 headed serpent
machine gun in hand she want the people
to embrace her soft white fingers/to save us
from death/the compulsion of fascists to kill ...

I have read no finer modern poet, and it is most noticeable that when she makes references about something, everyone in the United States will understand. She has been to Paris, she has been everywhere and she is a great success in the United States, particularly her play *For Coloured Girls*. It was played here in London. Did any of you see it? It wasn't successful here, but it was a rave hit in the United States.

So that's what I recommend to you, Ntozake Shange's *Nappy Edges*.

'CULTURE AND *RACE TODAY*'
Darcus Howe, January 1983

In 1982, we extended the *Race Today Review* into the realm of concrete activity. Along with Bogle L'Ouverture and New Beacon Books, we organised the First International Book Fair of Radical Black and Third World Books. The Fair itself went on for three days, accompanied during that week by a festival of concerts, readings, exhibitions, cinema, forums and seminars. The event was an outstanding success. Over a hundred publishers participated. Artists, writers and political activists were drawn from Africa, the Caribbean, North America and Europe. We recorded more than six thousand people at our turnstiles, thereby establishing a sound basis for the development of an artistic and cultural movement.

In March 1983 (13–20), the Second Annual Book Fair takes place in Brixton, the centre of the mass black revolt in Britain. We bear in mind that mass revolt sharpens the sensibilities of existing artists, dumps the frauds and generates the presence of new personalities. From all accounts, 1982 was a good year. The dub poets have come into their own; the black theatre can no longer be dismissed as 'fringe'. Successful plays have been written by black playwrights and performed by casts of talented, young black actors. Fine Art is teasing its way, spearheaded by exhibitions rendered by Leslee Wills in textiles and the Pan African Connection, a group of young college students, in print, ceramics, painting, sculpture and drawing. A veritable deluge of books, pamphlets and leaflets have been published, ranging from the literary to the sociological to the sharply political. The music scene throbs with reggae vibrations, and we found our way to the top of the charts on two occasions during the year. Norman Cowans was picked for the England cricket team to tour Australia and six black footballers were invited to join the England team to play against West Germany.

A few words about sport. Are our sportsmen and women to be included into the community of artists? We take the lead from C.L.R. James, who stated the case in the acclaimed literary masterpiece *Beyond a Boundary*.

The aestheticians have scorned notice of popular sports and games to their own detriment ... Sir Donald Bradman's technical accomplishments are not on the same plane as those of Yehudi Menuhin. Sir John Gielgud in three hours can express adventures and shades in human personality which are not approached in three years of Denis Compton at the wicket. Yet cricket is an art, not a bastard or a poor relation, but a full member of the community.

We treat most if not all of these areas in the 1983 *Race Today Review*. More needs to be said about one particular inclusion in this year's *Review*. We have included an extract, 'Pawn Shops and Politics' from *Falls Memories*, an Irish publication written by Gerry Adams, who, at 34 years old, is the vice president of Sinn Féin, the political arm of the nationalist movement in the north of Ireland. Recently, he won a seat in the new Assembly organised by the Conservative government. *Falls Memories*, though no literary masterpiece, opens a window on the world of a section of the Irish working class in the Six Counties. It contains 17 stories and accounts of working-class life. Adams, in these stories and accounts, evokes the lore of a working-class community, vividly weaving portraits of personalities and historical events created by a vibrant, active and resolute population. Though the tracts are particular to the Falls Road area in Belfast, though the author's aim may be to strengthen the nationalist movement, he has, perhaps, unwittingly made a contribution to the international peoplehood of working folk. His 'Aunt Jane' describes a childhood which so many of us experienced in the far-flung colonies; his 'Pawn Shops and Politics' carries some elements of the Black Power Movement of the 1960s; 'The Union and the Unions' and 'Linen Slaves of Belfast' could be retold by millions of colonial workers in Africa, India and the Caribbean. Members of the *Race Today* Collective are moved by this publication. Like ourselves, Gerry Adams came to active politics in the late 1960s; like ourselves, he has abjured the bankrupt politics of established political institutions; like ourselves, he stands in marked contrast to those who content themselves with counting heads on the General Management Committees of local Labour parties with a view to manipulating a seat in Parliament. We could identify scores of activists who entered political activity at the same time and on the same issues as Adams who today busy themselves in Manpower Services Projects and Inner City Partnership hovels. The inclusion of the extract from *Falls Memories* is our way of extending solidarity to Adams and his comrades, to the working people of the Falls Road and the Six Counties. In embracing Adams, we embrace our own reflections.

'PAWN SHOPS AND POLITICS' BY GERRY ADAMS,
JANUARY 1983

Extract from *Falls Memories*, published by Brandon

*Time has triumphed, the wind has scattered all, Alexander, Caesar, empires,
cities are lost Tara and Troy flourished a while and fell. And even England
itself, maybe, will bite the dust.*

(Anon., translated from the Irish by Brendan Kennealey)

In 1960, I transferred from St Finian's School, via St Gabriel's to St Mary's
in Barrack Street. On our way home from school, we walked along Divis
Street and up the Falls, spending our bus fares in one of the many shops
which littered our route. On brisk autumn evenings, with leaves carpeting
the pavement and the road bustling with people, the great linen and flax
mills made a formidable backdrop while, facing them, cheek to cheek, the
rows of small shops served the miscellaneous needs of local customers.
There were a couple of stretches of the road which I particularly favoured:
from Northumberland Street up as far as the Baths, along the convent wall
by St Dominic's or alongside Riddell's field. Paddy Lavery's pawn shop at
Panton Street did a roaring trade in those days, its windows coming down
with family heirlooms, bric-a-brac, clocks; boots, even fishing rods and
inside, rows and rows of Sunday-morning-going-to-Mass suits, pledged
between Masses to feed the family or pay the rent. In Dunville Park, the
fountain occasionally worked, cascading water around those who defied the
wackey to paddle in the huge outer bowl. In Divis Street, a woman sold us
hot home-made soda farls and pancakes plastered with jam.

Brother Beausang packed us into the Ard Scol for oral exams to win
a place in the Donegal Gaeltacht; Ducky Mallon taught us our sevens;
and lunch breaks were spent playing football besides the glass factory and
afterwards seeing who could pee the highest in the school bog. We were
all part of a new generation of working-class Taigs, winning scholarships
to grammar schools and 'getting chances' which, as our parents and grand-
parents frequently reminded us, they never had. We wore school uniforms
– a fairly new and expensive luxury – and were slightly bemused to see
our mirror reflections in Austin's, the school outfitters. I always noticed
that the shop facing Austin's had its name sign painted in Irish. You could
buy hurling sticks in another shop just below that, while almost opposite
our school Wordle's kept their great shire horses in unique multi-storied
stables. Summer evenings were spent in the Falls Park playing hurling and

football and during the winter we cadged money for the Clonard, Broadway or Diamond picture-houses or for the baths. Exams to one side, life was pleasant and uneventful.

We learned little of local or national history at school and had no sense of it as we passed through streets as historic as any in Ireland. From the school at Barrack Street we passed by the Farset and we regularly dandered up Pound Street, knowing nothing of its history or even the old barracks which gives Barrack Street its name. There were three R.U.C. barracks in our day: one at Hastings Street, one at Springfield Road and another at Roden Street. A fourth, at Cullintree Road, had only recently been replaced. Not that we were worried or even interested in such places. Nowadays, of course, with heavily fortified British Army and R.U.C. barracks and forts dotted strategically throughout West Belfast it is difficult to remain disinterested or neutral about their existence. It is especially so, in wet wintry times, when the Falls Road, washed grey by drizzling rain and suffering from the ravages of war and redevelopment, appears bleak and shabby, with the omnipresent foot patrols of British soldiers treading carefully through back streets, a threatening intrusion into an area hostile to their presence. Not that British soldiers are a new feature of the scenery in West Belfast. Since its days as a country lane raids and harassment have been occupational hazards suffered by residents of the Falls Road. The *Belfast Newsletter* of 23 May 1797 records for example:

At four o'clock in the evening Lieutenant General Lake directed Colonel Barber and Mr Fox [town mayor] to proceed with as much expedition as possible to the cotton manufactory of Robert Armstrong on the Falls Road. Arriving there before two persons, who were on the watch, could give an alarm, they caught a smith and his assistant forging pikes and, on threatening them with immediate death, they produced sixteen they had secreted in an adjacent house, newly forged. A detachment from the Monaghan militia, and some yeomanry who followed, were so incensed at seeing those implements of destruction that they smashed the forge and levelled it to the ground. The pikes were then hung around the villains who were marched prisoners to the town.

A better known testimony of such raids is an expression which is often used even today by older Belfast people when unexpected visitors arrive: 'They're in on us and not a stone gathered.' It harks back to the days when cobblestones, locally known as kidney pavers or pickers, were used against British Army and R.U.C. raiding parties. My first personal recollection of such raids was in 1964 when carefree and sleepy-headed I noticed on the way to school a tricolour displayed in a shop in Divis Street. That evening a character, better known now than then, by name of Paisley, threatened to march on Divis Street and remove the offending flag. Our curiosity, further aroused by a warning from our Christian Brother teachers to go straight home and not dilly-dally in Divis Street, led dozens of us to gather and peer into the window of what we were to discover was a Sinn Féin election office. Further encouragement was supplied by the R.U.C. who sledge-hammered their way into the premises and seized the flag. It was with some satisfaction, therefore, the following day that we witnessed a large crowd replacing it, an occasion for a most defiant rendering of 'Amhran na bhFian' and the subject of some schoolboy speculation upon what would happen next. What happened next, of course was the Divis Street riots, an exercise which we found most educational, though in truth it wasn't much of a spectator sport, with the R.U.C. being unable or unwilling to distinguish between curious scholars and full-blooded rioters. Some of us learned quickly that it was as well to be hanged for a stone as a stare and thus I found myself after homework had been cogged, folding election manifestos in the Felons Club, above Hector's shop in Linden Street. The republican candidate, Liam McMillan, lost his deposit as did all the Sinn Féin candidates – but I suspect with hindsight that the electioneering was geared more to canvassing recruits than votes and in that it undoubtedly succeeded. In the months afterwards children playing in the streets parodied the then current Perry Como song, 'Catch a Falling Star', to rhyme during hopscotch and skipping games:

Catch a falling bomb and put in your pocket, Never let it fade away.
Catch a falling bomb and put it in your pocket, Keep it for the I.R.A.
For a peeler may come and tap you on the shoulder some starry night,
And just in case he's getting any bolder, you'll have a pocket full of
   gelignite.

Of course, youngsters are still parodying popular songs and turning them into their own little songs of resistance. In back streets and school yards throughout the Six Counties you'll hear rhymes which instruct British soldiers on how to dispose of their plastic bullets, and popular I.R.A. actions are committed to verse with a speed which amazes many adults.

In the build-up and aftermath of the Divis Street riots there was some awakening of national consciousness and a few of us began to query, with candid curiosity, the state of the nation. We were puzzled by our description in official forms as British subjects and wondered as we passed the customs posts on our way to Bun Beag for a summer in the Gaeltacht what exactly the border was. We were beginning to get a sense of our essential Irishness and events on the Falls Road served to whet our political appetites. Before the 1960s were over, we would be canvassing the streets of the Loney for support for our efforts in opposing the building of Divis Flats. 'Low rents not high flats' would be the cry as we picketed the corporation. From that agitation would arise the West Belfast Housing Action Committee, the West Belfast Unemployment Action Committee, the Civil Rights Association, the Central Citizens' Defence Committee and all that grew from it, from barricades to today.

But that was all in front of us. By the end of 1964, I was merely an interested part of a small group which gathered in a dingy room in a Cyprus Street G.A.A. Club to learn about Fenians and Fenianism, colonialism, neo-colonialists, partition and British imperialism. Sinn Féin, then an illegal organisation, was beginning to expand once again and I was happy to be part of this new expansion. The Special Powers Act, the ban on Sinn Féin and on the *United Irishman* newspaper, the lack of adult suffrage, discrimination in jobs and housing, the gerrymandering of local government boundaries and the sectarian divisions which were built into the Stormont structures all became real and deeply felt grievances.

'Do you know', I remarked to Jamesie Magee as we stood at the corner of Leeson Street and Getty Street, 'that you can be imprisoned for singing a rebel song?'

'Sure, everybody knows that', he replied with indifference. 'Sure me Da got six months once for burning a Union Jack.'

'I didn't know that.'

'Ah, you see', he retorted, 'you don't know everything, do you?'

'I never said I did!' Mortified at his suggestion I glared down towards the Varna Gap.

'Well, if I ever get time it'll be for more than burning a Union Jack', he continued. 'Josie had the right idea: he's in Canada. If I don't get a job soon I'm going to Australia. There's nothing in this place for anyone. If you had to pay for a living we'd all be dead.'

'Ach, it's not as bad as that', I asserted. 'A few changes here and there and we'd all be happy.'

'It's okay for you, still at St Mary's learning to be whatever you're learning to be. I've left school six months now and still no sign of work. If your ma or your granny weren't keeping you, you'd soon know your master. You jack in school and you'll see the difference.'

'You're putting the scud on me. C'mon and we'll go for a wee dander. Did you know that you can be whipped with a cat of nine-tails under "the Special Powers Act"?'

'And you want me to stay here? Your head's a marley: if me da can raise the money I'm taking myself off out ofit.'

And so he did. And shortly afterwards I jacked in school, and from then on *mar a detear, is e sin sceal elle* (as they say, that's another story). In the meantime, by some unnoticed, the Loney, Leeson Street and all that they meant have been erased and, the likes of it, as Tomas L. Criomthain wrote in *An t'Oileanath*, will never be seen again.

'THE POET IS DEAD'
Race Today, October 1983

Following the brutal murder of Michael Smith at the hands of supporters of the ruling Jamaica Labour Party, a wide and varied international protest movement has flowered. Within days of his death, Creation For Liberation, sponsors of Smith's first British poetry tour, along with the Alliance of the Black Parents' Movement, the Black Youth Movement and the *Race Today* Collective organised a picket at the Jamaican High Commission. It was done by word of mouth and close to two hundred people responded.

At the same time, the organisers put out an international appeal for protest telegrams to be sent to Edward Seaga, leader of the JLP and Prime Minister of Jamaica. And they rained down on the PM's desk. Prominent personalities from the world of radio and television added their weight; a veritable deluge of poetic tributes came from native dialect poets in Britain; sharply worded protests from the radical intelligentsia in France, Holland and Switzerland; clear and straightforward demands from the president of the Oilfields Workers' Trade Union, Trinidad and Tobago and from the Writers' Union. Memorial tributes were held in Jamaica, Brooklyn (NY), Wolverhampton and West London and an international tribute will be held in Brixton, London on 3 November.

Mikey, as we called him, was born 29 years ago in Kingston, Jamaica of working-class parents. In his teens, he began writing what is referred to as 'nation language poetry'. He was not the first. Louise Bennett had preceded him in pre-independence days. She met with the powerful opposition of the middle classes for whom the use of dialect was objectionable, but once it was established that independence from Britain meant having something of our own, Louise Bennett was home and dry.

By the late 1960s and early '70s, popular hostility to the hollowness of independence was fundamental to the new political thrust. Michael Smith, Oku Onuora, Mutabaruka and Linton Kwesi Johnson emerged out of this new movement to fashion the speech established by Bennett to revolutionary ends. So when Smith arrived in England in April 1982, the ground had been prepared. The language of reggae had burst upon the world via the Bob Marley train, and Linton Kwesi Johnson had established its poetic form here in the UK and in Europe. Mikey's first appearance was at the international poetry evening of the International Book Fair of Radical Black and Third World Books.

Wherever Smith went he captivated audiences with his unique delivery and performance. To a world falling apart at its seams, Michael Smith brought the uncompromising voice of the oppressed and the dispossessed. Such talents are rare. That is our loss.

When the telegrams of protests came cascading down, Seaga called one of his leading cultural bureaucrats and enquired of her, 'Who is Michael Smith?' We are certain that when he was told that Mikey's murderers were the Grey brothers, he further asked, 'And who are they?'

'FALLEN COMET: A TRIBUTE TO MICHAEL SMITH'
John LaRose, October 1983

'He came across our sky like a comet. And vanished.' That was the thought that came to me after the first shock of hearing about Michael Smith's death.

I had first heard of Michael Smith from Edward Kamau Brathwaite, the poet, literary critic and historian. Then others told me of him and I first saw him in the flesh on the *Arena* television programme about four Jamaican poets. This built Michael a fan base and his reputation in Europe was established from that moment. It was an audience of people, including writers and artists, from Britain, Africa, Asia, and other parts of Europe, the Caribbean and the US.

He came to the First International Book Fair of Radical Black and Third World Books in London in April 1982 and electrified the International Poetry Reading. Then he made his long-playing record *Mi Cyaan Believe It* with Island Records in London, and later toured with Gregory Isaacs. He performed at UNESCO in Paris in November 1982, then in Amsterdam and Milan. There was later another television programme with that magnificent performance of a Shelley poem in Westminster Abbey.

And now he is dead. The circumstances of his death highlight what seldom strikes us, except when someone as talented and outstanding as him, dies: the brutalisation of everyday life in Jamaica and most other modern societies.

Michael Smith had attended a public meeting in Stony Hill, St. Andrews, Jamaica on Tuesday, 16 August, the night before he died. He had confronted the main speaker at that meeting, the Minister of Education in the Government of Jamaica. The next day, Wednesday, 17 August, as he was passing the ruling Jamaica Labour Party local office in Stony Hill, he was stopped by four men who asked what he was doing there. He was chased, stoned and robbed. The attackers were seen by witnesses to enter the JLP constituency party office. Michael Smith became unconscious from the battering and was taken to the public hospital. He was dead on arrival. It was sheer barbarism. He belonged to none of the parties in Jamaica and he scorned the partisan politics there.

Michael Smith did not read his poetry – he performed it, with considerable skill. He had studied drama at the Jamaica School of Drama. He followed an oral tradition of patois poetry and contributed to its renewed popularity in the Caribbean. Michael Smith was a Dub poet, a poet using the rhythms of reggae and the resources of the common language, the language of the peasants, domestic and working people out of which context he sprang and wrote.

Derek Walcott, the Caribbean poet and playwright, has a line in his book *The Castaway* when he says: 'To change your language you must change your life.' With Michael Smith, his language was his life. And the poetry was his language and his life. I end this tribute with some lines from one of the poems by which we will remember him: 'Mi Cyaan Believe It'.

Mi seh mi cyaan believe it
mi seh mi cyaan believe it
room dem a rent
mi apply widin
but as mi go in
cockroach rat an scarpian also come in
waan good

RACE TODAY REVIEW
Akua Rugg, January 1984

The developments that have taken place in the cultural life of blacks in Britain during the last year indicate that we are now beginning to see the end of black artists floundering as isolated individuals in British society without a solid social, political and economic framework. Up until now, our performing artists have had to clutch at bit parts in the stream of popular entertainment or make do with fleeting appearances in more serious productions straining to be avant garde. Those working in the area of the fine arts have had to wait on some gallery owner deciding on a whim to mount the odd 'ethnic' exhibition. Until recently, British publishing houses, with the exception of the feminist presses have shown little interest in black writers.

Recently, however, there has been an explosion of the performing arts. Works by black playwrights have been staged throughout the year and not just in community or 'alternative' venues; a West End theatre held a three-month season of black drama. The Black Theatre Cooperative can command airtime for *No Problem*, a popular situation comedy series revolving around young West Indians, and Asian youth were represented in *Come to Mecca*, short stories by Farrukh Dhondy adapted for television. Creation for Liberation, a black cultural organisation, sponsored the first-ever open exhibition of work by black artists. And a British newspaper appearing in August without a photograph of a carnival reveller would be as unseasonable as one appearing in December without a picture of Father Christmas.

The Second International Book Fair of Radical Black and Third World Books, initiated by three radical black publishing houses drew to its forums, exhibitions and concerts an even larger audience than the first one. This is important because artists need to be nurtured by a receptive and critical audience if their work is to mature. They require cultural institutions – publishing houses, bookshops, art galleries, theatres and public festivals to ensure their work is constantly exposed. These institutions, which have emerged as a result of the social and political struggles waged consistently over the years by blacks, have created the space for black artists.

The establishment has now taken note of this and has set up bureaucracies to administer black art and culture. The danger is that the art forms developed by this patronage will prove to be as irrelevant to the lives of the mass of blacks as the pet projects of the Arts Council – the National Theatre, National Gallery, National Opera – are to the mass of whites. A line of defence against this threat has already been drawn up. Some of our cultural activists have formed organisations which assist people to transcend and transform the bankruptcy of cultural and intellectual life. The *Race Today Review* provides them with a formidable weapon for their arsenals. The *Review* for 1984 contains extracts from a short story and play, views and reviews of novels, essays, an anthology of poetry, music and film. There is nothing in this collection of work that serves to reconcile us to the status quo, neither here in Britain, nor in Somalia, Kenya, Jamaica, France, or the Caribbean. Rather, the contributions serve to expedite the struggles of radical and progressive elements in these societies against reactionary politics. John La Rose's observation that the death of Michael Smith highlights 'what seldom strikes us ... the brutalisation of everyday life in Jamaica and most other societies' is reinforced by the character sketch of a corrupt and arrogant politician drawn by Barbadian Austin Clarke in 'The Funeral of a Political Yard-Fowl'. A similar disregard of rulers for the ruled is revealed by Wanjiru and Wanyiri Kihoro in their review of Ngugi wa Thiong'o's essays. And Nuruddin Farah from Somalia, Grace Nichols from Guyana and the women of the Sistren Theatre collective from Jamaica, lift the whole debate about the particularities of women's oppression above the trivial level at which this subject is often discussed.

'IN SEARCH OF A SOLID FOUNDATION: BLACK THEATRE IN BRITAIN IN 1983'
Imruh Bakari, January 1984

There is a scene in the widely acclaimed play, *The Nine Night* by Edgar White in which the lead character, an elder Afro-Caribbean called Hamon Williams, in a reflective moment, casually remarks to his long-time friend and confidant Ferret Christian, 'You know, sometimes ah feel they have us here watching graveyards.' The disillusionment expressed here, speaks of a state reached by some older-generation Caribbean people in Britain who now experience the accumulated effect of alienation from their children, British society, and their homelands. The scene also seems an appropriate metaphor for the present state of black theatre in Britain; the next step will be a most decisive and possibly precarious one.

It will be unanimously agreed that 1983 has been a boom year for black theatre. Plays have been staged at regular intervals. Actors and actresses, both old and young, have been provoking all kinds of responses at well-attended performances. As it now stands, black theatre is pregnant with dynamism, optimism and controversy. We have most certainly arrived at the point where debates like 'where are the black writers, can they write?' and 'where are the black actors, can they act?' are redundant. The issue is now black theatre – what future and what steps are necessary to ensure its development and survival? Judging from the productions which I have seen in London, and the off-stage noises which speak of a (national) venue for black arts, it is obvious that a lot is at stake.

In March at the Bush Theatre, Edgar White's masterpiece, *The Nine Night* marked the return of director Rufus Collins to the London theatre scene. Collins had worked with White at the Keskidee in North London, but since the tragic end of that establishment about five years ago (more of that later), he has been based in Amsterdam. In *The Nine Night*, the Afro-Caribbean wake ritual for the dead becomes the context within which the conflicts in a Caribbean family in Britain are explored. In this production, the intuitive Rufus Collins was at his most disciplined and managed a very subtle and piercing interpretation. T-Bone Wilson, as the lead character, Hamon Williams, the father, turned in a memorable performance with the able support of Jason Rose as his friend Ferret Christian, and Donna Croll as his wife.

In July, Collins also directed Trevor Rhone's *Smile Orange* at the Tricycle Theatre. This is a farce which was first performed in Jamaica in 1971 and later adapted for a film by the same name. Its subject is the way tourism has warped Jamaican society. The play successfully highlights the day-to-day runnings at a not-so-prosperous hotel where the staff play out their fantasies of success while awaiting the arrival of the tourist who will give their lives some meaning. With the arrival of the tourist, there are a few benefits, but also disaster and disappointment. The production was a tour de force of raw Jamaican humour, and Sylvester Williams, as the epileptic Busboy, proved to be the most promising talent to emerge this year. Interestingly, among the responses was one by a well-respected theatre critic for whom most of the dialogue came across as a high-pitched buzz in which the occasional 'my dear', would emerge to establish the fact that the character was speaking English. The character referred to is the receptionist played by Cassie McFarlane who has not been seen much since her appearance in Menelik Shabazz's *Burning An Illusion* which came out in 1981. The critic in question seemed perturbed about the Jamaican dialect of the play, recommending 'why not speak "English" so that we all can understand?' This raises one issue which has to be decisively dealt with, which is whether certain influential individuals and groups in Britain are willing to accept a high quality of theatre from the black community on its own terms. In addition, it raises the question as to whether black theatre is willing to defend its own authenticity.

Tooth Of Crime by Sam Shepard was performed at the Bush Theatre in September. This production excelled beyond all expectations and broke new and important ground. It provided a rare opportunity to appreciate the multi-talents of Victor Romero Evans and Chris Tummings, two young actors who, despite being frequently side-tracked into media buffoonery, have a lot to contribute to the future of black theatre. *Tooth Of Crime* is a musical fantasy which was first performed in London some ten years ago. In the play, Hoss, the ageing superstar, is being challenged by the younger Crow in a world where artists and their art are conditioned and moulded by technology and the market. *Star Wars* in the world of the music industry.

In addition to these productions, there was a production of Ntozake Shange's *For Coloured Girls* and Michael McMillan gave us *On Duty* which focused on the experience of a female hospital worker. Writers Tony Dennis and Caz Phillips were disappointing. Their plays *Beyond the 'A' Penny Steps* and *The Shelter* seemed to be nothing but indulgent posturing, although provoking and controversial. Outside of what would be considered black theatre, individuals distinguished themselves, notably Alison Limerick in the musical *Labelled With Love* and Calvin Simpson in *1983*, a play about cruise missiles.

Clearly, then, Caribbean (black) Theatre in Britain has established high standards of professionalism. It has also proven, simply by audience response, to have some degree of authenticity. This seems to indicate that a firm basis exists for a dynamic and creative future. For a perspective on this, I refer back to a proposition floated some time ago by another theatre critic who said that with the growth of black theatre and the improving [*sic*] standard of black acting, black performers should form a company 'to do classics', no doubt English or European works. For varying reasons, the critic was severely trampled upon when he attempted to advance his argument at a forum at the Battersea Arts Centre. However, the issue still remains a pertinent one and is directly related to how some people see the future of black theatre, and its development.

Along with this debate have come thoughts on a National Black Theatre and a National Black Arts Centre. We are now at the point where the black community is being seriously offered the Roundhouse in Chalk Farm (probably the last relic of the 1960s) as a black arts centre. The idea has the backing of the Greater London Council (GLC). Unfortunately, I find myself at odds with some of the arguments and justifications being put forward, mainly because the answers to the questions raised are generally unconvincing and confused. A recent GLC report, in support of the arts centre idea, speaks of 'a monument and symbol of black achievement, a venue of high repute to rank alongside the major European art institutions'. In another instance, it is assumed that a centrally located black arts centre is essential for the growth of black arts in Britain. There are no grounds for believing that this is obvious. What seems more likely is that such an establishment will provide an atmosphere of exclusivity and self-importance for some. Having worked at the Keskidee Arts Centre for a number of years, I can testify to the fact that the idea of a National Black Arts Centre and/or National Black Theatre was systematically destroyed by a lack of foresight and clarity as to the role of such an institution on the part of those who ran the Keskidee; and by an endemic indifference to the idea by the arts bureaucracies of London. The dance company Maas Movers, the most promising beginning so far for a national black dance company in Britain, was also destroyed by a similar indifference and insensitivity.

It is clear to me that in 1983 the inherent lessons of these experiences have not been learnt. The Roundhouse has served its purpose well as a venue for mass events. At present, however, like the Riverside Studios, it has proved to be uneconomical. In addition, anyone who knows the requirements of artists and their work will know that the Roundhouse space is unsuitable, and the massive funds needed to renovate it could be much better spent.

Unfortunately, the idea for a black arts centre is presently tied to a stream of narrow sentiments which are seen as ends in themselves, and as such are inadequate and short sighted. As it stands, it seems that instead of facilitating the dynamic growth and development of the existing theatre companies, attempts are being made to stifle their efforts with the burden of a white elephant. Yes man, we not only watching graveyards, dey digging we grave too.

7

For Black and Third World Liberation

INTRODUCTION: 'TOWARDS A NEW SOCIETY'
David Austin

Reading these pages of *Race Today* so many years after they were published, we are reminded that it was not simply an important 'Black paper' but was one of the most important political journals in Britain at the time. We are also reminded of the depth and scope of its contents and the astute analysis of local and international events that were connected by threads of humanity and political possibility. From Brixton to Bombay, St. Georges to Georgetown, people, and particularly working-class people, were on the move and, as we sift through the popular journal's pages we are both transposed back in time and space, and left to wonder what happened to the political promises of that time.

This section fittingly begins with an article by Walter Rodney and ends with another, about Rodney, written by C.L.R. James. Rodney was one of the most important intellectuals and political figures of his generation and his ideas continue to resonate in our time, from London to Cape Town. In fact, it could be argued that his thoughts are more relevant today than they were then, as we struggle to forge political identities within a fractious environment in which difference is justifiably recognised, but then ossified into an essence. Rodney was a Black man from the Caribbean (the South American nation of Guyana) who ideologically and politically was associated with Pan-Africanism and socialism. Rather than understanding them as contradictory, his ethno-racial background and association with the African continent nourished his political perspective and informed his appreciation of the confluence of race and class.

Rodney was consistently critical of the African and Caribbean petty bourgeoisie in a manner that was reminiscent of Frantz Fanon. He would have no doubt been equally critical, had he been alive, of Obama's tenure in the White House, and most notably the former president's neglect of the underclass at home and America's imperial role overseas. Rodney was clear: to speak about race and nationalism divorced from class politics was to commit a cardinal sin, an unforgivable heresy that amounted to a plea to the powers that be for a seat at the table without challenging the table's legitimacy.

The thread that binds these articles can perhaps be summed up in a word that still elicits derision and fear, but nonetheless has regained traction in recent years – socialism. Divorced from its Stalinist past, socialism represents a call for a more just and egalitarian society in which the reins of economic and political power are shared equally. In opposition to the crass accumulation and concentration of wealth and power that is even more characteristic today than in the 1970s when these articles were first published, socialism demands that so-called 'ordinary people' play an active, creative and defining role in the (re)organisation of society.

It is this vision of a new society that binds these articles, regardless of whether they are about the fight for freedom against Gairyite tyranny in Grenada or about Detroit's Black underclass – an article written by white workers in Detroit and Windsor (Canada); the struggle against xenophobia, police brutality and predatory employers in Toronto, or against the collusion of big unions with corporations at the expense of workers; or in response to white left political groups attempting to make political mileage off the backs of Black struggles – as opposed to a genuine show of solidarity with them – a reality that brings to mind Linton Kwesi Johnson's call for Black self-activity in the face of white complicity in Black degradation in 'Indepedant Intavenshan', a poem that was likely first published in *Race Today*.

These texts also speak to the challenges inherent in political organising, as well as its necessity. James recalls how the he cautioned Walter Rodney's political associates to do their utmost to protect Rodney from assassination in Guyana. We also learn how the US deployed instruments of the state to disrupt and ultimately destroy the dissent of leading figures in the Black Panther Party, including that remarkable leader Fred Hampton in Chicago. As security files in the UK, Canada and the US attest, we should not be surprised to discover that the state intervenes and makes use of any means at its disposal to protect its interests. Indeed, any attempt to organise for change today should appreciate this as a point of departure.

But rather than being paralysed by fear and stupefied by the belief that any popular political efforts are ultimately futile, the state's response to Black self-organisation, ironically, attests to the viability of Black politics, especially in our time, if we are willing to learn from the past. This is why these texts are so important today. They recall a time when the vision of politics was more expansive in scope, more incisive, and predicated on the hope and belief that social change was both a possibility and a political imperative; a time in which the local and international converged in ways that, despite the prevalence of the Internet today, seem more distant and remote.

As we observe the public carnival that is big 'P' politics in our time, these texts remind us that it is the politics from below that most matters, and justifies our mistrust of officialdom with its parade of unfulfilled political promises. They remind us that our hope lies in a politics from below; a politics that crosses borders, and local engagement that is rooted in an international consciousness that is cognizant of the reality that we are interconnected across time and space.

'CLASS AND NATIONALISM IN AFRICA'
Walter Rodney, April 1974

Race Today: As we go to press the Sixth Pan African Congress in Dar es Salaam, Tanzania, is in its final session. In the preparations leading up to the Congress, the organisers – TANU (the ruling party) and the temporary secretariat – went along with Caribbean governments, particularly the Guyanese, who succeeded with their demands that Caribbean revolutionary activists be reduced to the status of observers. Below we publish extracts from Walter Rodney's paper to the Congress in which he draws a line of steel between Pan-Africanism, as espoused by the new black international technocracy, and revolutionary Pan-Africanism, i.e. the unity of Africa under socialist rule.

Since the Fifth Pan-African Congress held in Manchester in 1945, the political geography of Africa has been transformed by the rise of some forty constitutionally independent political units presided over by Africans. This is to state the obvious. Yet, following in the wake of the great pageant of the regaining of political independence, there has come the recognition on the part of many that the struggle of the African people has intensified rather than abated, and that it is being expressed not merely as a contradiction between African producers and European capitalists, but also as a conflict between the majority of the black masses and a small African possessing class. This, admittedly, is to state the contentious; but the Sixth Pan-African Congress will surely have to walk the tightrope of this point of contention.

Independence Movement

Pan-Africanism in the post-independence era is internationalist insofar as it seeks the unity of peoples living in a large number of juridically independent states. But it is simultaneously a brand of nationalism; and one must therefore penetrate its nationalist form to appreciate its class content. This exercise is made easier by the fact the nationalist movements in Africa which led to the regaining of independence in more than three dozen states constitute a phenomenon which has already received considerable attention. These movements were essentially political fronts or class alliances in which the grievances of all social groups were expressed as 'national' grievances against the colonizers. However, while the workers and peasants formed the overwhelming numerical majority, the leadership was almost exclusively petty bourgeois. Understandably, this leadership placed to the fore those 'national' aims which contributed most directly to the promotion of their own class interests; but they voiced sentiments which were historically progressive, partly because of their own confrontation with the colonialists and partly because of pressure from the masses. Pan-Africanism was one of these progressive sentiments, which served as a platform for that sector of the African or black petty bourgeois leadership which was most uncompromising in its struggle against colonialism at any given time during the colonial period.

Virtually all leaders of African independence movements paid at least lip service to the idea that regional freedom was only a step towards the freedom and unity of the whole continent; and the most advanced nationalists were usually the most explicit on the issue of Pan-African solidarity. Nkrumah and Kenyatta were both at Manchester; while Nyerere, Kaunda and Mboya were the driving forces behind the Pan-African Movement for East and Central Africa (PAMECA). Within the Francophone sphere, several leaders took Pan-Africanist positions in one form or another. The radical *Union des Populations de Cameroun* refused to accept colonial boundaries in Africa; Senghor espoused a culturally oriented doctrine of black internationalism, comparable to Pan-Africanism; and even Houphouet-Boigny was initially associated with a political party which was Pan-Africanist in thrust: namely, the *Rassemblement Democratique Africaine*, which addressed itself to the whole of French West Africa.

Class Limitations

It would be unhistorical to deny the progressive character of the African petty bourgeoisie at a particular moment in time. Owing to the low level of development of the productive forces in colonized Africa, it fell to the lot of the small privileged educated group to give expression to a mass of grievances against racial discrimination, low wages, low prices for cash crops, colonial bureaucratic commandism, and the indignity of alien rule as such. But the petty bourgeoisie were reformers and not revolutionaries. Their class limitations were stamped upon the character of the independence which they negotiated with the colonial masters. In the very process of demanding constitutional independence, they reneged on the cardinal principle of Pan-Africanism: namely, the unity and indivisibility of the African continent.

The petty bourgeoisie of Asia, Africa and Latin America are a different breed. They cannot be described as 'entrepreneurs', 'pioneers', 'captains of industry', 'robber barons' or in any of the other swashbuckling terms coined to glorify the primary accumulation of capital. Frantz Fanon flays them unmercifully but truthfully when he points to the shoddy, imitative, lacklustre character of the African petty bourgeoisie. Their role in the international capitalist system has always been that of compradors. Their capital outlay might often be greater than that of a factory owner during the Industrial Revolution in England during the early nineteenth century, but in the present era of monopoly capitalism it suffices mainly for chicken-farms. In any event, most of the African petty bourgeoisie is not directly involved in economic enterprises – their real sphere being the professions, the administration and the military/police hierarchy. They lack both the vision and the objective base to essay the leap towards continental unity.

Failure to Challenge Imperialism

A close scrutiny further reveals that the failure of the African ruling class to effect meaningful unity is not merely due to weakness. Recalling once more the dismantling process which took place in Francophone Africa at the time of negotiated independence, it can be seen that the pusillanimity of the African petty bourgeoisie in the face of the deliberate creation of non-viable dependent mini-states by France attests not merely to the strength of the colonisers but also to fear on the part of the presumptive African rulers that larger territorial units might have negated their narrow class welfare. Throughout the continent, none of the successful independence movements denied the basic validity of the boundaries created a few decades ago by imperialism. To have done so would have been to issue a challenge so profound as to rule out the preservation of petty bourgeois interests in a compromise 'independence' worked out in conjunction with international capital.

If the weakness of the present petty bourgeois leadership of Africa were the only problem, then they could be dismissed as passive bystanders who cannot make operational the potential of Pan-Africanism as an ideology of liberation. However, they maintain themselves as a class by fomenting internal divisions and by dependence on external capitalist powers. These policies are antithetical to Pan-Africanism. The record since independence confirms that the interests of the African petty bourgeoisie are as irreconcilable with genuine Pan-Africanism as Pan-Africanism is irreconcilable with the interests of international capitalism.

Most African mini-states are engaged in consolidating their territorial frontiers, in preserving the social relations prevailing inside these frontiers, and in protecting imperialism in the form of the monopolies and their respective states. The capitalist superpowers, directly and indirectly, individually and collectively, guarantee the existence of the African petty bourgeoisie as a ruling class and use them to penetrate and manipulate African society. This has been done so crudely and openly that one does not have to be specially informed or specially aware in order to perceive what has been going down.

Pan-Africanism has been so flouted by the present African regimes that the concept of 'Africa' is dead for all practical purposes such as travel and employment. The 'Africanisation' that was aimed against the European colonial administrator soon gave way to restrictive employment and immigration practices by Ivory Coast, Ghana (under Busia), Zaire, Tanzania, Uganda, Zambia and others – aimed against Dahomeans, Nigerians, Burundi nationals, Malawians, Kenyans and all Africans who were guilty of believing that Africa was for the Africans. Of course, it was said that unemployment among citizens of any given country forced the government to take such extreme steps. This is a pitiable excuse, which tries to hide the fact that unemployment is the responsibility of the neo-colonial regimes, which can do nothing better than preside over dependent economies with little growth and no development. In many respects, one African has been further shut off from another during the present neo-colonial phase than was the case during raw colonialism. Even within the context of the existing African nation states, the African ruling class has seldom sought to build anything other than tribal power bases, which means that they seek division and not unity at all levels of political activity, be it national, continental, or international.

Socialism: The Enemy

It is not surprising that Socialism has been enemy number one for so many African states. African leaders fight the bogey of Communist threat rather than the reality of capitalist/imperialist oppression. Even the more progressive of this ruling class harbour and protect local reactionaries while neutralising or eliminating Marxist and other left-wing elements. In ten, twelve, or fifteen years of constitutional independence, the various parts of Africa have scored no victories in ending exploitation and inequality. On the contrary, social differentials have increased rapidly and the same applies to the amount of surplus extracted by foreign monopoly capital. In the spheres of production and technology, the so-called 'development decade' of the 1960s offers the spectacle of decreasing agricultural production, a declining share of world trade, and the proliferation of dependency structures because of the further penetration of multinational corporations. All of these matters are highly relevant to a discussion of Pan-Africanism.

The transformation of the African environment, the transformation of social and production relations, the break with imperialism and the forging of African political and economic unity are all dialectically interrelated. This complex of historical tasks can be carried out only under the banner of Socialism and through the leadership of the working classes. The African petty bourgeoisie as a ruling class use their state power against Socialist ideology, against the material interests of the working class, and against the political unity of the African masses.

Both Socialism and Pan-Africanism are of the utmost importance with respect to this. In one sense, the unwillingness of the petty bourgeoisie to manifest overt hostility to Socialism and Pan-Africanism is a testimony to the development of mass consciousness and to the level of confrontation between progressive and reactionary forces on the world stage. But it is also very insidious in so far as pseudo-revolutionary positions tend to pre-empt genuinely revolutionary positions. For instance, the existing African regimes have helped create the illusion that the OAU represents the concretisation of Pan-African unity. The OAU is the principal instrument which legitimises the forty-odd mini-states visited upon us by colonialism. Obfuscation of the notion of class in post-independence Africa has made Pan-Africanism a toothless slogan as far as imperialism is concerned, and it has actually been adopted by African chauvinists and reactionaries, marking a distinct departure from the earlier years of this century when the proponents of Pan-Africanism stood on the left flank of their respective national movements on both sides of the Atlantic. The recapture of the revolutionary initiative should clearly be one of the foremost tasks of the Sixth Pan-African Congress.

Pan-Africanism and the Caribbean

Although New World black representation predominated at all Pan-African Congresses and Conferences in the past, the agendas were usually devoted almost exclusively to the affairs of the African continent. It can be assumed that the Sixth Pan-African Congress will not be substantially different, but the creation of independent Caribbean nation states does introduce a new dimension with regard to the participation of this part of the black world. Having sketched the main outlines of the petty bourgeois position in Africa, it is unnecessary to elaborate on the Caribbean scene, because of the numerous similarities. It is to be noted, however, that that which appears as tragedy against the vast backcloth of Africa reappears as comedy in the Caribbean. Early this year, the people of the then colony of Grenada took to the streets to express in uncompromising terms their opposition to the exploitative and oppressive system of Anglo-American colonialism, which is manned locally by a certain petty bourgeois clique. At the same time, the British government carried on regardless in its plans to grant independence to the said petty bourgeois clique, expressing reservations only on the point of whether or not it was safe to send a member of the Royal Family to preside over the independence ceremony. As it was, militant striking workers deprived the independence celebrations of telephone services, port services and electricity, but the petty bourgeois regime managed to find some fireworks to mark the auspicious occasion. What term other than 'comedy' can describe such a situation? The ruling class in each given British Caribbean territory usually takes pains to create a 'national' identity, which amounts to little more than glorifying the fact that some Africans were sent to slave plantations in Jamaica or Trinidad rather than Barbados or Antigua, as the case may be. On the basis of this 'nationalism', the petty bourgeoisie can continue the former British colonial policy of preventing trade unionists and progressives from moving freely amongst the people of the Caribbean.

The Sixth Pan-African Congress

Yet, the realities of state power have predetermined that when the Sixth Pan-African Congress meets in Dar es Salaam in June 1974 it will be attended mainly by spokesmen of African and Caribbean states which in so many ways represent the negation of Pan-Africanism. One immediate consequence of the rise of constitutionally independent African and West Indian states is that for the first time such a gathering will be held on African soil and will be sponsored, directed and attended mainly by black governments rather than by black intellectuals or by small black protest organisations, as was the case up to the Fifth Congress in Manchester. Already it is clear that states will be represented as states and that the OAU will play some role. When a few individuals began to contemplate this Congress some three years ago, it was felt that it should be a coming-together of black political movements, as distinct from governments. One school of thought envisaged that it would be a select conference of the most progressive elements in the black world. To a large extent, this was the significance of the All African People's Conference held in Accra in 1958. However, plans for a similar meeting in the 1970s would be hopelessly idealist. The African radicals of

Figure 7.1   Race Today, August/September 1985.

1958 are by and large the incumbents in office today. The radicals of today lead at best an uncomfortable existence within African states, while some languish in prison or in exile. The present petty bourgeois regimes would look with disfavour at any organised programme which purported to be Pan-African without their sanction and participation.

None of the progressive African regimes, which are already isolated and exposed to internal and external reaction, would dare to host a Congress which brought together only those who aggressively urge a unity of the African working masses and the building of a Socialist society.

In the light of the above considerations, any African committed to freedom, Socialism and development would need to look long and hard at the political implications of participation in the Sixth Pan-African Congress. The purists might be tempted to eschew any association whatsoever; but revolutionary praxis demands that one should contend against class enemies in theory and in practice, by seizing every opportunity to utilise all of the contradictions within imperialism as a global system – in this instance, contradictions born of economic exploitation and racist oppression.

'BLACK AND WAGELESS IN DETROIT: "THE EMBERS ARE STARTING TO BURN AGAIN"'

Race Today, November 1975

In the last two years, *Race Today* has sought to make known, and act upon the rebellion of young unemployed blacks throughout the world. For us, the struggles of these wageless brothers and sisters in Brixton, Trench Town, East Dry River, Detroit, New York, Toronto, Bulawayo, Lagos and Nairobi are constituent parts of a total thrust against the bankruptcy of modern civilisation. Where they have been able, through mass education, to articulate their rejection of modern society, to explain and develop what they are against and what they are for, they have managed to rally millions to their cause. Huey Newton, Bobby Seale, Eldridge Cleaver, George Jackson, Johnathan Jackson, Malcolm X represent the fact that the rebellion of this social grouping has penetrated the consciousness and influenced the ideas and actions of millions of blacks everywhere.

It would follow that the power of this section of the international working class would, at some historical juncture, penetrate the consciousness of white workers and influence them in the same way. It was only a matter of time.

Below we print an article written by white male workers in the auto industry in Detroit (USA), and Windsor (Canada) about the rebellion of young unemployed blacks in Detroit. The writers report on a particular conflict and draw conclusions about the impact of the rebellion on themselves.

On Monday, July 28, 1975, Andrew Chinarian, a white bar owner in Livernois on Detroit's west side, shot and killed Obie Wynn, an 18-year-old black, unemployed youth. The shooting took place at 8 p.m. on one of the hottest nights of the summer and provoked the black youth of the neighbourhood into action: looting, burning and rock throwing began immediately and continued for two nights. The conflict has created both a new political climate in this city and a new terrain on which the working class will be moving this winter and for many hot summers to come.

The conflict took place in the city's vast north-west ghetto, which is primarily black residential. Detroit is now a predominantly black city. After the massive riot which took place in 1967, much of the white working class and many businesses abandoned the city for the white suburbs which surround it. Essentially, the only companies left are the major auto companies and those who are too poor to move out. When the white people left, they took their money with them, so the city has experienced massive cutbacks in services from all levels of government.

Detroit's economy, which has for many years been built almost exclusively around the auto industry, has been hit very hard by the industry's current international crisis. Unemployment is high, running around 15 per cent. And in black neighbourhoods, in the inner city, unemployment is as high as 30–40 per cent (or higher, because the government counts only people 'looking' for a job).

The Protagonists

Andrew Chinarian is a white man who owns a bar in the neighbourhood. He is friendly with the white police in the neighbourhood and has been involved in at least two similar shooting incidents in the past.

Obie Wynn was an 18-year-old black youth who lived with his family in a house behind Chinarian's bar. He dropped out of high school but got his diploma later, through a General Educational Development test. He was unemployed and awaiting a job interview at the time of his death. After his death, his arrest record became well publicized – 'charges of robbery both armed and unarmed, carrying a concealed weapon, larceny, car theft, and destruction of property'. The white media in town stopped just short of using his arrest record as justification for his murder. To us, the record looks like the consequence of struggling for the wage in the ghetto instead of the workplace.

The Event: Monday

It's still unclear exactly what provoked the shooting. Chinarian stated later that Wynn was breaking into a customer's car. Friends who were with Wynn at the time said that Wynn was simply sitting on the car and that Chinarian went back into the bar to get his gun when Wynn refused to move. The only facts we have are that Wynn was shot in the back of the head, some distance from the car.

Within minutes, a crowd estimated at three hundred gathered outside the bar. They were prepared to lynch Chinarian and to burn the bar, but the police arrived and carted Chinarian away. The black youth in the area moved onto the streets, tipping over, smashing and burning cars. Youths from other areas arrived, along with about seven hundred police who tried to clear the areas with nightsticks and tear gas canisters, which the youth threw back. Eventually, the police managed to make 63 arrests.

Coleman Young, the black mayor, and Phillip Tannian, the white police chief, tried to cool the situation down, even appearing on the 11 p.m. news saying that the rumours of burning and looting were all false. However, on a special 11.30 recap of the news, they displayed films of the cars being burned and black youths milling about the street.

Sometime after 11 p.m., Marian Psyzko, a white immigrant bakery worker who was driving through the neighbourhood on his way home from work, was dragged out of his car and beaten with a piece of broken concrete. He was taken to the hospital in a critical condition. Police arrested a 15-year-old black youth and held him without pressing any charges or granting him bail. Later, they were to openly admit he was not the 'major perpetrator' of the beating.

The Bail Situation

In contrast to the gestapo-type arrest of the 15-year-old youth, Chinarian was arraigned on second-degree murder charges and released on $500 bail. The police accepted at face value Chinarian's version of the shooting – i.e., that Wynn was committing a crime at the time of the shooting. In the words of the police lieutenant who released Chinarian, 'I released the man because he was a bar owner, a businessman, and a citizen of the area.' The 63 people who were arrested during the disturbance were mostly charged with malicious destruction of property, a misdemeanour, but they were released on the same $500 bail as Chinarian. The black community was angered by this – even Mayor Young had to air his disapproval of the privileges given to Chinarian and in response a judge ordered Chinarian rearrested. He was later released on $25,000 bail.

Tuesday

Late Tuesday afternoon, there was a tactical dispute between Mayor Young and the police department as to where police should be positioned. Young wanted them at the bar but Commander James Bannon wanted to cover a wider area and avoid pinning his troops down.

Bannon moved on his own, and when he left the bar unprotected the crowd of about five hundred came together. They rammed a stolen car into the front of the building, entered it, and destroyed the inside. More cars were burned and the area around the bar was looted. The police moved in with tear gas and 43 more people were arrested.

Campaign Cool It

Mayor Young and others, including Baptist ministers, black businessmen and black officers of civic and community organisations set up after the '67 riot, attempted mediation. Mayor Young considered ordering all white police officers to be moved out of the area, but he simply didn't have enough black officers to control the crowd.

The self-professed goal of Mayor Young and the rest of this black bourgeoisie was to 'avoid violence'. The cornerstone of their credibility with the black working class has always been their ability to obtain results by 'working within the system'. They could cut bureaucratic red tape and provide housing projects, jobs in the city government and basketball courts. Getting blacks into the police department in large numbers was the most outstanding example of their success.

During the disturbance, these black officers were forced to directly confront the black youth. The black bourgeoisie could do nothing more than front for the police. As one white police official put it, the purpose of Campaign Cool It was to 'go ahead of the police lines to tell the crowd: the pigs are coming and they mean business.' Mayor Young approached the crowd with 'We cannot win by using violence.' The black youth responded directly by stoning Young off the car from which he had been speaking. Mayor Young and Campaign Cool It retired, and the police moved in with nightsticks.

Wednesday

On Wednesday, Livernois slowly began to return to 'normal' and adjust itself to the new political climate which had been created by the disturbance. Early in the day, Mayor Young was quoted as saying the disturbance had more to do with unemployment than a racist bar owner. And later on in the day, Chrysler, the city's largest employer, announced it was rehiring all its laid-off Detroit-area workers. It was all an attempt to re-inspire confidence in their ability to lead the city back to prosperity (and at that moment, to cool the city off).

Thursday

On Thursday, the post-riot analyses began. The most common was a comparison to the '67 riot, about how the city was mostly white then, with a white mayor and a white police force; about how it is mostly black now, with a partially black police force and a black mayor; about how most of the participants in the '67 riot were older, employed blacks; about how this time the participants were almost all unemployed youths; about how the police responded much more quickly this time round; about how the damage was much less extensive this time.

Psyzko's Death

The post-riot analysis became a lot more potent when, late Thursday afternoon, Marian Psyzko died of his wounds. Young went into action immediately. He visited the families of both men, stating over and over again that he was pursuing the law equally in both cases. At Psyzko's funeral he said, 'I think the bishop drew a good parallel between Obie Wynn and Marian Psyzko. The deaths of both men were senseless and tragic.'

The newspapers scrambled to make Psykzo's death the main topic of discussion. The *Press*: '[Psyzko] represents the worst fears of many whites: a man caught in circumstances he knew nothing of – a victim of black mob action on a dark city street.' Their big scoop was discovering that Psyzko had spent some time in a Nazi prison camp. He became a heroic 'World

War II Freedom Fighter' and the irony of his death became that 'he fought for freedom over there but died over here.'

The Following Week

The following Tuesday, the 15-year-old youth who had been held in connection with Psyzko's beating was released from custody and it was announced that he would testify against three young black men. They were immediately arrested and are being held without bail, charged with first-degree murder.

Meanwhile, Chinarian is free on bail and awaiting a second-degree murder trial. The prosecutor's office stated the charges were different because they felt there had been premeditation in the death of Marian Psyzko, but none in the death of Obie Wynn. When Chinarian was arraigned, his lawyer immediately asked for a change of venue, claiming his client has already been tried and convicted by 'mob rule'. It is almost certain that the trial will take place in the safety of the white suburbs.

Confused State Reaction

The rulers of the city (and the nation) remain bitterly split over how to deal with the black wageless – terrorism à la Commander Bannon or mediation à la Mayor Young. This is an important split, one which is reflected across the land in the various debates the ruling class is conducting about how best to deal with the working class.

The Left

There was a small organised left presence during the disturbance. A few white leftists who went down there got chased off. On Thursday, a group of black militants from the Republic of New Africa held a march which many people from the area joined. They presented to the police three demands: that police be removed from the area, that Chinarian be jailed until his trial, and that the charge against Chinarian be increased to first degree murder. They also said that the 15-year-old youth who was being held in connection with Psyzko's death should be bound over to the citizens of the area and 'judged – and punished – by his peers. No sane man would willingly submit to the justice of the white courts.' The RNA march seemed to get support from the people in the neighbourhood but it didn't push the struggle forward in a direct, tactical sense.

Lessons

The main lesson of the disturbance is its reiteration of the unbroken autonomy of the struggle of the black wageless. Everybody in Detroit was talking about it: that the conditions which provoked explosions in the ghetto haven't changed very much in the last decade; that but for a small set of fortuitous circumstances this relatively small disturbance could have exploded into a repeat of the massive '67 riot; that the city could explode again (and much more severely) at any time. Also, significantly, similar disturbances took place in other US cities. In the words of one Windsor autoworker, 'The embers are starting to burn again.' There is no question that these disturbances are moments of the daily struggle of the black wageless. They're struggles not so much against unemployment, against the low standard of living which capital attaches to unemployment, against the police who attempt to enforce that low standard of living. Through the crisis, the state is attempting to re-impose on the black wageless waged work (and low wages) as the only condition for their survival. The black wageless are resisting this, creating other sorts of wages, preserving some of the freedom which unemployment makes possible.

For White Male, Waged Workers

This increases the power of us white male, waged workers in three ways: 1) If Chrysler's response to the disturbance is to rehire people (and it's hard to tell if they're actually doing that), a lot of us will return to work. And we'll go back not devastated by layoffs but in a position of strength. 2) Even if these people aren't rehired, the political implication of the Livernois conflict is clear: layoffs are only a limited weapon for the capitalists in attacking the power of male waged workers at the plant. 3) The power of the black wageless is teaching us as white male, waged workers something about ourselves.

We've long shared in the various 'social wage' programs which the black wageless have demanded. But the content of this struggle is clear: black people didn't win those wages in return for work they did for capital; they won the wages when they were strong enough to leave capital no other choice. And they didn't restrict themselves to their power in the workplace either. They struggled everywhere and they worked only when politically they were given no other choice if they were to survive. These are important lessons for us to learn as white male, waged workers. One of our main weaknesses is that our efforts are often channelled into union struggles, which are always based on the assumption that first we work and then we bargain with the capitalists.

But we have to be clear that the struggles of the black wageless give us this power and teach us these lessons even though it is directed against us. When Andrew Chinarian shot Obie Wynn, he was exercising power he had over him. This power wasn't just defined in terms of business over unemployed youth. It was defined in terms of a *white* businessman over a *black* unemployed youth. That's what provoked the disturbance.

Many of us don't share in Chinarian's sort of power over black people. But there's a large issue here which shouldn't be mystified by dismissing Chinarian as petty bourgeois. Marian Psyzko might have been 'just an ordinary white worker', but when those black kids were on the rampage during that first night of the disturbance, he was the closest thing to the state that they could get their hands on. How was his power defined over them? The power to own a car, the power to expect protection from the police, the power to drive out of the neighbourhood when the police go berserk, etc., etc.

As white male, waged workers who are coming to grips with the material struggle of the working class both within itself and against capital, we don't chastise the black movement for this. We don't ask them to cool off these sort of attacks. We don't ask them to recognise that certain among us 'have our shit together' about these sorts of things. Instead, we are trying to move on the power which that struggle gives us in our struggle against capital. This perspective on the Livernois disturbance and the black movement is a small force within the white male working class. We are beginning to see the strength which the black movement actually does give us in our struggle against capital. But most of us continue to see the black movement as a totally negative force, as something which must be resisted. There can be no reconciliation of these two perspectives, only struggle within the white male working class which results in the victory of one or the other. The clarity which the Livernois disturbance gives to this debate is for us one of its most important consequences.

'THE MILROD 34: WEST INDIANS ON STRIKE IN CANADA'
John Huot, March 1976

Between 1970 and 1973, Italian, Greek and Southern European workers in Toronto engaged in a series of strikes against the low-paid, overworked status to which employers and the government have tried to confine them.

Immigrant workers are highly concentrated in the light manufacturing industries which have been created in the suburbs following the closure of factories. Of more than 6,200 industrial plants, only 300 now employ more than 200 workers. Many of these plants are owned by large multinational companies who locate and relocate wherever in the world they can find the cheapest source of labour – often, as in Toronto, recent immigrants. On average, these workers are paid 15–20 pre cent lower than Ontario workers as a whole.

The mass sackings, police brutality and arrests between 1970 and 1973 were sufficient to deter the workers from taking any major strike action until recently, when Toronto's newest immigrants, West Indians and Asians, have taken up the struggle. Between May and October 1976, West Indian and Asian workers, at the LTT, a subsidiary of Milrod Metal Products, in Mississauga, Toronto carried the fight to management over the issue of speed-up on the assembly line.

Milrod Metal Products is a typical Toronto area plant. It employs two hundred unskilled workers drawn from five different immigrant groups (West Indian, Indian, Greek, Italian, Portuguese), with few native-born workers. The workers produce dashboards, bumpers and window frames for General Motors and other auto companies. The majority of workers operate punch presses; others do spot welding, feed the lines with materials and pack the finished products, or work in the machine shop. The comparatively low investment in plant and machinery means not only that workers operate old and often dangerous machines which can malfunction unexpectedly and cut off a finger, but that the company stays there only as long as it has a steady supply of low-cost workers. Immigration policies ensure that such low-cost labour is available. They bring in new groups of immigrants as groups get stronger and demand better wages and working conditions. Until the late 1960s, they employed mainly southern European male immigrants, then they started hiring from the first generation of West Indian and Asian workers to be admitted to Canada under the revised 1967 immigration regulations.

In 1974, Milrod reached further into this new source of workers by hiring its first women workers. By mid-1976, about two-thirds of the workforce were black (mainly Jamaican and Indian), and one-fifth were women. Most of these workers are in their thirties and forties, supporting families in Canada, and often sending money to dependants in their home countries.

This is how Mrs Ena Smith, one of the fired workers, described Milrod's use of race: 'Most of the time the black workers are put on the hardest jobs. They know that black people don't have the franchise here as whites do.

When you're white, it's easier to get another job in Canada. Most of the time when black people get the hard job, you've got to stick it.' The fired workers say there was no racial tension among workers when black workers first came into the plant, but the company has promoted racial tension by treating blacks and whites differently in job assignments, shift changes and disciplinary measures.

In 1975, management even adopted an old trick from the days of slavery by appointing, as supervisor, the local union president, a Jamaican with a reputation for being tough. He became the company's number one slave driver during the speed-up campaign.

Unlike most small plants employing immigrant workers in the Toronto area, Milrod has a union – the International Association of Machinists (IAM), one of the oldest US-based skilled workers' unions. For Milrod's unskilled immigrant workers, the IAM seems to function mainly as a negotiator of mediocre contracts, a collector of $8 monthly dues, and as a straitjacket on shop-floor struggles, channelling them to arbitrators and the Ontario Labour Relations Board. At shop-floor level, the Milrod workers have elected stewards who are responsive to workers' needs, but any struggle which goes beyond the narrow bounds of the contract throws the workers into the hands of the IAM executive.

For a considerable period of time, Milrod's racist policies appear to have been relatively successful. Milrod had a hard-working labour force, and many of the fired workers had worked there for several years, even receiving letters of commendation from management. Few had ever been disciplined. Wages were about average for unionised plants employing immigrant labour: $4.35 an hour with no cost-of-living allowance and few benefits. Management retains complete power to assign workers to any job or shift without notice, regardless of seniority, which leaves the door wide open to arbitrary and discriminatory decisions affecting the workers' day-to-day life.

If Milrod's racist practices towards black workers were the key to forcing their workers to work harder for less money, then the rebellion of the black workers against these racist practices has been the key factor in challenging this situation for all workers. The black workers' rebellion in 1976 was sparked by a speed-up campaign which increased production quotas by up to a half, causing workers to injure themselves. Workers were switched to unfamiliar machines and a male supervisor pushed his way into the women's washroom after he had complained about the time women workers were taking. 'We are killing ourselves trying to meet production quotas', said Rahim Siraj, president of the Milrod union local. The company stepped up harassment to force workers to meet the new quotas and delayed payment of compensation for injury.

The hardest jobs were on the truck line which produces dashboards for Chevrolet trucks. The slave-driving former union president was in charge of this, and in May 1976, plant workers circulated a petition to have him removed. When the company failed to respond, day-shift workers held a half-hour stoppage in the plant. Later the same day, four Jamaican workers were suspended indefinitely and subsequently fired. Their cases are still being dealt with separately in arbitration. In late August, Rahim Siraj was suspended for a day 'for low production'. Night-shift workers stopped work and refused to leave the plant until the police showed up. The workers decided to start a plant-wide strike to demand realistic production quotas, safe working conditions, and Siraj's re-instatement with full compensation. The strike and the demands were decided upon by the workers themselves, without consulting the IAM business rep or other union higher-ups.

Support for the eleven-day strike was almost 100 per cent from both black and white workers; no picket line was needed. This unity meant that the company dared not attempt to bring in scabs, unlike in the early 1970s Toronto strikes, where militant picket lines and police intervention were common. The workers also successfully demanded that the IAM allow them to choose their own lawyer to represent them at the Labour Relations Board hearing at which the company eventually won a ruling that the strike was illegal. Faced with the threat of heavy fines, the workers decided to end the strike without winning any concessions from the company.

After the return to work on 9 September, harassment of black workers intensified. The Chevy truck line became almost entirely black, as those referred to as trouble makers were transferred there, if not already there. Plant superintendent Evans demanded that production quotas be met. Several workers testified at the Labour Board hearing that Evans told them: 'You are all immigrants here and you have to work hard. If you don't want to work, go back to your country.' Other workers have testified that Evans boasted: 'I'll soon get rid of all you black niggers out of here.' In the following weeks, workers on both shifts of the Chevy line received disciplinary warnings for low production. On 19 October, 34 of them, all but two black, representing almost the entire line on both shifts, were fired. The company charged them with conducting a deliberate slow-down.

The next morning, the fired day-shift workers and more than half the workers met and were ready to strike immediately but were talked out of it by the IAM business rep. 'He told us that the lawyer told him it would be a harder case for him to fight. He would have to be fighting for an illegal strike and for the 34 fired workers. So he persuaded the workers to go back to work, and they'd handle our case through the Labour Board, which would be easier for him', one of the fired workers recalls.

The IAM limited itself to hiring a lawyer, filing a complaint with the Human Rights Commission and arguing at the Labour Board that the firings constituted an illegal lockout. It has been the fired workers themselves, assisted by the Black Workers' Group, a local black organisation, who have begun to organise a broad movement of support around four demands: immediate re-instatement of all fired workers with full compensation for lost wages; an end to victimisation and racial discrimination; realistic production standards; a safe and healthy place to work.

To build support, the workers have mobilised the strength of the black community in Toronto. They have publicised their struggle in the black and white press and on television, and held a benefit dance strongly supported by the black community and many Indian and white immigrant workers from the plant.

The most dramatic display of the fired workers' strength has been at the Labour Board hearing. Normally, workers are intimidated by these hearings, where company and union lawyers use the workers' testimony to argue fine points of law, while the three-man Labour Board panel sits in solemn, 'impartial' judgement. But now most of the fired Milrod workers attend the hearing and shout 'Right! Right!' when one of their fellow workers describes working conditions and 'No! No!' when a worker gets a hard time from the company lawyer. The chairman has tried several times without success to instruct the workers to remain silent. When Winston Mauricette, one of the fired workers, was questioned about his work by the company lawyer, he retorted, 'Don't get on a high horse. Don't shout at me. If you want to talk to me, do so as a human being.' Workers shouted their approval. At one point, the hearing had to be adjourned for thirty minutes.

The respect which the Board, company and union displayed towards the workers at the hearings was perhaps sharpened by a dramatic incident in mid-January in Windsor, Ontario, Canada's car-manufacturing capital. A fired black auto worker, who was angry at the union's failure to get him re-instated, calmly walked into the union hall, cleared everyone out except the branch president, and then methodically shot him dead. Following this, a number of plainclothes cops began attending the Milrod Labour Board hearings.

In early February, the Ontario Labour Relations Board, unsurprisingly, found that the mass firing was not an illegal lockout, though management had acted in a 'high handed way'. However, the attitude of black workers at the hearing certainly demonstrated to all workers, black or white, that labour boards and lawyers are not so all-powerful when confronted with the workers' organised strength.

The Milrod workers are now moving to deepen the mobilisation of the black community. They have distributed leaflets in the black community, organised two demonstrations in front of the Labour Relations Board and sought support at the Congress of Commonwealth Caribbean Immigrants in Montreal in the belief that their struggle is important for workers in the Caribbean as well as in Canada.

The fired workers are also moving to win support from white workers in Toronto, both immigrant and native-born, with the slogan, 'The job of no immigrant is secure unless the jobs of all immigrants are secure.' Union branches have passed resolutions but done little else and the Milrod workers have made it clear they do not need missionaries from white left organisations. One such group, calling itself the Canadian Communist League, has already jumped into the fray, attempting unsuccessfully to set up its own 'Milrod Defence Committee', separate from the fired workers' own organisation. This group has succeeded in creating a certain atmosphere of distrust for white activists, which makes the Milrod workers' goal of soliciting white workers' support more difficult.

In all the activities of the black Milrod workers, there is a living illustration of a section of the working class feeling its way forward in unfamiliar surroundings, discovering who its friends and enemies are in relation to its own concrete needs. As a member of the Black Workers' Group put it:

Right-wing whites say blacks have a chip on their shoulder, left-wing whites say we are racist. They feel they have to control black people all the time. We say we have a legitimate right to organise ourselves. Your struggle can't be like my struggle because we have a completely different history. We hope that people in the white community will recognise this and come up with a show of solidarity. Some white leftists are running around saying they want to organise us. We can organise ourselves. What we want from whites is for them to get out into their own community and mobilise support.

'HOW THE US GOVERNMENT SUBVERTED THE BLACK PANTHER PARTY: THE FBI REVELATIONS'
Leila Hassan, March 1976

The Black Panther Party, formed in the United States of America in 1966, represents the most determined and organised stage of opposition to that government's failure to satisfy the hope and aspirations of the black unemployed. Leila Hassan, Assistant Editor of Race Today, *documents the reactions of the American state to the challenge presented by the Black Panther Party, and its implications for the unemployed black youth movement in Britain.*

When the facts of Watergate were dramatically exposed before the world, the major response was one of surprised horror at the depths to which politicians and state officials in America had sunk. The section of the population which had no difficulty in accepting the level of corruption unfolding day by day was the black community. They knew that Watergate was not the first time such 'dirty tricks' had been used. When the black community protested and made allegations that politicians, state bureaucrats and their agencies had embarked on a programme of gangsterism aimed at destroying the black movement in the US, the allegations were dismissed as incredible. When they claimed that the FBI murdered, framed and instituted provocative activities aimed at eliminating activists within the black movement, this was seen as hysteria. Such reactions gave the politicians and bureaucrats growing confidence to pursue their course. The result was Watergate. Now, from the mouths of ex-FBI agents, and FBI documents, the truth is out. Not only does it prove that the black community was correct, it clearly shows what the modern state is capable of today.

In 1966, The United States saw the formation, in Oakland, California, of the Black Panther Party, a revolutionary organisation consisting mainly of the urban unemployed and a minority of black students. One of the major issues facing the community was police brutality, particularly against the unemployed ghetto blacks, so the Panthers took advantage of an American law which gives its citizens the right to bear arms in public. They began patrolling the Oakland community in an effort to reduce police activity. This resulted in several daring confrontations with the police and succeeded in winning them the support of the community.

They formulated a ten-point programme demanding:

1. The power to determine the destiny of their community
2. Full employment
3. An end to robbery by the capitalists of the black community
4. Decent housing fit for the shelter of human beings
5. Education for their people that exposes the true nature of the decadent American society and which teaches them their true history and their role in the present day society
6. Exemption of all black men from military service

236

7. An end to police brutality and murder of black people
8. Freedom for all black men held in federal state, county and city prisons and jails
9. Black people be tried by a jury of their peers
10. Land, bread, housing, education, clothing, justice and peace.

In response to this programme, unemployed blacks flocked to join and support the BPP and by 1968, it had chapters in every black community throughout the US. Come 1970, a top secret report to US President Richard Nixon submitted that 25 per cent of the black population had 'a great respect for the BPP, including 43 per cent of blacks under the age of 21'.

The extent to which the US state sought to eliminate the party has only recently been brought to light. Documents from the FBI's Counterintelligence Program (COINTELPRO) have been made public and ex-FBI agents have testified to the US Senate's Intelligence Committee as to the corrupt practices and methods employed by them aimed at destroying the BPP. FBI infiltration resulted in the deaths of leading members of the BPP in Chicago and California and the FBI succeeded in exacerbating conflicts between the BPP and other black organisations.

The Murder of John Huggins, Alprentice 'Bunchy' Carter, John Savage and Sylvester Bell

In the late 1960s, the black movement was preoccupied primarily with what relationships, if any, they should have with white groups. The BPP publicly stated its willingness to work in a coalition with white groups. Black nationalist groups took the opposite position. In California, the conflict was particularly sharp, between the Panthers and the black nationalist group led by Ron Karenga, the US Organisation.

Political differences were manifested in personal abuse and slander. When members of the opposing groups met, they would insult, threaten and 'murder mouth' each other. In May 1968, the BPP issued a directive that its members should refrain from these petty squabbles, naming in particular, the US Organisation and Ron Karenga. COINTELPRO documents reveal that the conflict was closely followed by the FBI and manipulated to its own advantage, as demonstrated by the following quotation from a document of 2 December 1968, from the offices of J. Edgar Hoover to 13 cities in the United States:

For the information of recipient offices a serious struggle is taking place between the Black Panther Party (BPP) and the US Organisation. The struggle has reached such proportions that it is taking on the aura of gang warfare with attendant threats of murder and reprisals. In order to fully capitalise upon BPP and US differences, as well as to exploit all avenues of creating further dissension in the ranks of the BPP, recipient offices are instructed to submit imaginative and hard-hitting counterintelligence measures aimed at crippling the BPP. Commencing December 2, 1968, and every two-week period thereafter, each office is instructed to submit a letter under this caption containing counterintelligence measures aimed against the BPP. The bi-weekly letter should also contain accomplishments obtained during the previous two-week period under caption program.

Six weeks after this document was issued, two leading members of the BPP, Alprentice 'Bunchy' Carter and John Huggins, were gunned to death by members of the US Organisation on the Los Angeles campus of the University of California. Two members of the US Organisation, George and Larry Stiner, were subsequently convicted and sentenced to life imprisonment. However, on 31 March 1974, both 'escaped' from San Quentin Prison by walking away from a family visitors' area during a weekend family visit, and have not been seen since.

Following these murders, leaflets arriving at the BPP offices in Los Angeles showed a drawing of Ron Karenga looking through a list of 'things to do today'. This contained the names of John Huggins, Bunchy Carter, Bobby Seale and Walter Wallace with ticks next to Huggins' and Carter's names implying they were taken care of and the next to go were Seale and Wallace. More leaflets arrived, all drawings, and all threatening death to Bobby Seale and Huey Newton (the founder members of the BPP), and David Hilliard, chief of staff of the BPP.

Investigations have since uncovered that all these leaflets originated from COINTELPRO and they succeeded in inciting further violence against the BPP.

On 23 May 1969, BPP members John Savage and Jeffrey Jennings were walking towards their office when a member of the US Organisation called 'Tambozi', grabbed John Savage by the shoulder, jammed a .38 automatic pistol into the back of his neck and shot him dead.

On 15 August 1969, BPP member Sylvester Bell was murdered by Ron Karenga's men, in an attempt to intimidate him from giving evidence at the trial of the Stiner brothers, charged with the killings of Bunchy Carter and John Huggins. The murderers of John Savage and Sylvester Bell have never been brought to trial. Another COINTELPRO document dated 18 September 1969 states:

> In view of the recent killing of BPP member Sylvester Bell, a new cartoon is being considered in hope that it will assist in the continuance of the rift between the BPP and US. This cartoon, or series of cartoons, will be similar in nature to those formerly approved by the Bureau and will be forwarded to the Bureau for evaluation and approval immediately upon their completion.

The Murder of Fred Hampton and Mark Clark

Fred Hampton, aged 21, the chairman of the Chicago chapter of the Black Panther Party, was widely respected as one of the organisation's leading cadres in the community. Seen as a threat by the FBI, the Chicago BPP became a target for their 'imaginative, hard-hitting, counterintelligence measures'. In January 1969, the FBI made an unsuccessful attempt to create friction between the powerful and violent black Chicago gang, the Blackstone Rangers, composed entirely of unemployed youths, and the BPP. Their memo of 16 December reveals that the FBI composed and handwrote (with the appropriate misspellings) the following letter sent to Jeff Fort, the leader of the Blackstone Rangers:

> Brother Jeff: I've spent some time with Panther friends on the west side lately and I know what's been going on. The brothers that run the Panthers blame you for blocking their thing and there's suppose to be a hit out for you. I'm not a Panther or a Ranger, just black. From what I see these Panthers are out for themselves not black people. I think you ought to know what their [sic] up to. I know what I'd do if I was you. You might hear from me again. A black brother you don't know.

On 4 December 1969, in a pre-dawn raid, the Chicago police attacked an apartment where Fred Hampton was staying. They murdered him in his sleep, together with another party member, Mark Clark. Seven other members were also in the apartment at the time; some were severely wounded. The police attack was one of the most savage ever launched in Chicago. The police justified their actions by claiming that BPP members had fired back; the party, then and since, maintained that this was not true. The COINTELPRO documents now confirm information first uncovered in 1973, that William O'Neal, chief of Panther security, and personal bodyguard to Fred Hampton, was a paid informer for the FBI. He gave them a detailed floor plan of the apartment, told them that there were illegal firearms in the apartment, and it is alleged, drugged Hampton the night before the raid. Even after the raid, O'Neal continued to work for the FBI, reporting on the meetings between the Hampton family, witnesses and lawyers. He was paid $10,000 for his services.

In Britain, we have seen counter-intelligence activity operating against the Irish unemployed and their political organisations. British blacks, particularly the unemployed, have no difficulty in accepting the fact of Special Branch activities frame-ups, informers and agents provocateurs. They know intimately the nature of the British state.

In Britain, no organisational force to compare with the Black Panther Party has yet emerged. A large number of unemployed blacks are only now in the process of emerging here. As capital develops, in our era, the level of unemployment increases, and all developed societies are faced with trying to find a solution to the demands that the unemployed are making.

The life of the unemployed in Britain is similar to that of their counterparts in the US. Once they leave school, they are faced with menial jobs or no jobs at all – a miserly wage from the state of between £6 to £11 – if they are lucky. On the streets, they supplement their income through petty crime, and by involving themselves with one of the many state-funded 'self-help' projects, dropping in and out of the various hostels, community industries and the like. Hostels are usually slums through which 'self-help' youths renovate themselves and through which community industry employers get cut-price black labour.

So far the British state has looked to these specially created job programmes and special post-school skilling projects, crash typing courses and the provision of semi-skills, to sap the revolutionary potential of this section of youth. The principal of Brixton College, John Sturgeon, spells this intention out: 'People who feel there is no purpose in typing won't fit in to any kind of society ... You can't keep people down with the police forever. I wanted to create a middle class among the West Indians in order to pacify the district.' The only other alternative that the state has to offer this section of the community is prison. Those organisations and individuals within the black community, who see these projects and schemes as the salvation for the unemployed, do so because they believe that this section is incapable of surfacing from within its ranks an independent, revolutionary alternative. If nothing else, the Black Panthers showed that it can.

'GRENADA: EVERY COOK CAN AND MUST GOVERN'
Race Today, March 1979

In one sharp thrust, the people of Grenada have completed the first stage of the revolutionary movement which raised its head in that island state in the early months of 1974. The historic seizure of power, which took place on the morning of 13 March 1979, was effected largely by the unemployed youth of the Grenadian working class. And it could have taken place in any one of the Caribbean islands.

The basis for this remarkable development in Caribbean politics and social life has been laid in the last 25 years, during which Caribbean societies have been dragged directly into the orbit of modern capitalist economy. Millions of dollars' worth of foreign capital have poured into these islands, disrupting old colonial patterns, transforming whole landscapes, uprooting small peasants, concentrating in urban centres an army of unemployed, increasing the exploitation, degradation and misery of the working class and disgorging large numbers of the native population into the cities of North America and Europe.

At the heart of this transformation is and has been the unceasing and endless rebellion of workers, peasants, the unemployed, schoolchildren and housewives in all the Caribbean islands.

In 1968, we experienced the first dramatic challenge to a modern Caribbean regime. Then, the people of Jamaica took to the streets, ostensibly to protest the banning of historian, Walter Rodney. Shortly to follow were the people of Trinidad and Tobago, whose rebellion all but toppled the Williams regime, then St. Vincent, St. Lucia, Dominica, Anguilla, Antigua, Guyana and St. Kitts.

These governments, without a single exception, face these insurrectionary movements with massive repression and state brutality, as best described by the former prime minister of Grenada, Sir Eric Gairy: 'In the last 24 years people have tried to get rid of me, but lots of them, that have tried, are lying in the cemetery.' Let us be in no doubt that this repression has had the backing and support of the imperialists in Britain and the United States, strengthened by Latin American reactionary forces. US gun boats and the Venezuelan military intimidated the revolutionary forces in Trinidad and Tobago into surrendering in 1970. The Chilean government, the most brutal of Latin American regimes, provided training, arms and ammunition for Grenada's fascist dictatorship.

Therein lies the counter-revolutionary power which has raised its head in opposition to the Grenadian revolution, forces which have been present since the emergence of the movement to rid the country of what is popularly known as Gairyism.

In 1974, while Britain was still the colonial power, a general strike had paralysed the island after Gairy had unleashed a gang of thugs, the Mongoose Gang, against the opposition. The British responded by dispatching frigates to the Caribbean. In the midst of this, the British government granted Gairy independence, funds for development and dignified this self-proclaimed crook with the title, Sir. It was a clear attempt to give legitimacy to one of the Caribbean's most corrupt and brutal regimes.

The fact that the British and American governments have not promptly dispatched troops to rescue Gairyism now owes little to charity. It is the determined, systematic and courageous opposition of the Grenadian people, supported by Caribbeans at home and abroad, and led by a skilful, political leadership which has succeeded in isolating Gairyism beyond recall. Short of rescuing Gairyism, the imperialists are determined to undermine the Grenadian revolution with the assistance of Caribbean governments.

Why else are these governments vacillating in their recognition of the People's Revolutionary Government of Grenada? Why else are they putting pressure on the Grenadian government to return to constitutionality as a quid pro quo for diplomatic recognition?

What therefore has to be done to protect the Grenadian revolution from imperialist interference, both overt and covert? A democratic state must replace the old colonial state machinery as a means through which the people of Grenada are to be mobilised. This is a precondition for the transformation of colonial production relations which have kept Caribbean peoples as hewers of wood and drawers of water. And we have no objection to a new state organised around Assemblies of the people and the National Assembly which the new Grenadian Prime Minister Maurice Bishop described to us in the May 1974 issue of *Race Today*.

It is this bold and revolutionary move forward that can and will galvanise Caribbean peoples throughout the world, in support of the Grenadian revolution and, through us, sections of the international working class with whom we have been socialised. Every cook can and must govern.

'THE GRENADIAN REVOLUTION'
Race Today, May 1979

In the 'Backlash' columns of this issue, the difficulties facing the Grenada Revolution are articulated by the participants themselves. Firstly, Grenadian Prime Minister Maurice Bishop tells us that the government of the United

States is dictating to the People's Revolutionary Government that they should seek no aid from Cuba. This has been followed, in the last few days, with an announcement by Prime Minister Bishop that the CIA is organising a three-stage plot against the new regime. The first stage takes the form of subversive propaganda aimed at dissuading tourists from visiting the island, thereby robbing Grenada of much-needed foreign currency. The second stage will take the form of a series of fires at major public buildings. Already, two such fires have been reported. And finally, leading members of the People's Revolutionary Government are to be executed.

This comes as no surprise to those of us here in the United Kingdom who have expressed solidarity and support for the revolutionary overthrow of Gairyism. Any social and political movement in the Caribbean which seeks to break the stranglehold of US imperialism in the region is bound to be faced with military subversion by the most powerful regime on earth. Through Prime Minister Bishop, the people of Grenada have given us the lead. They will seek assistance from whichever country offers it and to hell with the US. That is good enough for us. The alliance of organisations of which *Race Today* is a part will continue to mobilise opposition to attempts by the US and other forces to subvert the process which leads to workers' and peasants' power in Grenada and the rest of the Caribbean.

Of equal importance is the task of transforming the colonial economy inherited from the Gairy regime. Minister of Labour Selwyn Strachan has indicated the needs of the workers and peasants, who are demanding free education, medical care, subsidised food and housing, while thousands of the wageless are besieging the new ministers for a social wage. Being without the benefits of modern technology, as Minister of Finance Bernard Coard points out, the new government can only exhort people to work hard and produce more and more to satisfy these demands, even though throughout our history, Caribbeans have generated enough wealth through our labour to reduce the working day to near zero and avail ourselves of all the modern technology that exists. Alas, that wealth is concentrated in the developed countries of the West and in the hands of a few.

This is the major problem which the revolution faces and from which all other problems spring and no amount of self-help can break this vicious cycle. We are saying that we are poised, as never before, to tackle the problem at its roots. Here we are, Caribbeans, in our thousands, residing in the heart of capitalism. Many of us live within a stone's throw of the Bank of England, the City and Parliament. The same applies to our brothers and sisters in North America. We work, some of us, in firms which have grown fat off the sweat and blood of Caribbean peoples. It is for us abroad to mobilise ourselves and our white working-class comrades to demand a return, without strings, of the wealth we have created. We have to congregate in our thousands at the door of the British and American governments if we are to use our power to release our Grenadian comrades from yet another round of sweat and toil. The Alliance of the Black Parents' Movement, the Black Youth Movement, the *Race Today* Collective and the Bradford Black Collective is committed to this political task. Enormous though it seems, it is the fundamental historical task of we Caribbeans who presently reside abroad.

Figure 7.2   C.L.R. James and Darcus Howe at C.L.R. James's 80th Birthday Lectures, Kingsway Princeton College, Camden, 1981.

'C.L.R. JAMES ON WALTER RODNEY'
November 1980

This speech was delivered by C.L.R. James at a memorial rally for Walter Rodney held at Conway Hall on 20 October 1980, a week after his murder organised by the Committee Against Repression in Guyana (CARIG).

I regret that I'm a little weak owing to the years, but I'm weak down below in the legs, not in the head. Tonight I want to say a few words about my personal relations with Walter Rodney which were always suitable owing to the kind of person he was, and then to draw some outline of what we have lost, and the person whom he was and the person whom he could have been.

I left Trinidad where I had been working with Eric Williams in 1963. It became impossible to go on. I published one or two books in London, and Walter Rodney and some other young West Indians came to me and asked me if I would hold some classes. So my first contact with him was to hold classes for six months. At the end of the classes, I said, 'Now, look here, each of us has got to do something to show that although we have studied in general, we are able to concentrate this knowledge on some particular subject.' And people chose various subjects.

Walter Rodney interested me particularly. First of all, he was socially a very quiet man. Secondly, what he talked about was the slave trade in Africa, the beginnings of the slave trade. And he didn't complain about how the evil slave trade had treated the slaves; he spoke about the impact of the slave trade on Africans in relation to that period. I was immensely struck by it. I was struck though I knew nothing about the subject.

The next time I met him was in Canada where there was a meeting of black writers, and Rodney was chairman of the meeting. He handled the post with the necessary firmness, but with genuine understanding of the requirements of people, all of whom wanted to speak whether they could speak or not. I found it strange that he had left Jamaica. I was informed that Rodney knew it would be difficult for him to get back in. He had been going round in Jamaica talking every Sunday morning to black people about the history of Africa, and he didn't leave Jamaica and was prohibited to return by accident. He and his friends sat down and discussed whether he should go or not, and they finally decided that he should take the risk. He took it and the results were tremendous. There was an upheaval in Jamaica, not only amongst the students but among the black people to whom he used to talk every Sunday morning. Motor cars were burnt, houses were destroyed and so forth. All on account of Walter Rodney and the work that he had been doing in the University of the West Indies. That shows another capacity, that to move ordinary working-class people with the history of Africa and the fact that he represented some emancipation for the African people.

Then I saw a book that he had published – a book that represented the work he had done in Jamaica. It is called *The Groundings with my Brothers*, published by the Bogle L'Ouverture organisation here in London. And I want to recommend that book to you as one of the finest studies of the life and history of the African people in short form. It isn't very long, it isn't very expensive, but we have to keep that book going, not only because of what it represents and shows how Rodney used to think, but because it is of the greatest value in understanding the population of the African people today.

Well then, Rodney went to Guyana and he used to come to the United States quite often. There were universities in the United States which used to invite him to hold semesters there, and the University of Michigan, some years ago, devoted a week to the study of the work of C.L.R. James. That is me, and we invited a lot of people and Rodney was there. I remember him sitting up in the corner and I remember his intervention. That was first class, as usual. But later they began to speak of the necessity of getting the university to give me an honorary degree. And I remember very well Rodney up in the corner, saying, 'Now the question of the honorary degree, that we can work out, but what we can do is this: in Africa, a person who has reached the age and the experience and the reputation of James, is known as "Mzee", and I recommend that we give him that degree here and now.' And from that time, a whole number of people have called me 'Mzee'. And he introduced that.

Then he went to Guyana, and he wasn't able to get the post which all the scholastic people in Guyana wanted him to have. But he used to come to the United States regularly. I know, during the last two years, I have attended three meetings in which Rodney had been asked to speak about Africa and the African situation. And the last meeting at which he spoke I was the chairman, because my college, the University of the District of Columbia, invited Rodney to speak and asked me to take the chair. He was the same Rodney he had been in the years before, quiet, without demonstration, but solid with a mass of material, logically developed.

I could feel what he was talking about going home to his audience. Well, I was waiting to hear that something would happen to him. I went to Trinidad. Rodney would come to Trinidad to the Oilfield Workers' Trade Union.

Then I heard that the WPA had been formed, the Working People's Alliance. At once, I felt very nervous. You see, right through the Caribbean, the population as a whole is critical, sometimes very hostile to the existing regimes. In Trinidad, they are absolutely anxious that Williams and his party should get out of it, but they have nobody to represent them, and we have, strongly, the habit of being ruled by the colonial governor, the single person. We have lived that way for three or four hundred years and it isn't easy to get rid of it.

But the moment I heard that the WPA had been formed in Guyana, and I heard what was going on, I sent a public telegram to the WPA. I congratulated them on having been formed. I said that their victory was certain and I asked them please to take note of the danger of assassination of Walter Rodney. That was published in the Trinidad press and right through the Caribbean. It was published in Guyana. I was certain, only for this reason: in Trinidad, you could want to get rid of the Williams' regime and of Williams himself, but there was nobody else who we could put to represent the powers that wanted to take over. But in Guyana, Rodney was absolutely made to get rid of Burnham and take his position. He was a great scholar, he was an international scholar, and he hadn't been mixed up in Guyanese politics before. He was absolutely new and Burnham would know that, and therefore, I warned them to be careful – 'Be sure that you guard Rodney from assassination.' I thought that might have helped; it didn't help.

We face, in the Caribbean, over the next ten or twenty years, a tremendous difficulty in developing the country, to make the government and the people really recognise what they are, feel what they are and do the immense amount of work that we can do. And I know no single person of his age more suitable to carry on that work as Walter Rodney would have been.

That's the kind of loss we have had, that is the loss in Guyana, that is the loss in the Caribbean. But there is something else, something that is waiting. We in the Caribbean have played an important role in the development of the African revolution. I am not going to call the names, but I know that it is very important that we as black people and colonial people get together and are able to understand one another and contribute to each other. We have a lot to contribute to them, but they have a lot to contribute to people from the Caribbean too. I know nobody, no one more suitable for that position than Walter Rodney. That's what we have lost.

And I want to add this finally. When the time came for the conference that was held in Dar es Salaam [the Sixth Pan-African Congress], Walter could not attend, but he circulated a document and I read the document. A completely Marxist document, a beautiful analysis. Nobody with Marxist training or experience could have done it better and I was somewhat disturbed. I wrote him and told him, 'But look here, I agree with everything you say but it is of no use carrying this document to that conference.' As it is they have done nothing, but if they had got that document, they would have done still less. But as time has passed, I believe that the mistake I made was in thinking that that document should have been done another way, because that is what we require at the present time.

It is not only that we of the Caribbean would have had somebody in Walter Rodney who would have helped to knit the Caribbean to Africa and to the people in the United States. It is in that general unity of the working-class people, we had a representative who was able to meet any member of the opposite movement, any part of England, any part of Europe, meet them on their level and show them that he understood not only the African people and the people of the Caribbean, but he understood their movement as well. That is what we have lost, and we have to see to it that people recognise, not only what he has been, but what he would have been. I am writing my autobiography, and it is going to be dedicated to Walter Rodney. We have to do things of that kind so that people will know what Walter has been to us and what he could have been to the world that is crying out for people like him.

8
Legacies

RACE TODAY'S POLITICAL LEGACY: REMEMBERING HOW BRITAIN CAME TO US

Adam Elliott-Cooper

Despite having the most expansive empire in human history, one that shaped the racial borders which mark today's globalised world, Britain is still reluctant to discuss racism. Even much of the British radical left feels far more comfortable discussing 'class', implying that 'race' happens somewhere else – the United States, Johannesburg in the 1980s, or the West Indies in the 1700s, perhaps. But being the centre of Empire for so many centuries made Britain, in many ways, race's administrative capital.

After controlling much of North America and the Caribbean, amassing the lion's share of the transatlantic slave trade, Britain claimed victory in European competitive colonisation in the nineteenth century, dominating the carving-up of Africa, the acquisition of Australasia, and controlling the 'jewel in the imperial crown', India. Through diplomatic, economic, military and ideological means, Britain deployed this racial governance at arm's length, with direct racial violence exported to its outposts in the colonised world. It is this understanding, that resistance to racism in Britain is intrinsically bound with the workers' and anti-colonial movements in the colonies and former colonies, that makes *Race Today*'s work so fundamentally important to Black political action and thought in the twenty-first century.

For centuries, the resources and labour of the colonised world flowed towards Britain, and it was inevitable that the people eventually followed. Some were invited to rebuild the country after the Second World War. Those with the status of citizens of the Commonwealth were able to move freely, while others navigated bureaucratic barriers and physical borders to make it to the mother country. Despite the variety of channels these colonial subjects followed, their reception tended to be similar: an abrupt and undeniable racism. These, very different, societies of disparate people eventually found themselves side-by-side, united by their experiences in Britain. Unlike their distant cousins in the United States, Black people in

Britain didn't have a shared history of oppression and struggle. Though they were struggling against the same imperial power, the trade unions in India and Trinidad and the socialists in Grenada and Ghana were for the most part separated by land, sea, language and culture. When we take this into consideration, it is remarkable that Black people in Britain have been able to establish and sustain anything resembling a cohesive anti-racist struggle at all. The British Black Power movement had to be in constant conversation with Britain's colonies and former colonies, drawing on Britain's post-colonial communities and their links 'back home'. Indeed, many of its most influential organisers had been born under British colonial rule, leading the charge against the far right on the streets and the structural racism reproduced by state institutions.

Today, the British establishment prides itself not only on its imperial history, but its 'tolerance' of ethnic diversity. Britain is certainly more multicultural than any of the former European imperial powers, and selectively celebrates this through showcases such as the Olympic Games Opening Ceremony in 2012, spokespeople from its ever-expanding diversity industry, or a royal wedding. This ethnic diversity includes people who hail from a range of Caribbean islands, from cultural powerhouses such as Jamaica to tiny British Overseas Territories such as Montserrat. Communities that trace historical routes from the Indian subcontinent, often via Africa or the Caribbean have made an indelible mark on the social landscape of Britain. Increasingly, Black people in Britain have migrated from the African continent, from both former British colonies such as Nigeria or Zimbabwe and countries such as Congo or Ethiopia, travelling for a myriad of reasons, from fleeing conflict or climate change, to migrating in the hope of greater economic and social security. Importantly, Britain is now also made up of peoples affected by more recent imperial endeavours – communities with links to Afghanistan, Libya, Iraq and other nations affected by US or NATO-led 'interventions' in the post-9/11 period.

Thus, despite the cultural richness that is sporadically celebrated in post-colonial Britain, the key thing that unites Black Britain isn't their gratitude for British tolerance, but the racism and violence of Empire. The *Race Today* Collective helped Britain's Black communities trace the routes of colonial systems of control to the centre of Empire, by connecting colonialism to racism in policing, the prison system, housing, schooling and other state institutions. Recovering the Collective's legacy can aid us in not only remembering the extraordinary impact Britain's Black communities have had on Britain, but also critically reflect on Britain's position as the imperial centre of the world for so many centuries, and challenge the far-reaching influence it continues to have over Europe's former colonies. An unapologetically anti-imperialist, black Marxist appraisal of Black struggles in Britain and across the world was published in the columns of *Race Today*. Despite their revolutionary politics, the Collective maintained that *Race Today* was not set up to distribute vanguardist manifestos, but to enable Britain's Black communities to better understand the situation they faced, and enable them to stand up for their rights effectively. Acting on C.L.R. James's principle that 'every cook can, and should govern', it moved from the research-based Institute of Race Relations in central London to a squat in Railton Road, Brixton, among the people in the unofficial capital of Black Britain. In the years that the Collective wrote, published and distributed, Black people in Britain and across the world were struggling against apartheid, colonial rule and state racisms. *Race Today* was able to capitalise on this position, finding common ground in rebellions in Handsworth and Grenada, and strikes in Grunwick and Mumbai.

Through the years that *Race Today* was in print, its readers were given a sense of global struggles against racism and imperialism in every corner of the colonised world. Vitally, it connected these struggles to the campaigns addressing the racism which was in the immediate reality of Britain's Black masses. Squatters' movements helped black families find housing, while the black supplementary schools challenged the racism in mainstream education. Mass action came to a head when confronting the violence of the police – with revolts across Britain, such as Notting Hill in 1976, then Bristol, Nottingham, Brixton, Toxteth (Liverpool) and other parts of England in 1981. These spontaneous rebellions were often accompanied by more organised resistance. *Race Today* reported from youth centres and community meetings in Handsworth (Birmingham), and helped galvanise national campaigns against racial violence such as the 1981 Black People's Day of Action.

But despite such a rich narrative of Black mobilisation on British soil, maintaining international connections has proved difficult. The multiple routes which led Britain's colonial subjects to the mother country are separated by oceans or colonial borders, as well as histories, cultures and experiences. Thus, it is near-impossible to present a straightforward black narrative in Britain. Unfortunately, this can often lead to a focus on pre-ordained Black historical epochs: the US Civil Rights Movement or the fall of apartheid in South Africa (or worse, a liberal interpretation of King or Mandela respectively). We can all relate to people wanting to stand up to racism, and can be inspired by the achievements they made. But at the same time, neither of these stories reflects the routes Black people in Britain have made from colony to imperial centre. Further, what can often result from trying to relate to everyone, is a simplified narrative that doesn't really speak to our histories. Thus there are many people today who know about the Montgomery bus boycott in Alabama, but nothing about the bus boycotts in Bristol. We are likely to be familiar with the lynching in the Jim Crow South, but may be shocked to hear that the British hanged 312 enslaved Jamaicans and put their heads on sticks in 1831 for rising up against their masters. Many young people have heard about the ANC in South Africa, but not about the New Jewel Movement, the socialist coalition that led to the Grenadian Revolution. What this leaves invisible therefore, is that Britain had its own civil rights and anti-apartheid struggles – the overthrow of colonialism is, in many ways, a struggle for civil rights. Indeed, the battle for a passport to Britain and inclusion in the sharing of the resources it holds was, and still is, our movement against a global apartheid.

Today, state violence is the issue most immediate to Britain's black communities. Deaths at the hands of the state, including immigration detention centres, prisons, mental health institutions and the police, still dominate Britain's anti-racist narrative. While organisations such as the Monitoring Group assist with legal cases for those who have suffered racial violence, others, like the London Campaign Against Police and State Violence, support campaigns, popular protest and civil disobedience. The United Family and Friends Campaign still draws significant crowds at protests and public meetings. While campaigns against black deaths in the US have helped re-galvanise Black British protest among younger activists, equivalent cases here in Britain gain far less mainstream media coverage.

A cynic might argue that the focus on places such as the US or South Africa under apartheid plays conveniently into the hands of the British state, diverting our gaze from its own injustices. But such complexities are an opportunity as well as being a barrier. Unlike the United States, no one group within Britain's Black population owns the narrative of Black people. *Race Today* offered an analysis of Black politics in Britain and its former colonies which could not be collapsed into a single story or viewpoint, but encompassed multiple, yet interconnected, experiences, struggles and ideas. Owing to these complexities, Black Britain, more than our distant cousins in the US, needs publications like *Race Today*. Drawing the links between our geographically disparate, yet intimately connected, histories requires constant reflection. Pushing past the invisibility of racial histories on British soil, which the Empire has hidden away in its colonies, means that resistance, in action and in thought, must be a continual process if we are to understand how what was the world's biggest empire can so easily negate its destructive racial legacies.

Figure 8.1 '*Race Today*: A Visual Retrospective' – part of the 'Icons of Railton Road' art installation created by Brixton, Jon Daniels, and unveiled in October 2015 at Brixton Advice Centre in Railton Road.

COMPLEX COALITIONS: SEX, GENDER, RACE, AND CLASS
Leila Hassan and Deirdre Osborne

In a range of investigative articles, reviews, poetry and interviews by women contributors, *Race Today* stayed true to its founding statement 'From Victim to Protagonist' in terms of women's agency. It recognised, recorded and provided a platform for voicing woman's collective politics in confronting discrimination, in leading campaigns for improvements in housing, education and employment, and against police oppression.

Women's intellectual energies and activisms engender an invaluable insight into the specific interrelation between class, race and sexual politics in 1970s Britain, as contoured by the experience of post-war migration heritage and the magnitude of the lived consequences of colonialism. The

Black Power Movement, the Black Arts Movement, and Gay Liberation from the US influenced and informed the black movement in the UK. However, the British context produced conditions that were distinct from American experiences of racism and sexism. At the same time, evolving Black-centred discourses in Britain were susceptible to being overwritten by their American counterparts. This was especially so in the arts where scepticism existed in white-dominant critical reception well into the twenty-first century, as to whether a truly autonomous 'black British' writing/film/theatre/television/literature/music could be classed as possessing noteworthy aesthetic credentials. *Race Today* challenged this perception at the outset.

While figuring centrally at the time, women's participation in history often becomes submerged by the prominence of men's public visibility, and retrospectively eclipsed in cultural memory. Eight women formed the backbone to the production of *Race Today* in editing, contributing articles, typesetting and graphic design. Leila Hassan, Jean Ambrose, Patricia Dick, Mala (Dhondy) Sen, Barbara Beese, Lorine Burt, Akua Rugg and Marva Spencer were involved in radical politics in various capacities as campaigners and organisers. Their participation extended across a number of activist groups including the Black Unity and Freedom Party, the Black Panther Movement, the Indian Workers Association, the Black Women's Movement, the Alliance of the Black Parents Movement, the Black Youth Movement, Creation for Liberation, and Brixton Women's Group.

As Leila Hassan notes, the members of *Race Today* did not subscribe to a politics of integration into the status quo, but sought to change the socio-cultural structures that sustained oppression against minoritised groups,* and women were at the vanguard for impelling such change. Middle-class and educated people migrating from the Caribbean islands frequently found themselves re-classified as 'black' and working class upon arrival in Britain. Professionals could end up as cleaners or ancillary workers forced to do manual labour in contexts for which they were professionally qualified. Black and Asian working-class women, migrants predominantly, worked in the NHS, transport, service industries and factories.

In resisting oppression, women led strikes, and mobilised community action. The recording of women-led campaigns (the nurses' strike, the strike at Imperial Typewriters, the Grunwick strike, battles for better education and against police malpractice) as published by *Race Today* gave a voice to these women workers' struggles. In one of the last issues, a con-

---

* Conversation with Deirdre Osborne, 16 January 2019.

versation between Jayabean Desai and Arthur Scargill was featured on the Grunwick strike and its impact. As vividly captured in Buchi Emecheta's novels (reviewed by Leila Hassan in *Race Today*), women of the African and Asian diasporas living in 1970s Britain faced racist discrimination in social welfare, personal welfare and the attribution of 'second-class citizenship'.

A wealth of writing by, about, and for women, constitutes a key legacy of *Race Today*. As the journal's arts critic Akua Rugg prefaces her collection of arts reviews (1975–84), *Brickbats and Bouquets: Black Women's Critique Literature, Theatre, Film*, 'writing for the journal brought me into contact with the work of artists from Africa, Asia, the Caribbean and America.'* Notwithstanding Rugg's pioneering arts coverage of events, publications and performances invisible to white-mainstream critical circles, it was through the attention given to the arts, and women's significant contributions that comprised much of the content. Black American women writers Toni Morrison, Ntozake Shange, Alice Walker and Maya Angelou profoundly influenced and catalysed black women in Britain and the journal was a harbinger for recognising women's cultural impact, and from a British perspective. As Rugg recollects:

> In *Race Today* we have reviewed the work of African-American writers Alice Walker, Toni Morrison, Ntozake Shange, Rosa Guy and that of the Jamaican theatre company, Sistren. The work of these artists gives a voice to women in the societies they come from. It reveals their struggles which have hitherto been hidden and projects images of women who see themselves not as passive victims unable to change the circumstances of their lives but as protagonists willing and able to determine their own destinies.[†]

The inspiration and solidarity that women in Britain found in African American and Caribbean women's writing was one cultural lens by which to begin viewing and articulating the distinctive conditions of life in Britain. Living in Britain presented a unique manifestation of diasporic location to which women responded socio-politically and creatively. *Race Today* published a range of poems and short stories by women writing in Britain. Work by Jean 'Binta' Breeze, Janice Shinebourne, Grace Nichols and Marlene McLeary was also reviewed by fellow writers such as Rhonda

---

* Akua Rugg, *Brickbats and Bouquets: Black Women's Critique Literature, Theatre, Film* (London: *Race Today* Publications, 1984), p. 9.
† Ibid., p. 10.

Cobham and Valerie Bloom, showing how the journal provided an arena for arts critique and recognition of the significance of these women writers.

It was not only in the arts that women had the opportunity to reflect critically on representations of their experiences. The trajectory of women's collective political activism to be found in *Race Today* is shared by *The Heart of the Race: Black Women's Lives in Britain* (1985) co-authored by Beverley Bryan (Black Panther), Stella Dadzie (co-founder of OWAAD) and Suzanne Scafe (member of OWAAD and Brixton Black Women's Group). These three women developed careers as educators and scholars from the activism of black women's groups. Like the women involved in *Race Today*, they represent members of the pioneer diasporic generation. As academics and pedagogues, they entered Britain's cultural institutions and worked from within to effect changes in curriculum, scholarship and critical mass. This book set a firm foundation for many 1990s publications, namely the equally classic *Black British Feminism* (1997), edited by Heidi Safia Mirza.* The impetus behind *The Heart of the Race* was to collate black women's first-hand experiences, 'to tell it as *we* know it, placing our story within its history at the heart of our race, and using our own voices and lives to document the day-to-day struggles of Afro-Caribbean women in Britain over the past forty years'. The imposition of a 'triple oppression' upon black women's social positioning (sex, race, class) is memorably contested in this black British feminist classic: 'what matters to us is the *way* Black women have challenged this triple state of bondage ... we must take stock of our experiences, assess our responses – and learn from them.'†

In the same vein, a decade earlier Barbara Beese and Mala Dhondy identify how black women's critiques of oppression and organised resistances have always encompassed more than one basis for action. In their Introduction to Selma James's manifesto, *Sex, Race and Class* (1975) they write: 'As black women in our own collective we have no choice to make between the two movements – we are products of both and not in opposition to either. Our existence poses no division in the class. It poses instead the potential for a linkage of its power.'‡

Thus 15 years before Kimberlé Crenshaw's landmark coinage, an intersectionality between the Black Power and the Women's Movement is

---

* Heidi Safia Mirza (ed.), *Black British Feminism: A Reader* (London and New York: Routledge, 1997).
† Beverley Bryan, Stella Dadzie and Suzanne Scafe, *The Heart of the Race: Black Women's Lives in Britain* (London: Virago, 1985), p. 2.
‡ Barbara Beese and Mala Dhondy, 'Introduction' in Selma James, *Sex, Race and Class* (London: Falling Wall Press and *Race Today* Publications, 1975), pp. 1–8, p. 8.

articulated by these women in Britain as a crucial coalition, yet one that is mindful of the 'imperial mission of white feminism', as Valerie Amos and Pratibha Parmar expressed in 1984.* The Women's Movement's totalising tendencies did not take into account the privilege of whiteness as ideology and social experience. While the compass of the black women's movement could include feminism, it could also be not anti-men, even as it called out sexism. However, further gaps were also apparent in recording black women's experiences, such as black lesbians' perspectives, as the activist and writer Valerie Mason-John's edited *Talking Black: Lesbians of African and Asian Descent Speak Out* (1995) comprehensively addresses.†

All of the women who were the backbone of *Race Today* were active in the campaigns that were going on throughout the 1970s and '80s. This did not always intersect directly with feminist tenets. While the Black Women's Group – Barbara, Leila, Lorine, Pat, and Jean – met in Olive Morris's flat in Railton Road, Brixton and knew about OWAAD, they were not directly involved in the organisation. Publishing a journal that gave voice to and supported black working-class campaigns remained at the forefront of their politics.

It is important in retrospective accounts to chart such continuities that are detectable in the multiple forms of women's activism. The overlapping constituencies of sex, race and class identified by Selma James (1975)‡ continues with Angela Y. Davis's *Women, Race and Class* of 1981.§ *Race Today* was an important vehicle for Britain's first black woman MP Diane Abbott who describes, 'I've always been a race politician. Issues on race are very important to me, but so are issues of class. Obviously they often overlap, but they are distinct. Marxism has given me a theoretical basis to my politics, but race has given me an emotional one.'¶

In another forum, the journal *Feminist Review* published two ground-breaking issues. Both testify to the need for the interruptions to 'known narrative' that the centring of black feminist concerns and women's socio-cultural politics engenders. 'Many Voices, One Chant: Black Feminist

---

* Valerie Amos and Pratibha Parmar, 'Challenging Imperial Feminism' Special Issue, *Feminist Review*, 17 (1984), pp. 3–19.
† Valerie Mason-John (ed.), *Talking Black: Lesbians of African and Asian Descent Speak Out* (London: Cassell, 1995).
‡ Selma James, *Sex, Race and Class* (London: Falling Wall Press and *Race Today* Publications, 1975).
§ Angela Y. Davis, *Women, Class and Race* (New York: Random House Inc., 1981).
¶ Deirdre Osborne, 'Determination, Dedication, Dynamism: An Interview with Diane Abbott', Special Issue, Woman and Politics, *Women: A Cultural Review*, 24 (2–3) (2013), pp. 169–78, p. 171.

Perspectives' (1984) problematises the assumed authority of white feminism to speak for all women and foregrounded the complexity of the term 'black' as evolving into a multi-racial, transnational and anti-imperialist site for debate.* Thirty years later, 'Black Feminisms: Many Chants' as another Special Issue continues the discussion of sex, gender and race that both engages with and disengages from the terms and inheritances of the 1980s, in mapping black women's perspectives.†

In the last decade, a heartening stock-taking of the important task of handing on women's heritages, in order to sustain cultural longevity has gathered momentum.‡ Archives have played an important role in this.§ The Black Cultural Archives housed the Oral Histories of the Black Women's Movement and touring exhibition as curated by Mia Morris and Tamsin Bookey.¶ Britain's first and youngest black woman publisher, Margaret Busby, who compiled the majestic compendium *Daughters of Africa* (1992), launched the *New Daughters of Africa* on 7 March 2019, with over two hundred women contributors.**

However, lamentable figures of the low representation of black women across Britain's institutions continues to be a reality, even as this situation is strongly and persistently challenged by women.†† The radical tradition is maintained through militant young women's innovations in contemporary expressive arts, such as spoken word, rap and grime, and in journalism and polemic by writers including Reni Eddo-Lodge, Afua Hirsch and Lola Okolosie or through online platforms such as Media Diversified, founded by Samantha Asamadu and gal-dem, founded by Liv Little.

The leadership roles which black women occupy in Black Lives Matter and #MeToo in the US, is consistent with a myriad of women-led campaigns and struggles in the UK. For the last decade, black women have been the key

---

* Valerie Amos, Gail Lewis, Amina Mama and Pratibha Parmar (eds), 'Many Voices, One Chant: Black Feminist Perspectives', Special Issue, *Feminist Review*, 17 (1984).
† The Feminist Review Collective (eds), 'Black British Feminisms', Special Issue, *Feminist Review*, 108 (2014).
‡ Heather Marks, 'Black British Feminisms' https://blackbritishwriting.wordpress.com/2017/08/24/resource-black-british-feminisms/ (accessed 11 March 2019).
§ See www.nationalarchives.gov.uk/documents/archives/the-heart-of-the-race.pdf (accessed 11 March 2019).
¶ See http://heartoftherace.blogspot.com
** Margaret Busby (ed.), *Daughters of Africa* (London: Jonathan Cape, 1992); idem (ed.), *New Daughters of Africa* (London: Myriad Books, 2019).
†† Nicola Rollock, *Staying Power: The Career Experiences and Strategies of UK Black Female Professors* (London: UCU, 2019). Available on www.ucu.org.uk/media/10075/stayingpower/pdf/ucu_rollock_february_2019.pdf (accessed 11 March 2019).

organisers of the campaigns demanding justice for those who have died at the hands of the police, these victims include: Sean Riggs, Leon Patterson, Brian Douglas, Christopher Alder, Ricky Bishop, Roger Sylvester, Joy Gardner and Azelle Rodney. Likewise, women have organised in response to the growing numbers of fatal stabbings and shootings in Britain's major cities. Mothers Against Violence in Manchester and Haringey's Against Knife Crime are but two organisations formed to combat the gun and knife violence within those communities.

Race Today of course existed well before the globalised social media explosion. While unimaginable numbers of stages and sources for gaining information around the globe have been opened up, these are also vulnerable to the number of 'hits', 'tweets', 'views' and ever-increasing lengths of search lists, which affects a deep and sustained analysis derived from being a permanently available and known resource for perpetuity.

The tensions in social and political activism continue to be both binding and divisive. Historical perspectives and contemporary applications of the experiences of ongoing prejudice and discrimination towards women present multiple views regarding who has the right to speak with, to, and on

Figure 8.2 'Icons of Railton Road' art installation by Jon Daniel at Brixton Advice Centre, 167 Railton Road, formerly the offices of *Race Today*. The art work depicts C.L.R. James, Winifred Atwell, Darcus Howe, Linton Kwesi Johnson, Farrukh Dhondy and Olive Morris.

behalf of whom, in the struggle for equality. Comprising what has become popularised as the 'Windrush generation', the women of *Race Today* were at the heart of multiple activist struggles, aiming to pave the way to improved conditions for generations who followed. Conscious of power, and powerlessness, they knew that to get power to change things, working with black women in the community was vital. *Race Today*'s politics, which gave race, sex and class struggles equal weighting, was an organisation fighting for change, and its spokes*women* occupied and set agendas for important platforms.

'RACE TODAY AND THE STRUGGLE FOR RACIAL JUSTICE'
Gareth Peirce

When the warriors of revolutionary movements depart, taking with them their oratory, the power of their personalities and their tactical genius, can those movements ever be reproduced? Most recently, the death of Darcus Howe prompted the realisation that the history of the recent past is elusive – the strategic underpinning of social rebellion is often not recorded or too fleetingly to be accessible to later generations. Prompted by Darcus's death to revisit the history of the end of the last century causes a separate realisation – that the most famous initiatives of the small number of brilliant activists of whom he was part had simultaneously given birth to a myriad of less recognised collaborations. And that an understanding of these whilst facing the new nightmares of the twenty-first century can reinforce renewed respect for their universality and an appreciation of the urgent need that they be sustained.

Two extraordinary political actions are firmly embedded in the history of twentieth-century British society: the trial of the Mangrove Nine in 1971 and the march, 20,000 strong, of black Britons in 1981 from New Cross to Hyde Park in protest at the hideous deaths of 13 children killed in a likely racist arson attack but for which police in response were pressuring surviving children to confess – to having started the fire.

Using the tools honed a decade before, in protests at police treatment of the Mangrove, the same collective applied the same determination; that organisation for unprecedented mass action was essential, inspired by the true concept of equal rights and equal demands. Side-by-side with the bereaved parents, ideas were proffered and a formulation of demands evolved, together with the energy and determination to mark indelibly what every part of English society had ignored: '*13 dead and nothing said*'.

And beyond the march, when the inquest into the 13 deaths, presided over by a buffoon of a coroner allowed the mendacious police narrative to be aired, the opportunity for its demolition was as dramatically and publicly seized as a decade before, once the arrests of the Mangrove Nine and the progression of their trial had brought into court, explosively, the collective experience of black citizens in Britain, searingly differently treated, gratuitously beaten, falsely accused and repeatedly framed by the police.

In forceful resistance to the repeated targeting of the Mangrove Restaurant (a lightning rod for police attention as a loved and loving haven for its clientele), it having become a symbol for the exercise of police power, the activists had turned the tables and made it a symbol of black resistance. And when refusal, by forceful protest, to take any more from the state triggered in turn charges of riot, a second radical strategy was mandated within the court, a root-and-branch attack to the entire criminal justice system – the corruption and mendacity and criminality of the police, the bias of the judicial system and the racism of the media.

The exercise of radical refusal by black people to submit themselves to the tyrannies of the state was to become, for others, whether initially conceived of as such or not, an authentic methodology. In this, the same collective group could and did support and guide others – almost all young, most of whom had never heard of the Mangrove trial but who in turn found themselves at the epicentre of conflict and accusation. The political courage shared with them had been first triggered but thereafter enriched by the experience of successful rebellion – the concept of collective support and tactical thinking, of taking the accuser on and turning the tables, armed with the confidence to assert that the history of British rights in English law, some forgotten, was there to be reclaimed and used by all, equally, in this country.

On the day, for Bristol youth in 1980, no such intellectual weaponry was to hand when they fought police in pitched battles and drove them out of St Paul's. With no political grounding and no collective organisation, the Bristol uprising, as many others in the years that followed, was triggered by precisely the same combination of brutal, swamping, racist police practices as had demanded the Mangrove resistance in 1970. The spontaneous combustions in St Paul's represented the accumulation of state violence, arbitrary stops and searches and arrests, and the instinctive reaction of new generations who could not tolerate a daily diet of oppression.

The state's reaction? – To charge a dozen arbitrarily selected defendants with riot, the same ancient charge that carried a maximum sentence of life imprisonment. It was tempting for a young person in the dock to refute his claimed identification by police – for throwing stones or smashing the windscreen of an oncoming police car – and say the evidence was mistaken and whoever was involved, it was not him. What took extraordinary courage but was fortified by the experience of the Mangrove defendants, was instead to tell the jury, '*Yes, the police marched into our community to crush us, to harass us, to arrest us, to oppress us, to injure us, to beat us and we had to fight back. This was self-defence, our right.*'

And before the jury in Bristol Crown Court was empanelled, their lawyers could insist, just as the Mangrove Nine had a decade before, that the black youths to be put on trial in Bristol Crown Court had a further fundamental right: to a jury of their peers. If the random selection of the jury panel had in fact omitted summonsing jurors from the areas of Bristol in which black citizens predominantly lived, then the selection had to be undertaken again – and was. The history of the experiences of the youth of St Paul's at the hands of police was played out in court, before a representative jury. And the defendants' articulation of their right to self-defence and its acceptance by the jury meant that by the verdict of 'not guilty', the invading police from St Paul's could again be routed and sent packing.

Zigzagging across England, without orators or radical tacticians within their ranks, a front line of young resistance was propelled by urgent reactive necessity to act in the same way. In the north of England, in Bradford in 1981, twelve young Asians put together Molotov cocktails – rags stuffed into milk bottles filled with petrol – to be armed in case the broadcast warning was true that fascists were on their way to attack the Bradford Asian community. Charged with having made bombs, each young defendant was reinforced in his courage to articulate the same fundamental concept – the universal right of necessary self-defence – and to explain to the jury the experience of Asians at the hands of the National Front, their homes set alight, their elders beaten or killed and, as for protection by police, '*nothing ever said or ever done*'. Tackling the unthinking racist structure of the criminal justice system, the beginning of the trial at Leeds Crown Court was delayed again and again when identical practices in the selection of jurors were exposed. No jurors had been summonsed from the court's catchment areas in which Asian citizens liable to jury service lived.

Two more trials in two successive years in East London, of the 'Newham Seven' and the 'Newham Eight' echoed the resounding Bradford 12 acquittals – of very young teenagers who physically took on fascists and, in one case, the police. The same collectivity of grass-roots support, mobilisation and wisdom was there to embolden them – to describe the history of attacks of Asian children even within school playgrounds, and why it was that Asian teenagers who had defended them were instead finding themselves in the dock at the Old Bailey. In a by-now-familiar precursor to their trial, the Snaresbrook court's pool of jurors had been identically exposed as having excluded areas for selection in which Asian citizens on the electoral register could be found. All these defendants could be justly found 'not guilty' if their rights could be established and the state could be taken on fairly, squarely and forthrightly.

Each of these confrontations played its part, to a degree, in checking manifestations of the state's multifaceted racism, or in so confident and overt a form – and fascist attackers paused, for a while at least, in their confident physical and on occasion fatal aggression.

But even the most triumphant of victories should never be assumed to be permanent; the courageous actions and political intelligence that created victories nevertheless required open-ended vigilance as well. Within a year of the Bristol victory, the most senior judge in England, Lord Denning, was to comment in his memoirs that the defendants in Bristol acquitted of riot, had been acquitted because they had *'Packed the jury with their own'* and came from *'Countries where the truth was not known'*. A week after the book's publication, two of those jurors had achieved Lord Denning's resignation and the recall and destruction of all copies of his book. But today, the right to challenge a jury in England has been abolished.

And a decade after the trial of the Mangrove Nine, the still seething resentment in the Notting Hill police canteen *'Mangrove 1, Notting Hill Police 0'*, fuelled a fresh Mangrove raid, no longer targeting vocal activists but adopting an easier recourse – the planting of soft drugs on a few old-timers. And when that trial had increased the score to *'Mangrove 2, Notting Hill Police 0'*, and a further decade later an even bolder planting of hard drugs resulted in a score of *'3 – 0'*, each successive trial had demanded the retelling of history to explain the motivation – revenge – by a police force expected to have learned from the bitter lessons of the past.

Repeated trials nevertheless took their toll – the Mangrove, albeit vindicated, struggling simply, peacefully, to serve food in a safe and tranquil environment, had been swamped by two decades of court hearings, trials and defence, and swamped too by the gentrification of Notting Hill, aided and abetted by its police. It is marked today by a blue plaque and the memories of the surviving foot soldiers. Yet every analysis, thesis, piece of organisation and learning that emanated from the ideas of a small organisation linked to that plaque, that found its place in the lives of ordinary people joining in their struggles and their formulation of the righteous demands that *'radicalism and reason in their proper proportion'* can be seen to have been even more urgently relevant and needed by the neglected Grenfell Tower residents and the betrayed Windrush generation – for all of whom equal rights and equal power were as ruthlessly ignored and destroyed as for others decades before.

It is the children of the Bradford and Newham defendants who are today part of a different suspect community, defined no longer as 'Young Asians' but as 'Muslims'. Stopped, questioned and searched in their tens of thousands at ports of entry under open-ended Terrorism Act coercive powers, they are accused on the basis of secret evidence of facilitating increasingly ambitious executive control, in juryless courts. Programmes aimed at their generation, at '*de-radicalisation*', targeting '*extremist*' thinking and requiring pledged allegiance to '*British values*', impose a statutory duty on teachers and doctors to report to the police signs of deviation. This is, of course, a moment of crisis in our history, a moment such as would have demanded the brilliant analysis and inspired reaction of the movement that embraced the Mangrove Nine and *Race Today*. The voice that was Darcus Howe's, after all, defined itself by the proud title of radicalism, daring to think as an 'extremist' and able to cut with an intellectual machete through the thickets of the different prejudices the UK now requires be formally accepted as essentially 'British'.

It is nevertheless quite wrong to think that that organisation has left us without recourse. In struggling to resist the breathtaking reach of new state oppression, to remember that the England of the 1970s and '80s too was intended to be, and was, a brutal, cruel and crushing experience, demands remembering and understanding equally the concepts and strategies by which it was combated – and the energy, courage and stamina that was demanded of the combatants. It is with gratitude that we can revisit what has gone before.

'SMALL INTERNATIONALISMS AND FUGITIVE THOUGHTS: AN APPRECIATION OF *RACE TODAY*'
David Roediger

I recently heard the music scholar Barry Shank present a family history based in large measure on the record collection he'd inherited from his father. He spoke of gauging the weight of a song's possible impact on his dad by the depth of the groove cut into the records by frequent re-playings. Some of my deepest grooves would be on the well-worn vinyl of Linton Kwesi Johnson's 1983 LP *Making History*. I must have bought it at the

Radical and Third World Book Fair in the mid-'80s, at the time of the miners' strike. As a young labour historian, I played the hell out of 'What About Di Workin' Class?' and had my US college students conjure with the meanings of the title track. The deepest grooves would have cut into the rebel song 'Di Great Insohreckshan' and the praise song to Walter Rodney, 'Reggae fi Radni'.

Before writing a bit in consideration of what I took and what we might today take from *Race Today*, I want to linger over the extraordinary good luck that had me at the book fair, at black support for the miners' demonstrations (sometimes including many South Asian, Cypriot, Turkish, and even Irish pickets), at C.L.R. James's Brixton lodgings (in the building housing *Race Today* as a collective) in one area where the great insurrection took place, and in the company of Walter Rodney's ideas. There is something to be said for the internationalism of delegations and conferences, but something too for the internationalism of small acts, of happenstance, and of fugitive inspirations.

I spent parts of years in London semi-regularly in the 1980s and '90s as part of the pattern of my partner's research on African history in archives in the US and Ghana. On leave from teaching, I was in the city, with and without my kids, far more than in libraries. The opportunity to experience political relationships I knew were bound to be episodic was great. All roads led to, but also then away from, *Race Today* and its milieu. We lived for months near the Grunwick plant whose labour struggles so figured in the imaginary, practice and journalism of *Race Today*. Because in the US I was so close to George Rawick, the radical historian and C.L.R. James's collaborator on whom I have later written extensively, I felt able to ask to see James on Railton Road in Brixton and where the *Race Today* Collective helped to organise his care.*

I failed to realise either of the two goals in that visit. One was to do an oral history of the sharecropper organising in the near-to-my-home Bootheel region of Missouri that James had done almost fifty years before; he instead wonderfully lectured me on Hegel. The other was to look at his papers and books with a view to getting the Herkovits Library at Northwestern University to buy some of them, a proposal that foundered on all sides. Living at one point in a university flat in Kensington, of all places, put me near one of the book fairs. We were often at Notting Hill. Mostly because of my surrealist activism in Chicago, I knew enough to visit

---

* David Roediger with Martin Smith (eds), *Listening to Revolt: Selected Writings of George Rawick* (Chicago, IL: Charles H. Kerr Publishing, 2010).

John La Rose at New Beacon Books; I bought and read current and back issues of the periodical there and at the legendary Colletts left bookshop in central London. Even watching television put me close to *Race Today*, via the Channel Four programming produced by Darcus Howe and Farrukh Dhondy. Overhearing my publishers at Verso talk about the journal *Race and Class* sent me to the Institute for Race Relations (IRR), the originator of *Race Today*. Working in Chicago in the collective running Charles H. Kerr, the world's oldest English-language radical publisher, in a left bookstore collective, and in the anti-Nazi initiative Workers Defense, I was also poised to appreciate just how much *Race Today* and associated groups were accomplishing on so many fronts.

Happening upon and seeking these presences with pleasure, I did not however try hard to systematise them. I only picked up and scoured the issues of the *Race Today* that came across my path, never subscribing. I played and replayed *Making History* – still do – but bought only one other of Johnson's recordings, plus a book of his poems. As both Rawick's and James's health declined, I never returned to Railton Road, save in showing the building to a friend much later. My experiences with the Jamesite Black left a little resembled surrealist idealisations of walking about in a city, discovering great things planlessly. The intellectual engagement with the ideas on offer was serious but neither daily life nor rhythms of relocations let me think I would be able to participate fully in the life of groups which, at their best, were so impressively rooted. I may also have suspected from Rawick and from experiences in the US left that to learn too much about the relations among groups and individuals broadly around *Race Today* might have surfaced sharp differences, and have therefore settled for more purely inspirational glancing contacts.

And yet, quite aside from the profound influence on my writing and thinking provided by the books of Rodney, of C.L.R. James, and of Selma James, the ideas and organisational forms encountered around *Race Today* influenced much of what I have subsequently tried to figure out and to act on. It was in those mostly 1980s moments and places that I first realised the import of British attempts to not only re-imagine race beyond Black and white but also to re-imagine Black as a category able to unite and mobilise a variety of people whom the sociologist Satnam Virdee would later call 'racialized outsiders'. When *Race Today* became a radical popular publication as opposed to a more staid and paternalistic academic one, such a view of race, by no means one confined to activists, was one of its founding principles. That is, as we learn from Robin Bunce's and Paul Field's superb *Darcus Howe: A Political Biography*, Ambalavaner Sivandan at IRR supported Howe's hiring as *Race Today*'s editor out of admiration for the latter's many skills, but also specifically because the latter 'saw "Black" as inclusive of Asians'.*

Such understanding of race as a political colour, tied not just to skin and continents cannot of course be called into being by intellectuals, and can go as well as come onto the scene. Indeed, it lasted only fragilely and too briefly in the British context, where it came under ruthless attacks from Thatcherism. But the ability of Howe, Sivanandan and others to see the expansive variant of 'Black' as a possibility to be fought for in that moment challenged and inspired me greatly. And a time when I was also in South Africa at significant junctures and heard from African National Congress veterans that 'the way to nonracialism was through race', transnational experiences led me to sharply question several varieties of United States left common sense regarding race and class. I doubted, increasingly if unevenly, that black and white were simple and necessarily enduring categories and that their clashing, as opposed to fostering interracialisms among people of colour was decisive to attend to at our moment. In the intervening years in the US, the question of how to build unity among those racialised outsiders who have recently arrived and those who arrived long ago but remain on the outside assumes increasing urgency. The realisation that some immigrants are African, or West Indian, and phenotypically black does grow but finding a broader basis for African American/immigrant unity remains meagre and tied tragically to Democratic Party electoralism.

Fascinating too, again in ways I could not fully appreciate at the time, were the *Race Today* watchwords: 'Here to Stay! Here to Fight!' Speaking plainly, they reflected a claiming of space and of rightful presence quite beyond mere citizenship. Such a slogan had antecedents of course – the US labour movement and Black freedom movement promise that 'We Shall Not Be Moved', for example – but they also proved to have a new centrality in animating struggles over the last forty years. The central slogan of the most combative US movement of the 1980s, the AIDS Coalition to Unleash Power (ACT-UP) would be 'We're Here, We're Queer. Get Used to It'. In 2006, the largest general strike in modern US history would oppose deportations chanting in Spanish '*Aqui Estamos Y No Nos Vamos!*' – 'Here We Are and We Are Not Leaving!'. This starting from the established capacities of the 'We', and not with appeals to the state, does not solve everything, nor tell us where to then go afterwards. But it is increasingly

---

*   Robin Bunce and Paul Field, *Darcus Howe: A Political Biography* (London: Bloomsbury, 2014), p. 144.

the starting point for mobilisations and re-reading *Race Today* reminds us of long creative traditions of listening to where communities are and where they might be ready to head.

Finally and perhaps unfashionably, it would be wrong to omit the firm and unorthodox Marxism of *Race Today* as a source of my attraction to it then and my excitement on returning to it now. That well-worn groove in Linton Kwesi Johnson's *Making History*, 'What About Di Workin' Class?' distilled a profound sense of ruling-class crisis cluelessness and the possibility and necessity of working-class response. The excellent coverage of strikes, of strike support, of gender and productive and socially reproductive labour, and of class in popular culture in the volume you hold bespeaks these same concerns. Perhaps no other venue was more outspoken than *Race Today* in its emphases on self-activity and self-defence among those racially oppressed and on the power of working-class action, nor more able to see how central racialised outsiders were to class militancy. The hope in its pages for new restiveness among white workers, sometimes realised, never took the form of waiting on or catering to such mobilisations, even as the periodical and the Collective firmly and consistently sought to reject all narrow nationalisms. At a time when some on the US left regard what is being called a 'both/and' approach addressing race and class together as necessarily a threat to class unity, *Race Today*'s body of work is useful not so much as antidote but as instead a source of grounding and subtlety in working through difficult matters.*

The Jamesite and *Race Today* tradition looked and looks to finding 'the future in the present'. But stepping back to this rich selection of readings remains quite useful in doing so. We see in these pages the wisdom, the method and the style of a group of organised rebels who together productively and restlessly looked for and to new motion among working people. The combinations of past and present and of confidence and searching in these pages speak therefore also to our moments of danger and of possibility.

---

* Melissa Naschek, 'The Identity Mistake', *Jacobin*, 28 August 2018, www.jacobinmag. com/2018/08/mistaken-identity-asaid-haider-review-identity-politics; Adolph Reed, Jr., 'Which Side Are You On?', *Common Dreams*, 23 December 2018, www.common-dreams.org/views/2018/12/23/which-side-are-you

BODY COUNT

Turn right out New Cross station
    left onto exhaust fumigated A2
        outpace inching traffic
            dodge a cycling youth
                barreling along the pavement

                look up at plaque
            down at how far each jumped
            chased by deliberate fire

    bass drives blood
    drum fuels pulse
lightning through brain
    blood writes history
        timed on pulse
            shock waves brain

                if one police in each station says
                    'no more chokeholds on my watch
                  no more hearts stopped on my beat'
                how many black lives will that save?

    Do the math
    add one to one hundred
take away ten black people
    divide that by two enquiries
        what do you have?

                Our children cry murder
                    mothers and fathers lower them
                        between two shifts balanced
                    on shuffled bills
                earth receives them
                as earth must without grudges
        balance sheets

our children fall
    through our arms
        held in entreaty
            we lose their names
                they become offerings
                    altars made on their behalf
                spray painted and smashed
            we lose them and lose ourselves

  along routes with too few signs
 marking where so-and-so fell
on such-and-such a day
  for no more reason than black
   skin to his or her or their name

    we turn on ourselves too
     from the wrong post code
      on divided council estates
     this crew against that
    we start each day nursing
   insults and reprisals
  blown up as big as history

we forget to answer to our names
  since we do not recognize ourselves
   you/me/I/we/they/us/them/their
    peel from our bodies
     left naked in public
      for eyes to cover
     nudity that stops traffic
    skin clothed with eyes
   pores smothered by hands

  history feeds on our bodies
history rolls our eyes
 dips our shoulders
  curves our backs

    we run on bones
     laid by history across oceans
      ask that child on that bike
     if history counts for much
    in a life lived at this pace
   standstill traffic
  web turnstiles
knife wars
 that child cuts eyes at you
  as if you spoke in tongues
   for the sacred whose bones
    pave Atlantic roads
     for those beaten
    choked
   by fire
  by police
breathe now

underground
  underwater
    over us all

      for the island borders
        our dreams of Africa
      the Caribbean
    South Asia
  Europe flows
through our veins
  we breathe spoors
    from Africa's Harmattan
      our tongues splinter
        to keep up with dialects
          stored in the roof of mouths
        in the small of our backs
      instep and crook of elbows

    cycling youth
  next time you pass the house
on New Cross Road
  stand on those pedals
    balance two wheels on the spot
      spit streetwise praise for those
      thirteen dead

        they move beside you as hard
      as your shadow your footfall
    as soft as your tongue

    bow your head to them
  look back Sankofa-style
along oceans
  whose roads
    call you
      by your name

Figure 8.3　The *Race Today* Collective, May 2019: Farrukh Dhondy, Michael Cadette, Jean Ambrose, Claudius Hilliman, Pat Dick and Leila Hassan.

Notes on Contributors

Gerry Adams was the leader of Sinn Féin between 13 November 1983 and 10 February 2018 and has been a TD for Louth since the 2011 General Election in the Dáil Éireann. From 1983 to 1992 and from 1997 to 2011, he was an abstentionist MP for the Belfast West constituency. He is the author of 15 books.

David Austin is the author of *Dread Poetry and Freedom: Linton Kwesi Johnson and the Unfinished Revolution* (Pluto, 2018) and the editor of *Moving Against the System: The 1968 Congress of Black Writers and the Making of Global Consciousness* (Pluto, 2018). He is the winner of the 2014 Casa de las Americas Prize.

Robin Bunce is a historian based at Cambridge University. He has written extensively on the history of political thought, and contemporary pop-culture. His most recent book, published by Bloomsbury, *Renegade: The Life and Times of Darcus Howe,* co-authored with Paul Field, was nominated for the Orwell Politics Prize in 2014.

Imruh Bakari Caesar is a film-maker, writer and creative industries consultant. He teaches Film Studies and Film Production at University of Winchester. From 1999 to 2004, he was Festival Director of Zanzibar International Film Festival (ZIFF),and is a founder/director of the Tanzania Screenwriters' Forum.

Adam Elliott-Cooper is a London-based academic and activist.His research focuses on post-colonialism, state power and resistance movements. He sits on the board of The Monitoring Group.

Fred D'Aguiar is a British-Guyanese writer and academic, best known for his poetry, plays and novels. He is currently Professor of English at UCLA. His most recent novel, *Children of Paradise*, is published by Harper.

Jayaben Desai (2 April 1933–23 December 2010) was a leader of the mainly Asian and female strikers during in the epic two-year Grunwick strike in

London between 1976 and 1978. Born in India, Desai moved to Tanzania before migrating to Britain in 1965 where she took low-paid work, first as a sewing machinist, then processing film in the Grunwick factory.

Farrukh Dhondy is an Indian-born award-winning writer, playwright, poet, screenwriter and political activist. He was appointed to the Central Core of the British Black Panther Movement in 1970 and was a founder of the *Race Today* Collective in 1973. Dhondy worked as a teacher in the East End of London before forging a career as a novelist and screenwriter. From 1984 until 1997, he was a commissioning editor at Channel Four.

Paul Field is a writer, lawyer and political activist. He has written extensively for *Labour Briefing*, and for international publications including *Jacobin*, *International Viewpoint*, and the *South African Labour Bulletin*. In 2014, he co-wrote *Renegade: The Life and Times of Darcus Howe*, with Robin Bunce.

Leila Hassan was employed by Institute of Race Relations from 1970 when it was still under the control of Chatham House. A member of the UK's oldest black power organisation, Black Unity and Freedom Party, at that time, Hassan was one of the staff members who helped overthrow the Institute's conservative management. Hassan went on to become a member of *Race Today* Collective, the deputy editor of *Race Today* from 1973, and editor from 1985.

Darcus Howe (26 February 1943–1 April 2017) was born in Trinidad, and came to Britain at the age of 18. A defendant in the trial of the Mangrove Nine in 1971, where he won his acquittal after defending himself for 55 days at the Old Bailey, Howe later conceived and helped organise the Black People's Day of Action in response to the New Cross Fire of 1981. Howe was editor of *Race Today* from 1973 to 1985, before going on to become a broadcaster with Channel Four and a journalist with columns in the *New Statesman*, *The Times* and *The Voice*.

John Huot is a retired teacher and union activist in community colleges in Canada. He is an active supporter in workers' movements, as well as of anti-poverty, anti-racist and climate justice movements. He recently published an article on the political perspectives which animated the movements in which he participated in the 1970s: 'Autonomist Marxism & Workplace Organizing in Canada in the 1970s', *Upping the Anti*, 18 (2016).

C.L.R. James (4 January 1901–31 May 1989) was a Trinidadian cultural and political historian, journalist, sports writer, novelist, philosopher and revolutionary Marxist. The author of such seminal works as *The Black Jacobins* (1938) and *Beyond a Boundary* (1963), James spent his last years living in a flat above the offices of *Race Today* in Railton Road, Brixton, South London.

Gus John is a Grenadian writer, education campaigner and human rights activist who moved to the UK in 1964. He has been active in campaigns around schooling and education in Britain's inner cities for more than fifty years. A distinguished academic, Professor John has held positions in Strathclyde, London and Coventry universities.

Linton Kwesi Johnson, world-renowned reggae poet and recording artist, was born in Jamaica. He moved to London in 1962 at the age of 10. While still at school, he joined the British Black Panther Movement. Johnson later joined the *Race Today* Collective. His poems first appeared in *Race Today*, which also published his first collection of poetry, *Voices of the Living and the Dead*, in 1974.

John La Rose (27 December 1927 – 28 February 2006) was a poet, essayist, publisher and trade unionist. Born in Trinidad, he was a leader of the Federated Workers Trade Union in the 1950s. After moving to the UK in 1961, he founded New Beacon Books in 1966 and helped establish the Black Parents Movement in 1975.

Ian Macdonald QC is one of the UK's leading human rights barristers. He represented Barbara Beese in the trial of Mangrove Nine in 1971. In 1981, Macdonald represented the families of those who had died in the New Cross Fire and in 1998 he was leading counsel for Duwayne Brooks in the Lawrence Inquiry.

Toni Morrison is an American author, who has won both the Pulitzer Prize and the Nobel Prize in Literature for her work. She was presented with the Presidential Medal of Freedom by President Barack Obama in 2012. Perhaps best-known for her 1988 novel *Beloved*, Morrison is professor emeritus at Princeton University.

Deirdre Osborne is a literary activist committed to decolonising politics and has taught in prisons, schools and universities. A Reader in English

Literature and Drama at Goldsmiths, University of London, she co-convenes the MA in Black British Writing. Her publications include (as editor) *The Cambridge Companion to British Black and Asian Literature (1945–2010)*, published in 2016.

Margaret Peacock taught English in a London comprehensive school in the 1970s and 1980s. The struggles of teachers at the time led to the formation of the group Teachers' Action, in which she was actively involved. Peacock spent 25 years as the head teacher of a mixed inner-city comprehensive.

Kennetta Hammond Perry serves as director of the Stephen Lawrence Research Centre at De Montfort University, where she is also a Reader in History. She is author of *London is the Place for Me: Black Britons, Citizenship and the Politics of Race* (Oxford University Press, 2015).

Gareth Peirce is one of the UK's leading human rights solicitors. For more than forty years she has represented victims of miscarriages of justice, including Gerry Conlon of the Guildford Four, the Birmingham Six, Judith Ward, the family of Jean Charles de Menezes, and Moazzam Begg. She is author of *Dispatches from the Dark Side: On Torture and the Death of Justice* (Verso, 2010).

Walter Rodney (23 March 1942–13 June 1980) was born in Guyana. Rodney was one of the leading thinkers and activists of the anti-colonial revolution, leading movements in North America, South America, the African continent and the Caribbean. Rodney's deportation from Jamaica in 1968 was a catalyst for that country's most significant post-war rebellion, the 1968 Rodney riots. Rodney's scholarship, including *The Groundings with my Brothers* (1969) and *How Europe Underdeveloped Africa* (1972), helped to inspire a generation of workers and student activists. Rodney was assassinated in 1980 shortly after the founding of the Working People's Alliance in Guyana.

David Roediger is Professor of American Studies and History at Kansas University. Among his books are *How Race Survived US History: From Settlement and Slavery to the Obama Phenomenon* (2008), and *The Wages of Whiteness: Race and the Making of the American Working Class* (1991). His most recent book *Class, Race and Marxism* (2017) is published by Verso.

Akua Rugg was culture and arts editor of *Race Today* and the *Race Today Review*. She was a member of the Black Parents' Movement, the Black Youth Movement, and a founder of the George Padmore Institute, and the Peter Moses Black Supplementary School, based on Shepherd's Bush, West London. Rugg's *Brickbats & Bouquets* was published by *Race Today* Publications in 1984.

Arthur Scargill joined the National Union of Mineworkers (NUM) at the age of 19 and became one of its leading activists in the late 1960s. He played a key role coordinating the strikes of 1972 and 1974, the latter of which helped to bring about the downfall of Edward Heath's Conservative government. He was elected President of the NUM in 1981.

Stafford Scott was a co-founder of the Broadwater Farm Defence Campaign in 1985, and many other campaigns since. He works for The Monitoring Group and Tottenham Rights and leads on the work on Undercover Policing at The Monitoring Group.

Mala Sen (3 June 1947–21 May 2011). Born in India, Mala Sen came to England in 1965. Originally a member of British Black Panther Movement, Sen later joined the *Race Today* Collective. She wrote *India's Bandit Queen: The True Story of Phoolan Devi* (1991), which led to the acclaimed 1994 film *Bandit Queen*. In 2001, she published *Death by Fire: Sati, Dowry Death and Female Infanticide in Modern India*.

Ntozake Shange (18 October 1948–27 October 2018) was an American writer, and black feminist. Some of her best-known poetry and plays include her Obie Award-winning *For Colored Girls Who Have Considered Suicide/When the Rainbow Is Enuf* (1976), and *Betsey Brown* (1985). She won numerous awards for her work, including the Paul Robeson Achievement Award in 1992.

Sarah White is a co-founder and the managing director of New Beacon Books. Her edited volumes include *Changing Britannia: Life Experience With Britain* (1999) and *A Meeting of the Continents: The International Book Fair of Radical Black and Third World Books 1982–95* (2005), which are published by the George Padmore Institute.

Index